Y0-CAJ-840

OLD ENGLISH PORCELAIN

OLD ENGLISH PORCELAIN

A HANDBOOK FOR COLLECTORS

By

W. B. HONEY

Of the Victoria and Albert Museum

NEW YORK

HARCOURT BRACE AND COMPANY, Inc.

Printed in Great Britain by
R. & R. Clark, Limited,
Edinburgh.

FOREWORD

By Bernard Rackham

The art of the porcelain potter—as practised in Europe, at all events—is frankly a minor art, but it is an art of which the products are very readily accessible to all who care to turn their attention to it. Even if all have not the good fortune to possess, or the means to acquire, specimens of old china, museums both national and municipal are so well endowed with them that a desire to enjoy their qualities is not difficult to gratify. But complete enjoyment even of specimens in a museum is not to be had merely by looking at them; even æsthetic appreciation can hardly be attained in this way, whilst to stop short at seeing and to ask no questions as to how or when or by whom these things were made is to miss a genuine intellectual pleasure. A work of art can only be enjoyed to the full if the circumstances of its creation are known and understood.

The handbook which it is my pleasure to introduce has just this straightforward and simple intention of enhancing appreciation of a very delightful if humble branch of English applied art. The devotees of old English porcelain, whether as collectors or merely as admiring visitors to museums, form a steadily growing body, and their first need is a manual which will give them reliable help in a study not altogether easy to the beginner. Just such help as they require will be found in the following pages. With constant reference to examples easily accessible in public collections the author explains the characteristics, technical and artistic, which distinguish the works of one factory from those of another. No statement is made that cannot be substantiated with good written or other evidence. Where plausible surmise must needs make good the lack of such evidence, the reasons for conjecture are clearly set forth and flaws in the argument are honestly taken into account—a noteworthy merit in a book upon a subject in the treatment of which sheer guesses have all too often slipped into the ranks of established facts and passed thenceforward unchallenged from author to author.

It is perhaps allowable here to draw attention to some of the features which should commend this book to collectors and students. The large volume of new facts which more scientific methods of investigation have lately established is here clearly detailed. Those who have been accustomed to turn for information to the older works on the subject will find here gathered together and summarised a quantity of new material—hitherto accessible only in recent volumes of several periodicals—from the study of which they will turn with fresh interest to their specimens, probably to discover that the classification of these will call for revision in many important particulars. Many of the suggestions put forward by the author are in the nature of pioneer work, as for instance with regard to the earliest wares of Bow, the dating of a certain much-debated class of Chelsea figures, the inscriptions on the "Chelsea toys", the relation of the enameller Giles to the Worcester factory, and the classification of the various Liverpool porcelains. Recent discoveries relating to early Derby and Bristol are also discussed. Perhaps only those familiar with earlier books will fully realise the extent of the material newly published in these pages. Further, the author has confronted the difficult task of indicating the peculiarities of paste and glaze, the subtleties of shape and of painters' mannerisms, which need to be grasped and understood if the great number of unmarked pieces are to be assigned correctly to their places of origin. Even marks are shown to be untrustworthy guides, and the author draws attention to all those other questions which must be taken into consideration before marks can be accepted at their face value.

If the reader, when he reaches the end of this book, lays it aside with a feeling of perplexity, amounting almost to dismay, let him take heart in the reflection that the new methods of study advocated by the author are a challenge to himself to join in the excitements of exploration and discovery. He will have learned that there are more secrets lurking among the specimens in his cabinets than he had been aware of. It may be his lot, by attentive examination and comparison, to make his own contribution to the recovery of the lost history of this branch of English applied art. If his faith in marks is shaken by the disclosure that a red anchor does not always mean Chelsea or a blue crescent Worcester—parenthetically it may here be pointed out that the tables of marks at the end of the book include a number that have never been published before—he may continue undismayed his favourite pursuit; for his sporting instincts will be aroused afresh when he becomes aware that the task of selection and classification is not so easy as he thought. On the other hand, with this new work at his disposal, he cannot justly complain of the lack of competent and trustworthy help.

AUTHOR'S PREFACE

The earlier history of English china is still very obscure. Official records such as are to be found in the princely archives of many Continental factories are here lacking, account-books and papers have vanished, and local chronicles are usually silent, with the result that unsupported conjecture has frequently been accepted in the place of ascertained fact. Much new evidence has, however, been brought to light in recent years, and the useful test of chemical analysis has been more extensively applied. It has accordingly been my intention to supply in this book a concise and up-to-date account of the first fifty years or so of English porcelain. With a few exceptions, nineteenth-century wares have been very briefly treated. In spite of technical excellence, the absence of variety in bodies and glazes and (as it still seems to us to-day) of artistic merit, make the later bone-porcelains decidedly unattractive to the collector who has any familiarity at all with the productions of the eighteenth century.

I have given the fullest references to the available documents, and it is important, now as ever, to bear these constantly in mind. Much is talked, and even written, of the *flair* of the expert, by which the make of a specimen may be recognised though no account could be given of the process of recognition. It is true that a sense of the whole quality and touch of a factory's work can be developed. But that power can only be acquired by familiarity with documentary pieces, and the evidence regarding these cannot be re-examined too often. For instance, the incised triangle was formerly accepted as a Bow mark, and the red and gold anchors were held to indicate quality and not date. Moreover, the anchor occurs also on Derby and Worcester china, and the expert's sense of dates and makes may have been derived from "documents" as misleading as these. Again in Derby, figures of the 1760's were until quite recently mistaken for gold-anchor Chelsea, whilst those of the previous ten years were generally miscalled Bow or Longton Hall, and many false attributions have been made in consequence of these and other initial errors.

I have endeavoured to assist the student by descriptions of typical specimens, by pointing out distinctive features of paste, glaze and decoration,[1] and by references to important pieces which may be seen by everyone in the National collections. Of these, the series at the British Museum, by the inclusion of the Franks Collection, is especially rich in documentary pieces, whilst the Schreiber Collection at South Kensington is unrivalled for high quality. Mr. Herbert Allen's collection, on loan at South Kensington, is wonderfully complete, particularly as regards that later porcelain which is scarcely represented at all in the others. The student should constantly refer to these collections. It is of course not easy to give in words a really adequate notion of the peculiarities of pastes and glazes, or of a painter's handling. Actual pieces must be seen.

The illustrations to this handbook necessarily include types that will be familiar to the experienced collector: the rare and exceptional would have failed to give a true impression of the work of the several factories. And where subjects and models are so largely

[1] In the index I have gathered together under some headings (*e.g.* "teapots" and "handles") all the references to peculiarities of form found in the different manufactures, and under the name of each factory will be found a brief summary of salient points.

common to all, photographs can convey but a small part of the "quality" of a factory's style.[1] I have therefore not attempted the impossible task of giving an illustration of every type, preferring rather to reproduce a smaller number of pieces which seem to me most characteristic, or admirable as works of art, giving them on a scale sufficient to show something of their charm. For it is by æsthetic virtues in the quarry that the collector's pursuit is finally justified, though delight in these may well be kept cleaner and fresher if it comes unsought in the intervals of another task, and for this last there can be nothing better than the difficult one of classification.

The importance of a study and comparison of the actual porcelain cannot be too greatly stressed. Collectors are apt to concentrate their attention on marks, though nothing is more likely to mislead. A mark may be copied, or even added to a piece long after its making, and can never be more than one of several items of evidence in favour of an attribution. The inquiries and disputes about the numbers said to have been used by the Bristol painters provide an excellent instance of the attractions and dangers of the short-cuts offered by marks. The study of the painters' styles is alone likely to be profitable. A painter's work should have as much character as handwriting, and no more absorbing task awaits the collector than the training of the eye to recognise a personal touch.

I wish to offer here my thanks to the collectors who have generously allowed me to reproduce specimens from their cabinets, and to the Officers of the British Museum and the London Museum for facilities so readily granted for examination and photography. My wife has given me valuable help in the tabulation of the marks and in the preparation of the unusually long

[1] For the same reason a list of the figure-models used at each factory would be useless for the purpose of identification.

index. To Mr. Bernard Rackham I am particularly indebted. It was his enthusiasm and unequalled knowledge of the subject that first led me to study it seriously, and he has given me invaluable advice and encouragement whilst this book has been in preparation.

CONTENTS

LIST OF PLATES

CHELSEA

BOW

DERBY

LONGTON HALL

LOWESTOFT

EARLY BRISTOL OR WORCESTER

WORCESTER

LIVERPOOL

CAUGHLEY

PINXTON

NANTGARW AND SWANSEA

PLYMOUTH AND BRISTOL

STAFFORDSHIRE

COALPORT

ROCKINGHAM

SELECTED BIBLIOGRAPHY

THE literature of English porcelain includes but few trustworthy books combining an appreciation of æsthetic qualities with impartial criticism and historical scholarship, and where so much is uncertain each partisan author in turn has appropriated for his favourite factory much that rightly belongs to others. Of the more general works, Nightingale's CONTRIBUTIONS (1881) is still indispensable for its reprinted catalogues and contemporary advertisements. Jewitt's monumental CERAMIC ART IN GREAT BRITAIN (1878) still remains an unexhausted store of facts. Sir Arthur Church's ENGLISH PORCELAIN (1904) contains much important technical matter though its critical judgements are sometimes a little odd, and Mr. R. L. Hobson's twenty-two-year-old CATALOGUE OF THE BRITISH MUSEUM COLLECTION is still a valuable work of reference. Almost everything that is known about the subject could be learned from Mr. Bernard Rackham's indispensable catalogues of the SCHREIBER COLLECTION and the HERBERT ALLEN COLLECTION, though that information is necessarily scattered in isolated notes, or only implicit in the attributions. The little book of ANALYSED SPECIMENS prepared by Mr. Rackham and Mr. Herbert Eccles is also invaluable.

The following list comprises most of the more important and readily accessible books. In a number of cases monographs have been included in the list for the sake of the repertory of examples afforded by their illustrations: it will be understood, however, that the ascriptions attached to these cannot always be regarded as trustworthy guides to classification. Where an abbreviated title has been used in the course of this book it is added in brackets after the full title.

GENERAL WORKS

W. BEMROSE, Bow, Chelsea and Derby Porcelain. London, 1898.

WILLIAM BURTON, A History and Description of English Porcelain. London, 1902.

Sir ARTHUR H. CHURCH, English Porcelain. London, 1904. (Church.)

H. ECCLES and BERNARD RACKHAM, Analysed Specimens of English Porcelain. London, 1922. (*Analysed Specimens.*)

R. L. HOBSON, Catalogue of the Collection of English Porcelain in the Department of British and Mediæval Antiquities in the British Museum. London, 1905. (Hobson, *Catalogue.*)

LLEWELLYNN JEWITT, The Ceramic Art of Great Britain. London, 1878. (Jewitt.)

WILLIAM KING, English Porcelain Figures of the Eighteenth Century. London, 1922. (King, *Figures.*)

MUSEUM OF PRACTICAL GEOLOGY (Jermyn Street): Handbook to the Collection of British Pottery and Porcelain. London, 1893.

J. E. NIGHTINGALE, Contributions towards the History of Early English Porcelain from Contemporary Sources. Salisbury, 1881. (Nightingale.)

BERNARD RACKHAM, Catalogue of the Schreiber Collection of English Porcelain, Earthenware, Enamels, etc. Vol. I. Porcelain (2nd edition). London, 1928. (*Schreiber Catalogue.*)

BERNARD RACKHAM, Catalogue of the Herbert Allen Collection of English Porcelain. 2nd edition. London, 1923. (*Herbert Allen Catalogue.*)

G. W. RHEAD, British Pottery Marks. London, 1910.

BOW

FRANK HURLBUTT, Bow Porcelain. London, 1927.

EGAN MEW, Old Bow China London, 1909.

CHELSEA

G. E. BRYANT, Chelsea Porcelain Toys. London, 1925.

WILLIAM KING, Chelsea Porcelain. London, 1922. (King.)

RAPHAEL W. READ, A Reprint of the Original Catalogue of One Year's Curious Production of the Chelsea Porcelain Manufactory. Salisbury, 1880.

THE CHEYNE BOOK OF CHELSEA CHINA (edited by Reginald Blunt). London, 1924. (*Cheyne Book.*)

DERBY

JOHN HASLEM, The Old Derby China Factory. London, 1876. (Haslem.)

FRANK HURLBUTT, Old Derby Porcelain and its Artist Workmen. London, 1925.

LONGTON HALL

W. Bemrose, Longton Hall Porcelain. London, 1906.

LOWESTOFT

W. W. R. Spelman, Lowestoft China. London and Norwich, 1905. (Spelman.)

LOWDIN'S BRISTOL FACTORY

W. J. Pountney, The Old Bristol Potteries. London and Bristol, 1920. (Pountney.)

PLYMOUTH AND BRISTOL (CHAMPION'S FACTORY)

Hugh Owen, Two Centuries of Ceramic Art in Bristol. London, 1873. (Owen.)

W. J. Pountney (*see* above).

WORCESTER

R. W. Binns, A Century of Potting in the City of Worcester. London and Worcester, 1865. (Binns.)

R. L. Hobson, Worcester Porcelain. London, 1910.

R. L. Hobson, Catalogue of the Frank Lloyd Collection of Worcester Porcelain of the Wall Period. London, 1923. (*Frank Lloyd Catalogue.*)

NANTGARW AND SWANSEA

William Turner, The Ceramics of Swansea and Nantgarw. London, 1897. (Turner.)

Swansea, Glynn Vivian Art Gallery, Catalogue of a Loan Exhibition, 1914. (*Swansea Exhibition Catalogue.*)

ABBREVIATIONS

B.M.—British Museum. The numbers are those on the labels, corresponding with those in Mr. R. L. Hobson's *Catalogue* (1905).

Schr.—The Schreiber Collection at the Victoria and Albert Museum, South Kensington. The numbers are those of the new *Catalogue* (1928).

V. & A.M.—Victoria and Albert Museum.

CHAPTER I

INTRODUCTION: HISTORICAL AND GENERAL

TECHNICALLY, the history of the earliest English porcelain [1] belongs to that of the numerous attempts made in Europe, from the sixteenth century onwards, to discover a secret for long known only to the Chinese. Attempts of this kind are believed to have been made at one of the Venetian glass-works at least as early as the end of the fifteenth century, but the first European factory to achieve any considerable measure of success was that established at Florence in 1568 by Francesco de' Medici. The material produced there was the first example of the type now known as artificial or soft-paste [2] porcelain, obtaining the quality of translucency from the presence of a substance of the character of an actual glass or frit,[3] and not from the use of the fusible

[1] The word porcelain is apparently derived from the Italian *porcellana*, a cowrie-shell, literally, a little pig. Marco Polo, who reported porcelain in China in the fourteenth century, used the word indifferently for both porcelain and shell.

[2] The name soft-paste is sometimes held to refer to the relative fusibility of the porcelain, in contradistinction to the highly refractory body of hard-paste. But its softness in material is equally characteristic, and the name has passed into common usage in this sense.

[3] In the early manufactures the ingredients forming the glass, sometimes with actual broken glass (cullet), were subjected to a preliminary fusing or "fritting" (the root of the word is the same as in *frying* and *fritter*), and the resulting substance was powdered before the admixture of the clay or chalk which gave the paste its "body" and the resulting china its whiteness. The purpose of this was to "fix" the alkali in the mixture, which would otherwise have crystallised on the drying of the piece and caused it to crumble: see the articles by Mr. Donald A. MacAlister in *The Burlington Magazine*, vol. li (Sept.-Oct. 1927), p. 134, which give a very full account of the

natural silicate of alumina (*petuntse* or china-stone) which combines with china clay (*kaolin*) to form true porcelain of Chinese type. The characteristic hardness of the latter is such that a steel instrument will not readily scratch it. Soft-paste, on the contrary, is easily cut or filed; it has usually but not invariably a sugary fracture, unlike the conchoidal or flinty fracture of true porcelain.[1] Soft-paste is porous and will absorb liquids and so become stained; hard-paste is impervious. In true porcelain the feldspathic glaze material is akin to the body [2] and may be fired with it; in soft-paste a lead glaze is added at a second firing in a "glost" kiln, at a lower temperature. The glaze of the early soft-paste made at Chantilly in France contained a considerable quantity of oxide of tin, the characteristic ingredient which gave whiteness as well as opacity to the glaze of *maiolica*, Delft earthenware and other *faïence*, which is called on this account *tin-enamelled* (or familiarly, *enamelled*). It is probable that varying small quantities of tin-oxide were used also in many English soft-paste glazes: the formula for the Worcester glaze offered to Derby by Richard Holdship [3] in fact included "tin-ashes", and the early Chelsea glaze often has a milkiness suggesting its use. The hard-paste glaze specified by Richard Champion of Bristol also included it.

The importation of tea by the East India Companies in the seventeenth century, with teapots and cups of Chinese porcelain, gave a new impetus to the search for the secret of the Chinese manufacture, but it was not until 1709 that it was re-discovered in Europe

materials used in soft-paste manufacture and their chemical properties. The Handbook to the Jermyn Street Collection (1893) also gives much useful information on the subject.

[1] In his evidence before the House of Commons, Richard Champion, speaking of his hard-paste porcelain, is quoted by Owen (p. 117) as saying "the *Seve* and several other kinds [of soft-paste] . . . when they are broke seem as dry as a Tobacco Pipe, that is the case with all the *English* China; but the *Dresden*, the *Bristol* and the *Asiatic*, China, have when broken a moist and lucid appearance".

[2] It is, in fact, found in association with it, and is the same material a stage removed in the process of decay.

[3] See p. 161.

by Johann Friedrich Böttger at Meissen, near Dresden in Saxony, and in the course of the next fifty years the method was passed on to many other factories in Germany, to Venice, St. Petersburg and elsewhere. Meanwhile, in France, soft-paste porcelain had been made for a short time by Edme and Louis Poterat at Rouen about 1673, and in the first half of the following century factories were in existence at Chantilly, Mennecy, St. Cloud and Vincennes. The last-named was in 1756 transferred to Sèvres, becoming the Royal factory, protected by high customs duties and the rights of monopoly. Soft-paste remained the characteristic French porcelain of the eighteenth century, and though true porcelain began to be made at Sèvres from 1769, the manufacture of the *pâte tendre* was not entirely discontinued until 1804.

In England, John Dwight of Fulham claimed in 1671 to have discovered "the mistery of transparent earthenware, commonly knowne by the names of porcelaine or china"; but the material made by him was almost certainly a thin stoneware,[1] and no porcelain of English manufacture can be ascribed to a date earlier than 1744.[2] A patent for the manufacture of porcelain was in fact taken out in that year by Edward Heylyn

[1] Certain white porcelain mugs in a form common in Fulham stoneware were formerly ascribed to Dwight's manufacture. Similarly, an English origin has been claimed for some white porcelain cups of the same form as the surviving specimen of the stoneware made by Francis Place (*d.* 1728) at York. This specimen, at South Kensington, is accompanied by a certificate in Horace Walpole's handwriting declaring it to be of "Mr. Francis Place's china": clear evidence of the dangerously loose way in which this word was used. These white cups and mugs, however, are all of Chinese origin, of the so-called *blanc de Chine*, from Têhua in the province of Fukien, made to order in European shapes. Chinese specimens in both these forms may be seen in the Museum at South Kensington. The "glass-house clay" mentioned in 1686 by Dr. Plot, Dwight's friend and contemporary (see D. A. MacAlister, *loc. cit.*, p. 139), was not used in the making of artificial porcelain in glass-works, but for the crucibles or pots in which the glass was melted. Opaque white glass owes its opacity to oxide of tin and not to the presence of white clay.

[2] The date 1742, erroneously stated by Church (p. 30) to be inscribed on an ink-stand of Bow porcelain in the Willett Collection at Brighton, is actually *1752*.

and Thomas Frye (who later, in 1748, became the manager of the factory at Bow), but no specimens made as early as this have been certainly identified amongst those surviving. The earliest date recorded in a mark or inscription (1745) occurs on specimens of the "goat-and-bee" jugs from the Chelsea factory.[1] By the middle of the century the Bow and Chelsea factories appear to have been well established, and others, also making soft-paste porcelain, were soon in existence at Bristol, Worcester, Derby, Longton Hall, Liverpool and Lowestoft. These were all conducted by private enterprise, unlike those of the Continent, which were usually subsidised by royal or princely households.

Soft-paste porcelain is of a fragile nature. Not only is the finished product liable to crack at the touch of hot liquids, but it was prone to collapse or lose shape in the kiln, even at the comparatively low temperature required for its firing. Its manufacture was therefore unlikely to prove commercially profitable, and the efforts of English potters were directed to the production of a material less unstable in the kiln and more durable in use. At Bow a novel ingredient in the ash of calcined bones was used with the effect of strengthening the porcelain, and the productions of that factory and of its offshoot Lowestoft were more largely of the character of "useful wares". The risk of breakage from sudden changes of temperature was also considerably reduced by the inclusion in the paste of soapstone (steatite), a substance first employed in England [2] at a Bristol factory, and later the distinctive ingredient of the porcelain made at Worcester, where useful wares always formed a large part of the total output. Soapstone porcelain, which at times approaches true feldspathic porcelain in hardness to the file, was also made

[1] See p. 17.

[2] In China, soapstone was used in the manufacture of the so-called "Chinese soft-paste" porcelain, a decidedly hard feldspathic material, quite distinct from European soft-paste.

for a time at Liverpool and at Caughley, both offshoots of the Worcester factory.

The Chinese method of making hard-paste porcelain was independently re-discovered in England before 1768 and patented in that year by William Cookworthy of Plymouth, whose establishment was transferred in 1770 to Bristol, and three years later purchased by Richard Champion. This manufacture was a precarious one commercially, and unable without subsidy or protection or fashionable patronage to withstand the competition of the cream-coloured earthenware made in Staffordshire in the flourishing industry led by Josiah Wedgwood. In 1781 the patent rights in hard-paste and its materials were sold to a company of Staffordshire potters. The manufacture was gradually discontinued, and by the second decade of the nineteenth century true hard-paste had virtually ceased to be manufactured in England.

Experiments had meanwhile been made, towards the end of the eighteenth century, by the second Josiah Spode of Stoke-on-Trent, by which the essential ingredients of hard-paste were combined in a certain proportion with bone-ash, the same material that had first been used, as already stated, nearly fifty years before as a strengthening ingredient in the soft porcelain of Bow, as well as later in those of Lowestoft, Liverpool, Chelsea and Derby.[1] Spode's hybrid composition, which proved a manageable one, was soon generally adopted, and during the nineteenth century Staffordshire bone-porcelain [2] followed Staffordshire

[1] Appendix B shows clearly the gradual but unfailing supersession of the various eighteenth-century pastes by a composition containing bone-ash.

[2] The distinction attempted by Mr. Harry Barnard (*Chats on Wedgwood Ware*, p. 29) between china (bone-porcelain) and porcelain proper (hard-paste) can scarcely stand. The word china has been in use as a familiar name for porcelain of all kinds, including "the Dresden", since the early eighteenth century. Unfortunately, the word china seems to have been used also, in the seventeenth and eighteenth centuries, for white earthenware painted in Chinese style, and this sometimes makes the contemporary advertisements rather misleading.

cream-coloured earthenware in supplying a world-wide market.

Though Spode's hybrid bone-porcelain remained the English standard, a glassy soft-paste of very beautiful quality but exceedingly unstable in the kiln was made between 1811 and 1819 at Nantgarw and Swansea in Wales and perhaps to a slight extent at Coalport in Shropshire, from the recipe of its inventor, William Billingsley. Amongst the few unusual bodies, introduced for special purposes, may be mentioned the unglazed "Parian porcelain", so-called from its resemblance to the Parian marble of antiquity, introduced in 1846 by the Staffordshire firm of Copeland, Spode's successors at Stoke-on-Trent, and soon adopted by several others. "Parian" was composed of the ingredients of true porcelain in slightly altered proportions. Like the earlier "biscuit" of the Derby factory, which it imitated, it was used principally for figures and the like. The "stone china" and "ironstone china", respectively introduced in 1805 by Spode and patented by Miles Mason of Lane Delph in 1813, were varieties of hard earthenware having some of the characteristics of porcelain.

THE USUAL MODE OF DECORATING ENGLISH PORCELAIN was by painting, most often in fusible enamels over the glaze. In the best artificial porcelains the customary lead glazes melted at a comparatively low temperature and allowed the colours to sink into them with pleasantly soft effect, unlike the refractory feldspathic glazes on which the enamels rest like a superficial incrustation. Of true underglaze colours, cobalt-blue alone was in general use, though rare instances of the use of manganese-purple occur on early Bristol and Longton Hall porcelain.[1] As a ground colour cobalt-blue was ex-

[1] Cobalt-blue, and in certain very difficult circumstances copper-red, alone of the colours known to the eighteenth century will withstand without alteration the high temperature needed for the running of most glazes. Nineteenth-century chemistry, however, brought other underglaze colours, and

tensively employed, both as a coloured glaze and as a "powdered" surface, the latter generally produced by blowing the dry pigment through a tube closed with gauze over the moistened surface of the piece. Printing began to be used soon after 1750. In this process, designs were reproduced by transferring to the surface of the porcelain an impression from an engraved metal plate taken in enamel pigment on paper. At first the colours were applied over the glaze, but the process was before long adopted for designs in underglaze blue.[1] Printing in various colours seems to have been independently invented at various places, and the actual priority of its use at any particular factory cannot yet be proved. It was in use at the Battersea enamel factory between 1750 and 1755, where the engraver Ravenet was employed;[2] at Bristol or Worcester[3] before 1757; and at Liverpool, where John Sadler and Guy Green established printing works about 1756.[4] Printing was also used on Bow china probably dating from the earlier part of the same decade.[5] Extensive use was made of the process at Worcester, where the well-known engraver Robert Hancock executed many designs. By a later method, adopted towards the close of the century, the copperplate was oiled instead of being inked, and the design transferred to the porcelain by means of a flexible glue sheet or "bat". The powdered colour was then dusted on, adhering to the design thus printed in oil. Stipples in the style especially associated with Bartolozzi and Angelica Kauffmann were well-suited to this method, which is still in occasional use, though the general practice has been to revert to the use of paper-transfers.

---

these are in common use to-day. The characteristic underglaze chrome-green was used at Meissen as early as 1817.

[1] At least as early as 1759. See p. 164.

[2] The process is referred to, as practised at Battersea, by Rouquet in *L'État des Arts en Angleterre* (p. 143), a book published in 1755 from notes made two years earlier. Horace Walpole in a well-known letter, dated September 1755, mentioned a printed Battersea enamel snuff-box.

[3] See p. 145. [4] See p. 192. [5] See p. 73.

Gilding was of course much used on the more ambitious pieces. At some early factories (Longton Hall, for instance) the gold was fixed, without firing, merely by oil or japanner's size: this gilding is especially liable to be rubbed away. On the best soft-pastes—at Sèvres and at Chelsea and Worcester in the 1760's and 1770's—gold leaf was ground up with honey and painted on the ware, and then fixed by a gentle firing; this gold had a rich and slightly dull appearance and could be applied thickly and chased with a metal point. Later on the cheaper method of mercury gilding replaced this; an amalgam was applied and the mercury driven off in a vapour by firing. The resulting dull surface then required burnishing, and an excessive brassy polish is the note of the later gilding.

THE FRAGILE CHARACTER OF THE EARLY ENGLISH SOFT-pastes to a large extent forbade their employment in objects of daily use, and their makers were generally content to produce decorative pieces which should compete in charm with the imported Chinese and Japanese wares. These last (particularly the contemporary Chinese *famille rose*, and the "Kakiemon" and "brocaded Imari" porcelains of Japan) were not only copied and adapted directly, but also at second hand from the productions of the older European factories, in particular those of Meissen, themselves often inspired by or copied from Far Eastern models.

But the chief amongst the inventions of the Meissen factory in the second quarter of the eighteenth century were porcelain figures. Figures in enamelled earthenware had been made in Italy in Renaissance times, and later in Holland, sometimes after Chinese models. In China, porcelain had of course for long been employed for this purpose, and statuettes were included in the earliest specimens of the hard brown stoneware made by Böttger in his first attempts towards the discovery of porcelain. But the distinction of first employing glazed porcelain in Europe for small original works of sculpture belongs to the Meissen factory, and in particular to the modeller Johann Joachim Kaendler (1706–1775), to whom can be traced most of the styles seen in mid-eighteenth-century china figures. Kaendler was a modeller of genius and was quick to understand the part which glaze and colour may play in the total effect of a porcelain model. Porcelain became the medium of a branch of *Kleinplastik* bearing the same relation to monumental sculpture as an etching or engraving bears to mural decoration. In Kaendler's hands, it was seldom, as in later times it tended to be, merely a means of reproducing marble or stone sculpture on a small scale. Kaendler's original genius, too, was responsible for the innovation by which porcelain figures came to be used as a satiric commentary on contemporary life. The many novel forms of table-wares with plastic decoration were also due to Kaendler's fertile powers of invention.

Suggestions for models may well have been obtained from the German school of ivory carvers, and some examples may in fact be traced to originals in this material.[1] But in the part they played in the social life of the time porcelain figures appear to have been the successors of those in wax, or in sugar (*Schauessen*), which had been in use for table-decoration at German court festivals. Such figures were often grouped on the tables at the conclusion of a banquet to form connected scenes, mythological or pastoral, with palaces and temples and accessories of various kinds.[2] Figures

[1] See B. Rackham in *The Burlington Magazine*, vol. xxx (1917), p. 168. Kaendler was a pupil of Permoser, and Lück, another Meissen modeller, had also been an ivory carver.

[2] In a Dresden inventory of 1753 a "Temple of Honour in 264 parts" is mentioned. In *The Public Advertiser*, March 1, 1756, were advertised "several very curious desarts used at the most elegant and great entertainments and now divided into proper lots: consisting of Domes, Temples, Triumphal Arches, Epargnes, etc., embellished with Trees, Arbors, Flowers, China Figures, Vauses, Girandols, Candlesticks, Branches, and other ornaments used at Desarts, with several sets of China Dishes, Plates and Tureens". See also King, p. 7, and Adolf Breuning, *Schauessen und Porzellan-plastik*, in *Kunst und Kunsthandwerk*, vol. vii (1906), p. 130.

were also mounted in *ormoulu* to serve as candelabra, and these were often decorated with porcelain flowers. The German fashion was soon brought to England, and Horace Walpole, writing in 1753, remarked that ". . . jellies, biscuits, sugar plumbs and creams have long given way to harlequins, gondoliers, Turks, Chinese and shepherdesses of Saxon china".[1] And these "symbolic, domestic and rustic statuettes" (as Church gravely called them) are the most charming and the most characteristically trivial of all English china of the century. The sale catalogues of English porcelain of this time make frequent mention of objects "for desart", and many figures carrying baskets or receptacles may have been used singly as sweetmeat dishes, rather than as part of a connected scene. Figures of animals and birds were commonly used in this way, and as tureens, in the Meissen style. A little later it became the fashion to use porcelain figures as mantelpiece ornaments, often in sets. To this class belong the numerous examples, for the greater part no earlier than 1760, with elaborate backgrounds of foliage and flowers (*bocages*), as a rule summarily finished at the back and thus obviously unsuited for table use.

In style, the vivacious *rococo* of the 1750's, which affected the forms of vases and ornamental pieces as well as of figures, and the more fantastic manner of the following decade, gave place in the last quarter of the century to the sentimental groups, classical figures and personifications associated with the French *Louis Seize* style. In conformity with the revived fashion for antique marble sculpture, unglazed white porcelain ("biscuit")[2] was often used for figures and groups for which in England the Derby factory was especially famous.

[1] Quoted by Mrs. Arundell Esdaile in *The Observer*, June 22, 1924.

[2] The name "biscuit" is inexplicably given to porcelain of which the body has been fired (once) but not glazed. The fashion for biscuit was led by Sèvres when Bachelier had introduced the material in 1751.

Useful and decorative objects assumed those "classical" forms which, like all too many of their Greek and Roman examples, suggest metal or stone rather than the plastic clay. At first these were commonly tasteful and sometimes beautiful, but pompousness was the note of their early nineteenth-century successors. When these in turn gave way before the "Brighton Pavilion" *chinoiseries* of the Regency and a revived *rococo*, ill-proportioned forms and tasteless extravagances of modelling were the rule; and for the next fifteen or twenty years, lavish decoration of applied flowers in full relief too often accompanied the ostentatious painting and gilding which were fashionable on all but the humblest wares in the second quarter of the nineteenth century.

IN PAINTED DECORATION, KAENDLER'S CONTEMPORARY at Meissen, Johann Gregor Herold, had by 1740[1] created a distinctive European style in porcelain painting. Not only were the characteristic "German" (as distinguished from the Chinese and Japanese, called "Indian") flowers an invention of Herold, but the fantastic *chinoiserie* was invented, or at least first employed, as porcelain decoration during his period of directorship at Meissen.[2]

In England the Meissen flowers were at first frankly copied, though in various highly individual manners, but distinctive English styles of flower-painting were quickly developed, at first at Chelsea and Bow, and afterwards at Worcester and Derby. Many designs, besides those copied from Chinese or Japanese examples, were adapted from engravings, particularly those after Boucher and Watteau, and by the decorative designers (*ornemanistes*) of the period, such as Jean Pillement. Collections of engraved designs of the last-named class

[1] Herold went to Meissen in 1720.

[2] It was in any case fully developed long before the publication of Sir William Chambers's *Chinese Architecture* in 1757, to which event it has sometimes been ascribed. See E. Zimmermann, *Meissner Porzellan*, pp. 66-73 for a full discussion of *chinoiseries* on porcelain.

were published in England under such titles as *The Artist's Vade-Mecum*, *The Draughtsman's Assistant* and *The Ladies' Amusement or the Whole Art of Japanning*. In these are conspicuous the fashionable pastoral subjects as well as the *chinoiseries* already mentioned. Designs after Rubens, Teniers, Wouwerman and Berghem, and engravings from drawings of animals and birds by Francis Barlow, were employed, amongst others, and it is probable that illustrations from botanical treatises were copied for a distinctive series of designs which appear on Chelsea and Bow porcelain.

In the last three decades of the eighteenth century the influence of Sèvres largely superseded that of Meissen. Many designs, such as the "exotic birds", as well as the use of coloured grounds—*gros bleu*, *bleu de roi*, green, turquoise and crimson—and the use of "biscuit" porcelain for figures, are directly traceable to the Sèvres fashions, though the credit for the actual innovation in most cases lies with the Meissen factory.

The "Japan patterns" which were particularly favoured from about 1760 onwards at Worcester, and to a slighter extent at Derby and elsewhere, were very free adaptations of Far Eastern originals, both Chinese and Japanese. In feeling they were of course far removed from their examples, but often fanciful and accomplished in execution. Soon after 1800, however, many coarse "Japan patterns" made their appearance on Spode's porcelain and "ironstone china", as well as on Chamberlain's Worcester and at Derby. The credit (if credit it be) for these patterns is often given to Bloor of the last-named factory, but these loud designs seem to have first appeared in Staffordshire. The phenomenon is sometimes unconvincingly explained by the cutting off of civilising Continental influences during the Napoleonic Wars.

Contemporary with the so-called "return to Nature" in English literature of the late eighteenth and early part of the nineteenth centuries, there appeared a naturalistic style of flower-painting, often associated with the name of William Billingsley. This flower-painting soon developed into a rather mannered style, which was carried to Coalport and Rockingham by the Steeles of Derby and imitated in the Staffordshire factories. This hardened into lifeless formality, and rather after the middle of the century a lax naturalistic style again appeared. About the time of the Great Exhibition of 1851, ambitious attempts were made to rival the finest work of Sèvres, and careful and highly finished painting is found on the best Coalport and Staffordshire porcelain. The subsequent history of English china lies beyond the scope of this book, but I may note here the potter's growing consciousness of "Art" in the period after 1850, the influence of Renaissance styles shown in motives drawn from *maiolica* and Limoges enamels, and the vogue for designs in the style of the Turkish and Syrian pottery called at that time Rhodian and Persian. The influence of Japanese naturalism and asymmetry is also noticeable in the third quarter of the century.

THE CLASSIFICATION OF ENGLISH PORCELAIN OF THE eighteenth century is made difficult by the common absence of factory marks such as were generally used on Continental china, and even where marks occur, they cannot be accepted as proof of origin without confirmation by other evidence. The marks of the larger factories were often employed by their minor rivals. For instance, the anchor of Chelsea was freely used at Derby and Coalport; the Worcester crescent at Bow, Lowestoft and Caughley; whilst even the most respectable establishments are found to have imitated the marks of famous Continental factories. Further, the addition of a mark in enamel-colour or gold at any time after the manufacture of a piece presents no technical difficulty, and this possibility sometimes adds a further element of doubt.[1] Another element of con-

[1] See p. 80 for an example of this.

fusion arises from the practice of several of the earlier factories of selling undecorated porcelain to enamellers working independently.[1] Similarity of painting, therefore, can only be regarded as a reason for grouping a number of specimens if supported by other evidence. Of these enamellers, William Duesbury, afterwards proprietor of the Derby factory, is known from a published work-book for dates between 1751 and 1753 to have painted porcelain from Bow, Chelsea, Derby and Staffordshire factories. Reference will be made[2] to certain examples believed to have been decorated by him. Duesbury apparently worked for several dealers, who purchased china "in the white".[3] Receipted bills from "Richard Dyer, at Mr. Bolton's, enameler, near the church, Lambeth", are among the papers of John Bowcockc, clerk to the Bow factory, but nothing further is known of him.[4] Another London enameller, J. Giles, of Kentish Town and Cockspur Street, is known from advertisements to have decorated Worcester and probably other porcelain to the order of his customers, between 1760 and about 1780. Two miniature-painters, John Donaldson and Jeffrey Hamet O'Neale, also decorated Worcester porcelain in this way, probably in London.[5] At a later date, white or slightly decorated porcelain from Nantgarw and Swansea was painted in London for the firm of Mortlock by Richard Robins and T. M. Randall and the painters in their employment, who also decorated white porcelain from Sèvres in the same way.[6] A similar establishment at Poolbeg Street, Dublin, was carried on about the same time by James Donovan and his son; their

[1] Migrant painters cause a similar difficulty.

[2] P. 62.

[3] A portion of the stock of Thomas Turner, who was among the employers named in Duesbury's work-book, was sold at Christie's in 1767, and included a large proportion of pieces described as "white Chelsea figures". See Nightingale, p. xxxviii, and Bemrose, *Bow, etc., Porcelain*, pp. 7-17.

[4] But see also p. 56.

[5] See p. 176.

[6] See p. 257.

productions, however, were usually marked with their name.[1]

The English porcelain bodies were of widely varied composition, and chemical analysis is sometimes of assistance in confirming attributions made on stylistic grounds; several instances of this will be mentioned in the course of this guide. The use of one particular ingredient, bone-ash, is readily ascertained from the presence of phosphoric acid,[2] and since it is known to have been adopted at certain factories at certain dates, its presence revealed on analysis often provides a last and convincing link in a chain of argument. The value of bone-ash in a porcelain body is sufficiently proved by the later history of English china.[3] We may be sure that once adopted at a factory it would never be abandoned.

Excavations on factory sites can provide evidence of the utmost value; but it must always be remembered that nothing short of an undoubted "waster"[4] can prove conclusively that a particular type was made on the factory site in question. Moulds may have been taken from pieces brought to be copied; and finished pieces, unless of a single type and found in great quantity, may perhaps have been made elsewhere. Excavations proposed at China Walk, Lambeth, may do much to clear up the relations between Bow and Lambeth, the last a factory of which no productions have ever been identified.

In spite of the foreign origin of most of the models employed for figures, and of so many of the usual decorative themes, the earlier English porcelain shows unquestionable originality in interpretation if

[1] A cup and saucer in the British Museum (No. XIV. 10) so marked has the Minton mark also. A vase in the Herbert Allen Collection (No. 588) is a pretentious example of Donovan's painting.

[2] Dr. Harold James Plenderleith has published in *The Burlington Magazine*, vol. li (Sept. 1927), a simple method of testing for phosphoric acid.

[3] See Appendix, p. 278.

[4] That is to say, a piece obviously not finished or fit to be sold.

not in invention. Borrowed styles of painting quickly acquired an individual and English quality, and the scope allowed by the processes of moulding and assembling of the parts of a figure and by its painting in many cases resulted in an entire re-creation of the subject, which assumed a fresh and novel character. This, with a beauty of material and colour, is the chief source of the charm we experience before the best Chelsea and Bow china figures. Even if we do not know the Meissen or other examples from which they were derived, there is probably in most cases an original either in porcelain or some other material waiting to be found. We may, however, ascribe to Nicholas Sprimont the whole invention of the exquisite Chelsea "toys", and many of the figures, alike "red anchor" and "gold anchor", were original in conception. In fact the Chelsea factory was pre-eminent in most respects. For the rest, one may note here the *naïveté* and colour of the early Bow, and the freshness and individuality of the best Longton Hall and Bristol figures. And if Duesbury's Derby china was the product of industry rather than art, and this is especially true of the figures, the factory has the credit of creating many beautiful things in the table-wares of the last thirty years of the eighteenth century. Worcester of the "Dr. Wall period" stands a little apart; its best and earliest work has something of the Bow simplicity, its later boasts much of the Chelsea splendour, and in all there is an especially English quality that endears it to the collector.

A

B

C

D E F

About 1745–50. C, E and F have the triangle-mark.
(*Mr. Wallace Elliot's, the Schreiber and the V. and A. Museum Collections.*)
See pp. 17, 19, 20.

A B C

D E F

G

About 1750. E has the raised-anchor mark.
(*Mr. O. Glendenning's, Mr. Alfred E. Hutton's, the London Museum and Schreiber Collections.*)
See pp. 23 to 26.

CHAPTER II

CHELSEA

THE earliest specimens of porcelain presumed to have been made at Chelsea are the famous "goat-and-bee" jugs, incised with the word *Chelsea*, the date 1745 and a triangle.[1] A specimen with these marks is in the British Museum (No. II. 16 A). Others, lacking the date and name and marked only with the triangle, are at South Kensington, in the Schreiber Collection, No. 117 (plain white, Plate 1 F), and in the Museum Collection (No. 2875—1901), painted in colours. These jugs are usually in the form of a vessel supported on the back of two reclining goats, with a twig handle and a bee in relief under the lip, though the bee is sometimes absent. The form is copied from a silver model, of which an example existing in 1912[2] was stated to bear the hall-mark for 1724. We have, however, no information whatever regarding the name of their maker and the date of foundation of the factory.

No earlier reference to the actual factory has yet been found than that contained in the *London Trades-*

[1] See Appendix A, p. 259, No. 1. An example with date, name and triangle (formerly in the collection of Mr. William Russell) was first described by Sir A. W. Franks in *The Archaeological Journal*, vol. xix (1862), p. 340; illustrated by Jewitt, vol. i, p. 193. The model has been reproduced in Staffordshire earthenware as well as in Coalport porcelain.

[2] Chaffers, 13th edition (1912), p. 947. An example stated to bear the London hall-mark for 1737, and the initials EW (for Edward Wood), was illustrated in *The Cheyne Book*, No. 14.

man of 1747,[1] speaking of attempts to make "Porcelain or China-ware" at Greenwich[2] and Chelsea. More definite evidence is contained in two newspaper advertisements of 1750[3] in which N. Sprimont, speaking for the "Chelsea Porcelaine Manufacture", disclaimed connection with a "Chelsea China Warehouse"; to which S. Stables, writing from the latter, replied that he was supplied by no other than Charles Gouyn, "late Proprietor and Chief Manager of the Chelsea-House". The factory has been shown by a lease to have been situated at the corner of Justice Walk, occupying also the houses at the upper end of Lawrence Street.[4]

Nicholas Sprimont (*b.* 1716, *d.* 1771[5]) was a silversmith of Compton Street, Soho, whose name had been entered at Goldsmiths' Hall in 1742 as that of a plateworker. A pair of oval silver-gilt dishes made by him, dated 1743–44, with scalloped edges and shells and coral in high relief, is now in the collection at Buckingham Palace.[6] In view of the early use of silver models, it seems likely that Sprimont was connected with the work almost from the first, and that the advertisements of 1750 were issued on the occasion of his assuming the management of a factory in which he had been previously employed as modeller or designer. Nothing is known of Gouyn, though he is sometimes considered to have been the silversmith who inspired the early models. The name, like that of Sprimont,

[1] Nightingale, p. viii.

[2] Greenwich porcelain (if it was ever made) has not yet been identified.

[3] *The Daily Advertiser*, May 15, 1750, and *The General Advertiser*, Jan. 29, 1750. See Nightingale, p. v.

[4] See map in *The Cheyne Book*, p. 20.

[5] He was buried in Petersham Churchyard, Richmond, Surrey. See an article by Dr. H. Bellamy Gardner in *The Connoisseur*, vol. lxv (1923), p. 159.

[6] Formerly at Windsor Castle and exhibited at the Special Loan Exhibition at South Kensington, 1862, Catalogue Nos. 5941-2. A pair of sauce-boats made by Sprimont, said to bear the hall-mark for 1746, were exhibited at Chelsea in 1924 (*Cheyne Book*, No. 11): they are not dissimilar to the triangle-marked sauce-boats mentioned below.

suggests a French or Flemish origin,[1] and an analysis of the paste of the earlier Chelsea porcelain shows a high percentage of lime (probably derived from chalk), a characteristic also of French soft-pastes. It may thus perhaps be conjectured that Gouyn was concerned with the technical part of the manufacture: he was possibly the chemist referred to in an unsigned document (evidently written by Sprimont) in the British Museum, entitled *The Case of the Undertaker of the Chelsea Manufacture of Porcelain Ware*.[2] Appealing for heavier import duties on "Dresden" (Meissen) china, the writer speaks of himself as a silversmith by profession who had begun to make porcelain after "a casual acquaintance with a chymist who had some knowledge that way". That Gouyn or someone connected with the Chelsea factory had been employed at the French works at St. Cloud [3] is suggested by a resemblance not only in paste but in the modelling of some grotesque figures, such as a teapot in the British Museum in the form of a seated Chinaman.[4] A similar teapot, delightfully modelled, with the spout in the form of a parrot, from Mr. Wallace Elliot's collection, is figured in Plate 1E. On the other hand, it is noteworthy that nothing resembling the characteristic St. Cloud painting in underglaze blue is found on Chelsea porcelain. The "chymist" may have been a technician only.

[1] See Church (*English Porcelain*, p. 18), who asserts that both Sprimont and Gouyn are Flemish names. Horace Walpole (*Letters*, ed. Mrs. Toynbee, vol. v, p. 291), writing in 1763 (see below, p. 45), spoke of Sprimont as a Frenchman; and Rouquet in *L'État des Arts en Angleterre*, a book published in 1755, but based on notes of a visit two years earlier, spoke of "un habile artiste françois" as director of the factory.

[2] Lansdowne MSS. No. 829, fol. 21. Quoted in full by Marryat, *History of Pottery and Porcelain* (3rd edition), p. 373, and Jewitt, vol. i, p. 171. See also King, p. 33.

[3] Of the other French factories, Chantilly and Mennecy were princely concerns, whilst Vincennes had by 1745 scarcely begun to make porcelain in any quantity.

[4] *Catalogue*, No. II. 12. Both St. Cloud and Chelsea pieces may, however, have a parallel derivation from the so-called Callot figures of Meissen porcelain.

THE EARLY CHELSEA PORCELAIN OF THE TYPE MARKED with a triangle is a very translucent material, resembling milk-white glass;[1] transmitted light reveals small flecks which show a greater translucency than the surrounding paste. In addition to the "goat-and-bee" jugs, we may single out as especially fine and characteristic specimens the teapots and cups and saucers in the form of overlapping strawberry leaves (Plate I C), of which there are examples at South Kensington and Bloomsbury. The saucer figured in Plate I B is a rare and charming piece. Sauce-boats with festoons and masks in relief (such as Schr. No. 129), and fluted dishes (Plate I A) are all in forms manifestly derived from silver. The well-known pattern of "raised flowers" is obviously of the same origin: examples are in the British Museum and Schreiber Collections (Plate I D). Where painting has been added to these early pieces, it is generally of a rather artless but not unattractive quality, the small detached flower-sprays and insects serving to conceal blemishes in the material. Rather laboured "Meissen flowers" are more rarely seen on triangle-marked pieces, as on a pair of cups in the London Museum.[2] A triangle-marked teapot in the Schreiber Collection (No. 130) is painted with a Japanese design in the style of Kakiemon,[3] but this decoration was probably added some years after the manufacture of the porcelain. That stock was kept in this way is shown by the occur-

[1] A marked strawberry-leaf jug in the Trapnell Collection was actually catalogued as Bristol Glass.

[2] Painting in precisely the same style occurs on two dishes in the Schreiber Collection (No. 180), marked with the raised anchor, and supplies evidence of continuity between the earliest and the later periods. Another style of painting in a style derived from Meissen is seen on two vases in Mr. Alfred Hutton's collection figured in an article by Dr. Bellamy Gardner in *The Connoisseur*, vol. lxxvi (1926), p. 232, where several other interesting painted specimens are reproduced.

[3] The potter Kakiemon, who worked at Arita in the mid-seventeenth-century, gave his name to a school of decoration of which the characteristic productions have slight painting mainly in red, blue, turquoise and green. Arita porcelain is usually known as "Imari", from its place of export Many copies of the Kakiemon designs will be noticed in this book.

rence in the catalogue of the sale of 1756 of two "beautiful crawfish salts". These are not uncommon (a pair is in the British Museum, No. II. 18), and are generally marked with the triangle. Horace Walpole in his description of Strawberry Hill made an often-quoted reference to a pair. Of figures belonging to this period we know very few, apart from the *Chinaman* teapots. But a group of *Lovers* in the British Museum (No. II. 6 A) may be put down to this time by the evidence of its mark, a trident intersecting a crown, in underglaze blue, which occurs also on a cup with "raised flowers" in Mr. Frank Hurlbutt's collection and on a strawberry-leaf cream-jug in Dr. J. W. L. Glaisher's collection.[1] Other figures are sometimes conjecturally given to the factory for this period on the evidence of a paste showing pin-holes by transmitted light, a feature of many triangle-marked pieces, but the evidence cannot be considered conclusive, since pieces apparently of different origin show a similar appearance.[2]

It is probable that the scratched triangle was used only on pieces made before 1750, when Sprimont became manager, though the milk-white porcelain of the dated jugs apparently gave place to a harder and rather colder-looking material before the models of the early period ceased to be employed. A coffee-pot in Mr. Alfred Hutton's collection,[3] marked with a triangle, with "raised flowers" of the kind just mentioned, is from the same mould as another (unmarked) at South Kensington (No. 3238—1853), which is of a colder white approaching the colour of the "raised-anchor" paste of the next period. It is possible that the later

[1] See an article by Dr. H. Bellamy Gardner in *The Connoisseur*, vol. lxiv, (October 1922). Chaffers (*Marks and Monograms*, 8th edition, 1897) also asserts that the mark occurs in combination with the incised triangle.

[2] The *Waterman with Doggett's Badge* and the *Fortune-telling Group* conjecturally ascribed to this period in Mr. King's *Chelsea Porcelain* (p. 22) would now be classed as Bow (see p. 68); for another series discussed by Mr. King, and ascribed to the factory in this period, see below, p. 23.

[3] *Cheyne Book*, No. 30.

cool white body was introduced, in preference to the earlier, more glassy porcelain, as more manageable, and in particular as more suitable for use in the thicker masses required for the figures which now began to be made in some quantity; and that the mark of an anchor[1] in relief on an applied oval medallion was introduced to distinguish this paste so soon as it was proved. It is very likely that the marks employed at Chelsea at first indicated different pastes. Since a glaze needs to be suited to the composition of a body, it would obviously be desirable for a factory to record the latter, for its own information, by a mark in the paste, especially when pieces of several varieties of body were stocked in biscuit condition over a long period. I have already mentioned two instances suggesting that stock was held in this way at Chelsea. The introduction of the mark of the gold anchor in the last period, though coinciding with a change of paste, could not of course have the same significance, since it was painted over the glaze.

Some Chelsea porcelain of this second period, however, seems to have been left unmarked, and its identification therefore depends upon resemblances in style to the marked pieces. I may mention as typical of the latter some pieces painted in the Kakiemon manner: for example, the pair of bottles in the British Museum (No. II. 20); a figure of a stork and the famous *Nurse and Child* copied from a late sixteenth-century earthenware model made at Avon, near Fontainebleau, and ascribed to Barthélemy de Blémont (or Bertélémy de Blénod), but sometimes erroneously attributed to Palissy.[2] Plain white examples of the two last

[1] It has been supposed (Church, p. 29) that the anchor mark indicates a connection with a glass-house said to have been started at Chelsea by some Venetians in 1676, under the patronage of the Duke of Buckingham, but this connection is a pure conjecture. The anchor in Chelsea is never as large as on Venice porcelain.

[2] See M. L. Solon, *History and Description of Old French Fayence*, p. 35, where a copy signed BB is mentioned; and M. J. Ballot, *Musée du Louvre: La Céramique française—Bernard Palissy et les fabriques du XVIe siècle* p. 31, Plate 47.

are in the Schreiber Collection (Nos. 121 and 122), and a *Nurse* in colours is at the British Museum (II. 34). The mark occurs also on some copies of the *blanc de Chine* of Fukien province: a plate in the British Museum (No. II. 10) is decorated with the applied sprays of plum-blossom more familiar on the rival Bow porcelain, as are the fine substantial cup and saucer in Mr. Alfred Hutton's collection, figured in Plate 2 E. In Mrs. Radford's collection is a figure of Kuan-yin, obviously moulded from a Chinese specimen in the same material. The raised anchor occurs on the exceedingly rare transfer-printed Chelsea porcelain, of which there is a specimen of very unusual character in the British Museum (an octagonal saucer, No. II. 244). It is not certain that this mode of decoration was ever actually employed at Chelsea, though at the neighbouring Battersea enamel factory it was much in favour. The existing specimens may well have been decorated there.[1] An advertisement in the *Liverpool Advertiser* for February 11, 1757, quoted by Mr. Hobson,[2] mentions "printing . . . upon porclane, enamel and earthenware . . . as lately practised at Chelsea, Birmingham, etc.". But probably Chelsea and Battersea were confused. The raised anchor also occurs on many pieces belonging by their decoration rather to the next period. In fact, it is scarcely possible to define a style of "raised-anchor" painting: some immaturity is perhaps noticeable more on these than on the red-anchor-marked specimens, but otherwise the styles are alike and will be discussed later.

A much-discussed class of pieces attributable to Chelsea and often considered to date from the first period may conveniently be described here. A *Girl in a Swing*,[3] a *Boy playing a Hurdy-gurdy*, and his dancing companion,[4] all at South Kensington (Nos. C 587—1922, C 689—1920, and C 328—1919), are typical

[1] See also p. 252. [2] *Catalogue*, p. 61.
[3] An example is reproduced in W. King, *English Porcelain Figures* Fig. 16.
[4] Figured in W. King, *Chelsea Porcelain*, Plate 11.

examples, left unpainted as are most of the class. A specimen of the *Boy* has been analysed by Mr. Herbert Eccles [1] and proved to contain an unusual quantity of lead, suggesting the use of flint-glass cullet in place of the usual mixture of sand, lime and alkali, and I think we shall be justified in conjecturing these pieces to be largely experimental productions, made as trials of new recipes before the final establishment of the raised-anchor paste. Some specimens are defective (one of *Ganymede* in Mr. Glendenning's possession has even received its glaze-firing, though the legs of the figure were damaged before it was fired to the biscuit state); some have partially collapsed in the kiln; and their undecorated state is also a confirmation of the view that for the greater part they were never considered to be worth finishing. For their identification as Chelsea productions we have, I think, sufficient evidence. Though the paste has proved different, the appearance of the glaze is very like that of "raised-anchor" Chelsea and quite unlike that of any other factory, whilst the tree-stumps and the form of the leaves on the support for the *Girl in a Swing*—thick and flat and rather stiff, with serrated edges—is exactly repeated in many raised- and red-anchor models (for example, the *Woman with a Basket* figured in Plate 12). For their date we have a figure of *Britannia* mourning the death of Frederick, Prince of Wales,[2] who died in 1751. The modelling of the head and slender limbs of Britannia in this figure is exactly that of many others. I reproduce a rare and unusually fine example of the class in Mr. Glendenning's *Europa* (Plate 2 G). The fine *Hercules and Omphale* in the Schreiber Collection (No. 120) shows similar

[1] See King, *op. cit.*, p. 23.

[2] Figured in King, *op. cit.*, Plate 8, and *Cheyne Book*, No. 213 (Plate 2). The figure in the British Museum (No. I. 3) of Britannia seated on a globe apparently also belongs to this class: it has been tested and found non-phosphatic—see *British Museum Quarterly*, vol. ii, No. 1, p. 31, where it is figured. The blank tablet in this is a confirmation of the view taken above that these are experimental pieces. Their collapsing was caused by too much lead-flux.

A

B

C

"Kakiemon" patterns. About 1750–56. C has the red-anchor mark.
(*V. and A. Museum and the Schreiber Collections.*) See p. 28.

A

B

A is painted in blue; blue-anchor mark. About 1755. (*Schreiber Collection.*)
B. "Kakiemon" design; red-anchor mark. About 1750–56. (*V. and A. Museum.*)
See pp. 28, 29.

A

B

About 1755. Red-anchor marks.
(*V. and A. Museum and Mr. Alfred E. Hutton's Collections.*)
See p. 31.

A B C

D

About 1755.

B, C and D have the red-anchor mark.

D is in *Mr. Alfred E. Hutton's Collection*; the others in the *Schreiber* and *V. and A. Museum Collections.*

See pp. 31, 32, 33.

A

B

C

About 1755.
A and C have the red-anchor mark.
(*Schreiber and V. and A. Museum Collections.*)
See pp. 32, 33.

A

B

About 1755.
Painting in crimson monochrome; B has the red-anchor mark.
(*Schreiber and Mr. Herbert Allen's Collections.*)
See p. 31.

A

B

A. Dish, *famille rose* style. About 1755.
B. Dish, "brocaded Imari" style. About 1755.
(*Mr. Herbert Allen's Collection.*)
See pp. 29, 46.

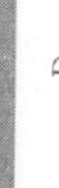

D

B

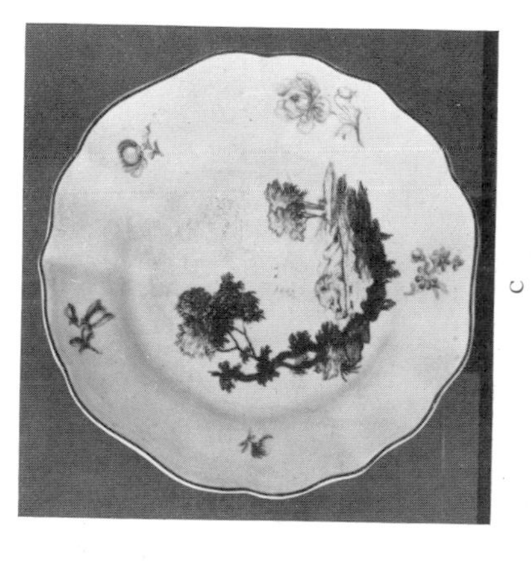

C

A

About 1750–55.

B and C are painted in crimson and have the red- and raised-anchor marks respectively; A and D are painted in colours.

(*Schreiber and V. and A. Museum Collections.*) See pp. 31, 32.

features in the head of *Omphale*. It has been conjectured by Mr. William King that the hollow tops of the tree-stumps in the *Girl in the Swing* were intended to hold porcelain flowers, such as were made at Vincennes. We have no evidence that these were made at Chelsea before 1755 [1] (when they are mentioned in a sale catalogue), though they may have been, and a date later than 1751 rather than earlier would be suggested by this feature. Coloured examples of this group are of rare occurrence. A figure of the *Dancing Girl* in Col. and Mrs. Dickson's collection [2] shows colouring decidedly late in style, resembling Bow work of about 1760–65. It is more than likely, however, that this is an example of the work of an outside decorator, added to a figure of earlier date.

Closely akin to the pieces just described are some others, represented here by a taper-stick from the London Museum (Plate 2 C) and by Mr. Hutton's white *Bird* (Plate 2 A) and *Girl with a Basket* (Plate 2 B). Mr. King has found an interesting link with admitted Chelsea in the correspondence between the last-named figure and a Chelsea toy.[3] A base with curved bevelling is found on pieces of this class: it may be compared with the simply chamfered bases of the others. The modelling of the figures shows the same slenderness. Besides the flat leaves, flowers of a peculiar convex form decorate the supports of these; they resemble, but are not identical with, those on a large white figure of a *Gardener's Companion*,[4] in Dr. and Mrs. H. Bellamy Gardner's collection, which is marked with the raised anchor. The glaze of all these is even closer to that of "raised-anchor" Chelsea than in the case of the *Girl in the Swing* family, and the painting on the examples I

[1] There are examples that are probably of Chelsea manufacture at the British Museum.

[2] Figured in F. Hurlbutt, *Bow Porcelain*, Plate 33.

[3] *Op. cit.*, p. 23.

[4] Figured in King, *English Porcelain Figures*, Fig. 17 and in the *Cheyne Book*, No. 215, Plate 1.

have reproduced is not far removed from the more primitive styles found on some "raised-" and "red-anchor" pieces. The finely modelled *Hound*, also figured in Plate 2, may be linked with the others on the showing of its paste and glaze.

A series of important white pieces dating from this time, and in their modelling standing apart from the others, includes busts of *King George II.* (Schr. No. 126), of George III. as *Prince of Wales* [1] and of the *Duke of Cumberland* (Schr. No. 127: Plate 2 D). There is every reason to regard these as Chelsea on the ground of paste and glaze. The traditional association with the factory of the French sculptor Louis François Roubiliac [2] has been discovered to have a foundation in fact, since Nicholas Sprimont is known to have stood as godfather to a daughter of the sculptor,[3] and an impressed R often found on certain later Chelsea models [4] was formerly believed to indicate Roubiliac's work, but marks of this kind are more probably those of "repairers", or workmen responsible for assembling the parts, rather than that of the artist responsible for the original model for a figure. It is quite likely, however, that these Royal portraits were modelled by Roubiliac, to whose work they show a distinct resemblance. A bust of George II. at Windsor Castle signed by Roubiliac shows considerable resemblance to the Chelsea piece, though different in detail. Some examples of the Royal busts were stated by Franks [5] to bear the raised-anchor mark (though I have never seen one), which is, however, found on the *Sphinxes* (such as Schreiber No. 125), which are usually of similar cool white porcelain. A beautiful bust of a *Boy* in Dr. and Mrs. Bellamy Gardner's collec-

[1] *Cheyne Book*, No. 212 (Plate 1), and King, Plate 15.

[2] Roubiliac was born in 1695, came to England about 1738 and died in 1762.

[3] Mrs. Arundell Esdaile has kindly pointed out a passage relating to this in the *Publications of the Huguenot Society*, vol. xxvi. Further particulars will be given in her forthcoming *Life* of Roubiliac.

[4] See p. 41.

[5] *Loc. cit.*, p. 345.

tion also belongs to this series. Dr. Gardner has also pointed out the resemblance borne by his white figure of a *Gardener's Companion*, mentioned in the last paragraph, to a statue of *Eloquence* by Roubiliac, on the monument to the Duke of Argyll in Westminster Abbey, erected in 1743.[1]

Another fine and important series, some Chinese groups,[2] for long assigned to Chelsea and apparently of this period, cannot be convincingly linked with the other productions of the factory, and they are probably of Derby origin.[3] The figures of Mrs. Kitty Clive and Henry Woodward, as the *Fine Lady and Gentleman*, and of Quin as *Falstaff*, sometimes ascribed to Chelsea, are now attributed to Bow for reasons stated on page 60.

MOST OF THE CHELSEA PRODUCTIONS OF THE FINE middle period of the factory may be readily identified by a cautious acceptance of the customary mark of a small anchor in red enamel.[4] This was sometimes painted over the raised mark, which as I have explained apparently continued in use for some time concurrently with the painted mark. We may assume that the raised anchor ceased to be used when it was no longer necessary to distinguish the reformed paste from that of the first period and those tried experimentally. Surviving catalogues of the second and third annual sales of the factory's productions, held in 1755[5] and 1756,[6] afford a pleasant opportunity for identifying many existing pieces. Sales were advertised in 1754,[7] but no copies of the catalogues are known to survive.

[1] *The Connoisseur*, vol. lxv (1923), p. 150. See also p. 36 below for another, rather later, class which may be Roubiliac's work.

[2] Such as the *Chinaman and Boy*, Plate 35.

[3] See p. 85.

[4] The inexperienced collector will often overlook the tiny anchor mark of Chelsea—raised, red and gold—which is often tucked away in the most unexpected places, and only occasionally appears on the base of a figure.

[5] Reprinted in W. King, *Chelsea Porcelain* (1922), pp. 69-130.

[6] Reprinted in R. W. Read, *The Original Catalogue of One Year's Curious Production of the Chelsea Porcelain Manufactory*. Salisbury, 1880.

[7] See Nightingale, pp. ix and x.

The exceptionally beautiful porcelain of the red-anchor period has a very soft paste of fine grain, often showing by transmitted light the round spots of higher translucency known to collectors as "moons" [1] and due to the presence of large pieces or aggregations of frit. According to Mr. William Burton the admixture of coarser frit was a device intended to prevent loss of shape in the kiln. The glaze is smooth and even, of a cool white, seldom crazed, and free from the black specks which sometimes disfigure the raised-anchor-marked pieces. The raised- and red-anchor pastes and glazes, however, appear to have been essentially the same. An almost constant feature of red-anchor pieces is the appearance of three or four small round "spur" marks on the base. These very distinctive characteristics greatly assist the identification of the relatively few unmarked Chelsea pieces of this period.

Chelsea painting in this period was almost always of great distinction and originality of handling, though many of the designs were of Japanese or German invention. Free copies of the Japanese designs in the so-called Kakiemon style (Plates 3 and 4 B) were especially popular and were designated in the Catalogues of 1755 and 1756 as "wheatsheaf and pheasant", "tyger and wheatsheaf", "tyger and rock", "nurl'd partridge pattern", and "octogon plate, Hob in the Well". The last was apparently the name of a popular play of the time, misapplied to a Japanese design illustrating the story of a boy who saved the life of a companion by breaking a water-jar into which he had fallen. A Chelsea example of the design is at South Kensington (C 1330—1924). The large hexagonal vases (Schr. Nos. 156 and 157, and B.M. No. II. 21), the bowls (Schr. No. 161), and the cups and saucers (V. & A.M. No. C 1067—1924, and Schr. No. 163: Plate 3) show the Chelsea treatment of these designs, which were all most probably copied at second hand, through versions

[1] These were first observed by the famous collector Dr. H. W. Diamond

made at Meissen.[1] The form of the bowls with outturned rim (as in the Schreiber Collection, Nos. 167 and 187: Plate 6) was also exactly copied from Japanese porcelain of this type. Why one of the Kakiemon designs was called the "old pattern" in the Catalogue is not clear. Chinese designs were more rarely used: a saucer-dish in the Allen Collection (No. 88: Plate 9 A) is a charming original composition only slightly resembling the *famille rose* design by which it was inspired. The decoration on a basin of Japanese form in the Schreiber Collection (No. 167) is a version of Chinese painting of the *famille verte*. Blue-and-white porcelain, which inspired so much of the decoration at other factories, seems to have enjoyed but little favour at Chelsea. The only known specimens in this mode are certain plates (examples are in both the National collections [2]), marked with a blue anchor and painted with a bird and plants in the Chinese style (Plate 4 A: Schr. Collection No. 128). They are of an extremely rare and pleasant quality in both colour and glaze. The "India plants" of the Chelsea catalogues were probably the *indianische Blumen* of early Meissen, adapted from Chinese designs. Like most Eastern things at this time, Chinese and Japanese were alike "Indian", from the name of the importing "East India Companies".[3] The familiar reddish-brown edge of the Chinese "export porcelain" was largely copied, with a totally different effect, on Chelsea china of this period. Gilt-edges are seldom seen, and gilding is in fact generally absent.

Meissen designs were at first quite frankly imitated.[4]

[1] Compare E. Zimmermann, *Meissner Porzellan* (1926), Taf. 5.

[2] Schr. No. 128 and B.M. II. 56.

[3] "India plants" may, however, have been a name for the exotics so delightfully copied on such pieces as that figured in Plate 7 C.

[4] It has been argued by Mrs. Arundell Esdaile (*Some Eighteenth-Century Literary Allusions to Chelsea China* in the *Burlington Magazine*, vol. xlvi, Jan. 1925), that Meissen examples were copied as early as 1744. The specimen cited, a "tankard" with a harbour scene, is of a type one would expect to find marked with a raised or red anchor, and we have no other evidence

It is known from a letter dated 1751[1] that pieces of Meissen porcelain, the property of Sir Charles Hanbury Williams, were lent for copying at Chelsea to Sir Everard Fawkener, who was stated in the letter to be "concerned in the manufacture of China at Chelsea . . ." The writer added, ". . . I find that the Duke is a great encourager of the Chelsea China". This is a reference to the Duke of Cumberland, whose secretary Fawkener became in 1744.[2] Scattered bunches of half-naturalistic flowers were directly copied from the *deutsche Blumen* of the Saxon factory, which also furnished the models for the moulded patterns of the rims, the "nurl'd [or gnarled] borders" of the catalogues. (It is noteworthy that silversmith's terms were often employed in descriptions in the Catalogue of 1755, even for pieces apparently not specifically of silver shape. "Chas'd", "wro't", "scollop't" and "nurl'd" constantly occur in the descriptions.) But before long the Chelsea painters developed several highly individual styles. On a seemingly early bottle of Chinese form

that pieces so marked can be ascribed to so early a date—a year earlier, it should be noted, than the "goat-and-bee" jugs. Crude versions of Meissen flowers on triangle-marked pieces have already been mentioned. Mrs. Esdaile further quotes a letter from Lord Chesterfield dated August 9, 1750, referring to a "little snuff-box", apparently of Chelsea china, and saying "how well we imitate the Dresden china, and for less than a quarter the price". About a year later, Lord Chesterfield sent "two china baubles", unspecified, to the same correspondent in Paris, who sent in return a present of china, apparently of French make, which "the manager" of "our manufacture" (presumably Nicholas Sprimont) begged to be allowed to borrow "for a pattern". One may guess that this was Mennecy or St. Cloud porcelain and served as inspiration for the Chelsea "toys". Nothing of Vincennes origin of this date seems to have been copied at Chelsea.

[1] See a letter from the Earl of Ilchester to the *Burlington Magazine*, vol. xx (1911–12), p. 361.

[2] It was stated by Mason, a workman at the factory (in an account quoted by Chaffers, 3rd edition (1870), p. 701) that the manufacture was at first carried on by the Duke of Cumberland and Sir Everard Fawkener, who employed "a foreigner of the name of Sprimont . . . at a salary of a guinea per day"; but the Duke's concern was probably limited to patronage only. Rouquet (*op. cit.*, p. 143) said of the factory ". . . un riche particulier en soutient la dépense". At a later date (1764) Sprimont, in an advertisement, contradicted the statement that the Duke of Cumberland proposed "to purchase the secret", "that so matchless an art should not be lost".

which belonged to Jewitt, and is now in the Schreiber Collection (No. 155), the rather immature painting of a landscape already shows an original touch. The bowl (Schr. No. 187) figured in Plate 6 C shows a scarcely modified Meissen style, whilst the plate of silver form in Plate 5 A illustrates the typical Meissen-Chelsea flowers of this period. In *The Case of the Undertaker of the Chelsea Manufacture*, already quoted, the writer speaks of the employment of ". . . . a nursery of thirty lads . . . bred to designing and painting", and the Chelsea painting may perhaps be indebted to these for its freshness, as much as to Fawkener and Sprimont for their taste in the direction of the work.

A gifted painter [1] with a manner all his own is associated in particular with a number of pieces with delightful designs illustrating Aesop's Fables (Plate 10). Dr. Bellamy Gardner has shown [2] that some of these designs seem to have been suggested by an edition of the fables illustrated by Francis Barlow. The pattern of some splendid large dishes (Schreiber No. 182), which combines the scattered Meissen flowers with vivaciously rendered border-panels of figures and landscapes by this "Fable Painter", is known as the "Warren Hastings pattern", from a set with this design having formed part of his effects at a sale at Daylesford House in 1818. (Plate 5 B shows a smaller example with charming groups of figures.) The same hand is seen in the attractive painting in crimson monochrome, the "purple landskips" of the catalogues, very well represented by a bowl (Plate 8 A) and a cup (Plate 10 B) in the Schreiber Collection (Nos. 168 and 169), and Mr. Allen's dish figured in Plate 8 B. This manner was a Meissen invention, and landscape styles from the same source, translated into English, are seen on the

[1] The names of the earlier Chelsea painters have never been discovered. The gossiping and inaccurate J. T. Smith in his *Nollekens and his Times* mentions one Paul Ferg, apparently the son of an artist of the same name but we have no means of identifying his work.

[2] *The Connoisseur*, vol. lxiv (Oct. 1922).

dish (Allen No. 84) and a charming cream-jug (Schr. 191: Plate 6 A), all probably by the hand of the same "Fable Painter". The river-scene on the pretty saucer shown in Plate 10 D depicts a church which it is tempting to identify with that at Chelsea.[1] A rare style of figure-painting, perhaps inspired by Meissen, is represented by a bowl in Mr. Bunford's collection[2] painted with cupids bearing a basket of grapes, in light brick-red; a cup and saucer similarly decorated is in Mr. Wallace Elliot's collection.[3] The charming piece figured in Plate 6 D, with figures of children framed in a *rococo* scroll, shows the red-anchor style of painting at its most gracious. A novel manner of flower-painting, first found on Chelsea porcelain of this period, was apparently borrowed from a botanical treatise still unidentified. This kind of decoration became common, and rather dull, on later English porcelain—at Derby and Swansea, for instance; but at Chelsea the freedom and feeling with which the painter interpreted his subjects entitle such examples as the plate at South Kensington (No. 2953—1901) and the cups and saucers in the Schreiber Collection (Plate 7 A and C) to rank among the finest achievements of the factory, beautiful alike in drawing and colour. Of the same high quality are the cups, tureens and sauce-boats of a very distinctive class (again suggested by Meissen), in which applied leaves and flowers and twig handles, beautifully painted in by no means natural colours, play an important part in many fanciful but always harmonious compositions. A masterpiece of this class is a large tureen in the collection at South Kensington[4] with forget-me-nots in relief, well described in the 1755 Catalogue as "a beautiful round tureen and cover, sprig handles, and a dish to ditto enamell'd with blue flowers". The mono-

[1] A similar picture of Battersea Church occurs in a gold-anchor piece painted in black and green (see p. 45).
[2] *Cheyne Book*, No. 24 (Plate 3).
[3] Figured in *The Connoisseur*, vol. lxxix (Sept. 1927), p. 9.
[4] No. 2062—1901.

A

B

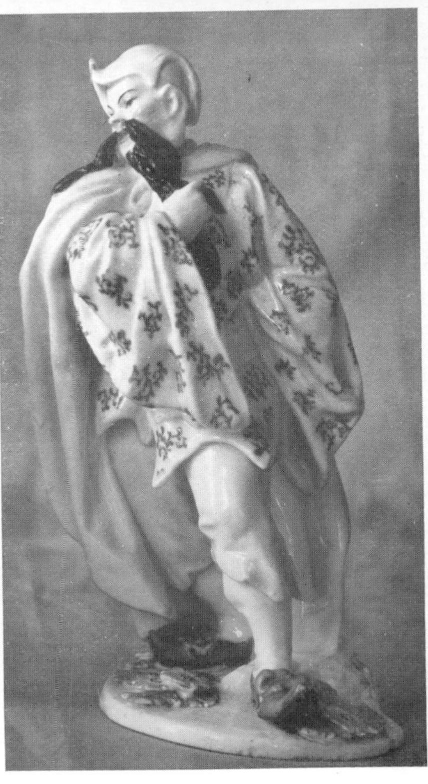

C

About 1755–56. Red-anchor mark.

(*Mr. Alfred E. Hutton's Collection.*) See p. 34.

A

B

C

About 1755. Red-anchor marks.
A is in the *Schreiber Collection* and B and C in *Lord and Lady Fisher's Collection.*
See pp. 34, 35.

A, B, C. Figures of birds, raised-anchor mark.
Height: $8\frac{1}{4}$ in., 6 in., $6\frac{3}{4}$ in. respectively. About 1750.
D. Tureen, red-anchor mark. Height: $8\frac{7}{8}$ in. About 1755.

(*Schreiber Collection.*)

See pp. 33, 37.

A

B

Gold-anchor mark. About 1760–65.
(*V. and A. Museum and Schreiber Collections.*)
See pp. 45, 46.

chrome-blue flowers are of exquisite softness. The characteristic applied leaves are seen by the handle of the beautifully painted jug figured in Plate 6 B (No. C 945—1924 in Mr. Broderip's gift at South Kensington). The painting on two finger-bowls in the Schreiber Collection (No. 190: Plate 7 B) seems to be an early example of the work of a painter who subsequently specialised in the "exotic birds" of later Chelsea porcelain. Of the fine tureens and dishes in the form of vegetables, fishes, animals and birds, all suggested by Meissen, the rabbit (Schr. No. 151: Plate 13) "big as the life", as the 1755 Catalogue described it, the swan (No. 2963—1901), the plaice (No. C 1451—1924), and the beautiful asparagus and cauliflower dishes (Nos. 2937—1901 and C 676—1925)—all at South Kensington—may be specially mentioned. A problem in classification is presented by a charming unmarked dish given to the Victoria and Albert Museum by Dr. and Mrs. H. Bellamy Gardner, decorated with ears of corn in relief and painted with feathers. An unglazed fragment apparently from the same mould was found on the site of the Bow factory;[1] but a similar dish in Dr. Gardner's collection[2] is marked with the red anchor, and the model is almost certainly that sold in 1755 to accompany a tureen in the form of partridge, such as that in the Allen Collection (No. 65), marked with the red anchor, which matches it in colour and painting. The Catalogue of 1755 mentions "Two fine partridges in a beautiful dish with corn etc.". The Bow fragment must therefore be regarded as a piece of a copy of the Chelsea dish.[3]

THE CHELSEA PORCELAIN FIGURES OF THIS PERIOD are by general consent among the finest ever made. And their due appreciation has driven their market price to a point at which an English public museum

[1] See *The Burlington Magazine*, vol. xl (1922), p. 224.

[2] See his article in *The Connoisseur*, vol. lxv (1923), p. 150.

[3] Tureens in the form of partridges were, however, made at Bow. See p. 69.

can scarcely hope to acquire them! Fortunately, a few choice examples have come to the nation by gift and bequest, and serve to illustrate their quality if not their range. Collectors, however, will recall with pleasure the astonishing assembly at the Chelsea Town Hall in 1924, of which the *Cheyne Book* is a very useful reminder. Meissen models were a chief source of inspiration (though it is rare to find exact copies as at Bow), and many examples were based on engravings, as in the case of the beautiful *Leda and the Swan* (Schr. No. 134), which is adapted from a composition of Boucher; and a group of a Chinese lady and boy in Mr. Alfred Hutton's collection, which exactly reproduces an engraving by J. J. Balechou after the same painter.[1] Some of them, such as the fine "*Carpenter* with his Tools", of which there is an unsurpassed example at South Kensington, appear to have been entirely novel creations, but all have the originality that can come with the fresh and spirited rendering of a borrowed theme. The Chelsea pair of *Masked* ("*Dutch*") *Dancers* (Schr. No. 137: Plate 12 A) far surpasses its model (though it was Kaendler's), and all have a clear soft colouring with a sparing use of gold that is quite peculiar to the factory. The slight colouring of the red-anchor figures gives especial importance to the delicious white material, which one is here tempted to describe as the most beautiful porcelain ever made. The *Nurse* already mentioned occurs in various colourings of most delicate quality. The three figures reproduced on Plate 11 are drawn from Mr. Alfred Hutton's fine collection, and well illustrate the delicate, bold and significant modelling of the best red-anchor specimens.

A well-known model of a flower-holder in the form of two boys struggling with a large fish (V. & A.M.

[1] See King, p. 38 and Plates 2 and 18. A similar model was also made at Meissen, it is true, but the closer correspondence of the Chelsea version with the engraving suggests that both were independently copied from it.

No. C 196—1926) bears a very close resemblance in style to certain Sèvres groups by La Rue, modelled about 1757.[1] It is unlikely, however, that La Rue worked for Chelsea, and all the models probably have a common origin in engravings after Boucher. Bronzes in the same style are also known. Another copy of the *Boys with a Fish*, in the Schreiber Collection (No. 824), is very different in colouring, and has sometimes been thought to be Spanish. But as a "fine white group of boys and fish" was included in the sale of the stock of Thomas Turner [2] (one of Duesbury's employers),[3] the Schreiber specimen is perhaps an example of his enamelling done outside the factory. Similar painting is seen on some specimens of the very pretty *Seasons*, and the two styles may be often distinguished [4] in the painting of other models, as if there were two "editions" of each. Perhaps the finest of all the red-anchor figures are the wonderful *Man and Woman seated beside Baskets*, of which examples from Lord and Lady Fisher's fine collection are illustrated in Plate 12 B. The *Madonna and Child* [5] is a unique instance of the treatment of this subject in English porcelain in the eighteenth century, whilst the *River God* and *Goddess* [6] in Mr. Alfred Hutton's collection are almost the only successful renderings of the nude figure.

The *Pantaloon* [7] and *Doctor* and others are specimens of the very popular figures after the Italian *Commedia dell' Arte*, first adapted at Meissen from designs (some of them by Jacques Callot) in Riccoboni's *Histoire du Théâtre Italien*, published in 1731. The Catalogue of

[1] Two of these are in the Jones Collection at South Kensington (Nos. 138 and A).

[2] Nightingale, p. xxxviii.

[3] Bemrose, *Bow, Chelsea and Derby Porcelain*, p. 8.

[4] Compare, for instance, the three specimens of the *Seasons* in Mr. Edmund Broderip's gift at South Kensington.

[5] *Op. cit.*, Plate 39. The 1755 Sale Catalogue included the item: "An exceeding fine figure of a Madonna and a Child with a cross in its hand".

[6] *Cheyne Book*, No. 137 (Plate 9), and King, Plates 35 and 36.

[7] V. & A.M. No. C 1327—1924.

1755 speaks of "Figures of the Italian Theatre". The *Carter*[1] is probably adapted from Teniers; several figures are so described in the Catalogue of 1755. Of the "Cupids for Desart" or "Love in Disguise", which appear so often in the lists, one may mention such amusing creations as the *Cupid frying Hearts* over a fire (No. C 1416—1924 at South Kensington), and another with a heart in each hand (No. C 692—1925). These are apparently original, though such figures were among Kaendler's numerous inventions. The figures of *Dwarfs* in the Schreiber Collection (No. 131) are of a type made at Meissen in the early years of the factory and afterwards known as "Callot figures". The male figure (which is the earlier of the two at South Kensington) is actually derived from an etching of Jacques Callot in a series done at Florence in 1616.[2] No Meissen version is known, and the Chelsea model was perhaps done directly from the print: the female is apparently an original creation, unless both were derived from examples in bronze or another material: there is a specimen of the male dwarf in silver-gilt in the Jones Collection at South Kensington (No. 295).

The association of Roubiliac with Sprimont has naturally led to much speculation regarding his work for the factory, and I have already indicated the white Royal busts as possibly his. Three unusually large figures, apparently intended for *Sight*,[3] *Smell*[4] and *Touch*[5] from a set of the *Senses*,[6] show remarkable similarity to

[1] V. & A.M. No. C 688—1925.

[2] Published at Nancy six years later under the title *Varie Gobbi figure di Jacopo Callot* (Meaume, No. 752). These figures were also much done at Derby and appear in the price list as "pair grotesque punches". See p. 96.

[3] Figured as *Ganymede and the Eagle* in *The Cheyne Book* (No. 221, Plate 1).

[4] King, *English Porcelain Figures*, Fig. 18.

[5] In the London Museum, represented as a woman with her foot upon a tortoise.

[6] They are probably the "large and beautiful" figure of "Smelling", etc., of the 1755 Catalogue. *Hearing*, in white, is in the British Museum.

some of his work.[1] They have an almost turbulent sweep that goes beyond the usual vigour of the red-anchor style, but it is questionable whether the *quality* of a porcelain figure—essentially a toy—is not lost in a model on so large a scale. The unusual size (approaching a foot high) may in fact be a sign of Roubiliac's only occasional and unaccustomed work in the material.

A set of Meissen figures by Kaendler, caricaturing the Saxon Court Orchestra and known as the "*Affenkapelle*", served as models for the three monkeys (No. 136) in the Schreiber Collection ("*Monkies in different attitudes* playing on musick" is an entry in the Catalogue of 1756). These provide a rare instance of the exact copying of Meissen models. The figures of birds, again suggested by Meissen examples and dating from the earlier part of this period, were apparently copied with some fidelity from a text-book of natural history. The charming *Blue Tits* in the British Museum (II. 52), and the *Barn Owls*, *Ptarmigan* and *Ducks* in the Schreiber Collection (Nos. 149, 143 and 142), are fairly exact renderings of natural species, but the brightly coloured *Finch with Cherries* (Schr. No. 146) is apparently a fancy of the painter's, and probably later in date. The three spirited birds figured in Plate 13 are all from the Schreiber Collection and show the delicious treatment of the bases. The "moss" on these is apparently peculiar to the "raised-anchor" decoration: it distinguishes the earlier from the later of the two *Dwarfs* mentioned on the previous page. A charming use of the miniature Chelsea birds appears in the pigeon houses, of which there is an example at South Kensington, evidently the "magnificent perfume pot in the form of a Pidgeon House with pidgeons, a fox, etc.", of the Catalogue of 1755. A similar piece with a dog and chickens, forming a clock case, is at the

[1] The question is discussed by Mrs. Arundell Esdaile in *The Cheyne Book*, p. 60.

British Museum (No. II. 32). A characteristic of the applied flowers on the bases of Chelsea figures of both the raised- and red-anchor periods is the ring of dots marking the centre and the distinct painting of the veins of the leaves in fine lines. Bases in this period were generally simple mounds.

No sale of Chelsea productions was held between 1756 and 1759, and Sprimont's illness, mentioned in an advertisement of 1757, may well have been the cause of inactivity, though another explanation is suggested by the financial difficulties of Sir Everard Fawkener, who died in 1758.[1] From this date Sprimont seems to have obtained complete control of the factory and the sales began to be held again.

A change in the composition of the paste apparently dates from 1758 or the following year, when bone-ash began to be used at Chelsea.[2] This ingredient had already been in use at Bow for the previous ten years, and it is probably no coincidence that in 1758 the use of calcined bones in porcelain manufacture had been described in an anonymous work attributed to Robert Dossie, entitled *The Handmaid to the Arts*. It is also possible, of course, that the use of this ingredient was suggested by a workman who had been employed at Bow during the period just before this date.[3] Sprimont was no doubt much concerned to make his manufacture as little hazardous as possible, and would readily have adopted the strengthening ingredient. The glaze of this period was as a rule thick and glassy ("juicy" is the collector's word), and especially liable to craze, collecting in pools and hollows and there showing a greenish tone. It was, however, no less soft than

[1] See the account of Mason, previously mentioned, in Chaffers, *op. cit.*, 3rd edition (1870), p. 701. Fawkener's family are said to have been left in poor circumstances (King, p. 32).

[2] See analysis in Church, p. 25, and *Analysed Specimens*, pp. 13 and 30. It is stated in Groseley's *Tour to London* (1772) that Cornish clay was used at Chelsea in 1763. See Donald A. MacAlister, *loc. cit.*, p. 139.

[3] Mason, the workman previously mentioned, had been so employed. See p. 55 for an account of the introduction of bone-ash at Bow.

before, and the colours sank into it with equally rich effect.

Sales of the Chelsea china were held in 1759 (when a different auctioneer—Burnsall—was for the first time employed in place of Ford), in 1760 and in 1761. In 1761 it was advertised that no further sales would be held, owing to Sprimont's "indisposition", and no sale was in fact held in 1762, though certain pieces may be quite definitely assigned to that year.[1] The seventh sale was held in 1763, when the moulds and premises and Sprimont's household furniture were also offered, as he proposed to "retire farther into the country". Some items have been found in auctioneers' catalogues for 1764 and the following years, but no further sale was held until 1769. The workman Mason declared that by this time Sprimont had amassed a fortune, and that little work was done at the factory after 1763. The reduction of the manufacture is implied in a dealer's advertisement of 1768, speaking of porcelain "even still brought from that noble manufactory". In advertising the sale in 1769, Burnsall spoke of the china as the work of "Mr. Nicholas Sprimont, the Proprietor of the Chelsea Porcelain Manufactory, he having entirely left off making the same . . .". The models and materials were again offered, and in August of the same year Sprimont actually sold the factory to James Cox, by whom it was in February 1770 re-sold to William Duesbury and John Heath, of Derby. The last sale of the Chelsea porcelain was held by Christie, beginning on February 14, 1770. The catalogue of this sale[2] alone survives of those of this final period. An inventory has been preserved[3] of certain porcelain disputed between Duesbury and Heath and the executors of the factory foreman Francis Thomas (*d.* 1770), who was accused of having embezzled it in 1769. The advertisements of the earlier sales, however, help us to

[1] See below, p. 45. [2] Nightingale, p. 1.
[3] Bemrose, *Bow, Chelsea and Derby Porcelain*, p. 45.

date the introduction of the richly coloured grounds which rank among the fine achievements of the period. The general use of the mark of a gold anchor assists in the identification of Chelsea porcelain of the last period, though it is sometimes doubtful whether a late piece was made at Chelsea or at Derby after the sale of the factory. Duesbury appears to have used the anchor mark freely, even before his purchase of the Chelsea concern.[1] The gold anchor, it should also be remembered, has often been added on Coalport, Tournay and modern German imitations of Chelsea and Derby models.

Accompanying the change in composition of the paste is to be noted a marked change of style, which may have been due to Sprimont's unshared management of the factory in this last period. A similar development is, however, to be noted in the productions of the German factories in the same period. The inspiration was shared by all. At Meissen, Kaendler had created before 1760 such models as the *Shepherdess with a Bird-cage*;[2] at Frankenthal, Konrad Link modelled his *Thetis* and *Oceanus*;[3] and these, amongst many others, show the same largeness of style with sumptuous colouring and profuse gilding such as are characteristic also of the best "gold-anchor" figures of Chelsea. The bases broke into a riot of scrollwork, and this last and most splendid expression of the *rococo* spirit produced in the porcelain which is its fittest embodiment works which may perhaps be considered the most important plastic sculpture of their time. The modelling of some of the large vases (such as those in the Jones Collection) is astounding in its wanton extravagance, and fascinating in the highest degree to one who has

[1] Compare the Derby *Lord Chatham* in the Schreiber Collection, No. 306. See p. 93.

[2] See M. Sauerlandt, *Deutsche Porzellan-Figuren*, Plate 18. This figure, as it happens, was copied at Chelsea late in the red-anchor period, within a short time of its appearance at Meissen. But in this it merely anticipates the "grand manner" of the later style.

[3] Sauerlandt, *op. cit.*, Plates 76 and 77.

Vase, mazarine-blue and gold, gold-anchor mark.
Height: 12½ in. About 1765.
(*Schreiber Collection.*)
See p. 43.

Vase, mazarine-blue and gold, gold-anchor mark.
Height: $14\frac{1}{8}$ in. About 1765
(*Jones Collection, V. and A. Museum.*)
See p. 43.

A

B

About 1760–65.
A has a claret ground, B a turquoise ground: gold-anchor marks.
(*V. and A. Museum.*)
See pp. 44, 48.

A

B

About 1760–65.
A has a gold-anchor, B a red-anchor mark.
(*Mr. A. H. S. Bunford's and the V. and A. Museum Collections.*)
See pp. 46, 47.

A

B

A has the gold-anchor mark and dates from about 1760. (*Mr. Alfred E. Hutton's Collection.*)
B dates from about 1765–70. (*Schreiber Collection.*)
See pp. 41, 42.

A

B

About 1760–65. Gold-anchor marks.
(*Mr. Herbert Allen's and the V. and A. Museum Collections.*)
See p. 47.

About 1765.
The Muse Melpomene. Gold-anchor mark and R impressed.
Height: $15\frac{1}{2}$ in.
(*Mr. R. W. M. Walker's Collection.*)
See p. 41.

About 1760.
Gold-anchor mark. Height: $12\frac{3}{4}$ in.
(*Schreiber Collection.*)
See p. 41.

fallen beneath its spell. The forms of "useful wares" (if the term may be used of such exquisite things) show the same extravagant fancy (Plates 15 and 17). Some of the best examples in the national museums are those in the Schreiber Collection, and there are very fine pieces in Mrs. Salting's Bequest at the London Museum. Typical of the period in their grand manner are the *Shepherd and Shepherdess* (Schr. No. 199) and the *Actor in Turkish Costume* (No. 201: Plate 22), and, above all, the *Reaper* (No. 196), all of them apparently original work by the same gifted modeller. The *Music Lesson* (Schr. No. 197), the pair of groups symbolising the *Seasons* (Schr. No. 198) and the *Fable Candlesticks* (Schr. No. 222: Plate 19B) show the extravagant development of the *bocage* at this time. They all bear the "repairer's" mark of an impressed R, mentioned above in connection with the sculptor Roubiliac, to whom they were formerly ascribed. The *Music Lesson* was evidently based on an engraving, probably by R. Gaillard,[1] after Boucher's painting *L'Agréable Leçon*, and it is highly improbable that Roubiliac, then aged at least sixty-three[2] and at the height of his fame, would have consented to model a porcelain group that was not even an original composition. Another version of the same subject, widely different in treatment, occurs also in Frankenthal[3] porcelain. The specimen in the Schreiber Collection is in astonishingly good preservation, and it is interesting to note that an example was sold in 1770 for £8. The Catalogue entry reads: "A very large and curious group of a shepherd teaching a shepherdess to play on the flute". A characteristic breadth of style distinguishes the superb *Apollo and Muses* (from which I reproduce in Plate 21 the stately

[1] Prints were engraved by R. Gaillard and J. E. Nilson after this painting; and an impression of one by the latter is exhibited as part of the Schreiber Collection (No. 1818). It is known that an engraving by Gaillard, *Le Berger Récompensé* after Boucher, was reproduced on the Chelsea vase given to the Foundling Hospital, mentioned below.

[2] He died in 1762, at the age of 67.

[3] See Hofman, *Frankenthaler Porzellan*, vol. i, Plate 35.

Melpomene), the *Una and the Lion* and the *Bacchus*. The curious *Roman Charity*, adapted from an engraving by Rubens, is no less splendid, and was evidently a popular piece, since it was singled out for special mention in the advertisements of the sale in 1769. The model of the great *Pièta*[1] was also used at Tournay,[2] but there is good reason to believe that it was adapted at Chelsea from a painting by Van Dyck or one of his school.[3] The *Hawker with Lantern* and his companion at South Kensington[4] are smaller but not less attractive pieces, to some extent following the traditions of the preceding period. A novel style first seen in this period is represented by the *Family Groups*, of which one is figured in Plate 19A. These are usually marked with the gold anchor and have a somewhat Bow-ish simplicity and charm, though often falling between the delicacy of red-anchor and the sweep and splendour of the more usual later style. The *Fortune Tellers* and the groups and candlesticks on large flat bases with scrolled feet also belong to this class.

Meissen styles had been by this time largely superseded by those of Sèvres, and the coloured grounds, brought to perfection by the latter though in most cases invented in Germany, apparently began to be imitated at Chelsea as early as 1755, when "an exceeding rich blue enamel" is mentioned in the Catalogue. This may have been the so-called "Mazareen" or "Mazarin"[5] blue, one of the chief splendours of the gold-anchor

[1] Figured in King, Plate 64.

[2] Compare Soil de Moriamé, *Les Porcelaines de Tournai*, Plate 11 (No. 691).

[3] Compare E. Schaeffer, *Van Dyck* (*Klassiker der Kunst*), p. 447, where a painting in the Hofmuseum at Vienna is reproduced; another painting, apparently a copy of the last, is in the Prado at Madrid, and is there ascribed to Rubens or one of his school. See Adolf Rosenberg, *P. P. Rubens* (in the series just cited), p. 391.

[4] No. C 698—1925, from Meissen models.

[5] There is no evidence to connect the word with Cardinal Mazarin, and its origin remains a mystery. It is sometimes used for "powdered blue" grounds, but in the Chelsea catalogues a dark-blue glaze or underglaze blue is meant—the *gros bleu* of Sèvres, or the *ta ch'ing* of Chinese porcelain.

period. A blue described by this name is in fact mentioned in the catalogue of the following year (1756), but most of the characteristic pieces surviving are evidently of later date. Evidence as to this is furnished by two large vases presented to the British Museum [1] in 1763 by an anonymous donor who stated that they had been made at Chelsea in the previous year. The Chelsea advertisement of 1763 specially mentions "the most rare and truly inimitable Mazarine Blue and Gold". Among the finest of all the specimens justly so described are the pair of vases in Mr. R. W. M. Walker's collection, now on view in the Loan Court at South Kensington. This type has always, from the time of its manufacture, been especially prized, and it is indeed a wonderful fancy. Specimens described as "Satyr bottles of the mazarin blue, embellish'd with burnished gold grapes, highly finish'd with gold birds, most curiously chas'd" were sold in 1770 for £10: 5s. and £13; and another of the same pattern was sold to "Esdail" for £38: 17s. at the sale of Queen Charlotte's effects in 1819. These vases were spoken of by J. T. Smith in *A Book for a Rainy Day* (London, 1845) as included in the treasures of Mr. William Esdaile's Collection, seen by him in 1829. Mr. Walker's vases may well be the same pair. The vases in the Jones Collection (Plate 16) are superb examples of *rococo* modelling, and their painting in gold shows a remarkable combination of refinement and vitality. Three fine vases with raised gilding and mazarine blue are in the Schreiber Collection (No. 207: Plate 15), as well as a mirror-stand (No. 208), which may be mentioned as showing especially original and successful application of the mazarine colour. The model of the last, with its amusing *rococo* scroll-work, is repeated in a complete mirror and stand in the Herbert Allen Collection (No. 54). The pea-green ground made its first appearance in 1759, and in 1760 the sale advertisement announced the production

[1] *Catalogue*, No. II. 28, Plate 8.

of "some new Colours which have been found this year by Mr. Sprimont, the proprietor, at very large expence, incredible Labour, and close Application": these were probably the turquoise-blue and the so-called claret-colour, the "crimson" of the contemporary catalogues. The last, though probably intended as an imitation of the very different pink or *rose Pompadour*[1] of Sèvres, has never been equalled as a sumptuous ground. Its unevenness adds a vibrating quality to a very rich colour. Perhaps the finest of all surviving examples are in the bequest of Miss Emily Thomson, exhibited at South Kensington in a case by themselves (Plate 17 A). The service to which this beautiful group of pieces belonged may well have been the "*very curious and matchless tea and coffee equipage*, crimson and gold, most inimitably enamell'd in figures from the designs of Watteau", sold for £43 at Christie's in 1770. Other good specimens are the fine dishes at the British Museum (No. II. 70), and in the Schreiber Collection (No. 215). The pea-green and the turquoise are not so often seen as ground colours on Chelsea china, but the vase in Plate 17 B is an example of the latter. A yellow ground, which had been one of the first to be introduced at Meissen, is seen surrounding some beautifully painted flowers on a fine chocolate-cup and saucer and on a pair of dishes, of the favourite heart-shape, with the rare mark of an anchor in blue enamel (Schr. Nos. 184 and 216). The yellow ground with panelled decoration is very rare in Chelsea porcelain, but occurs on a tea-service in Mr. Alfred Hutton's collection, exhibited at Chelsea in 1924.[2] As these are all examples decorated in the style of the German factory, it

[1] Often miscalled *rose du Barry*. Madame du Barry did not come to Court until 1769, by which time this colour had fallen into disfavour at Sèvres. The Chelsea ground now called "claret-colour" was at first called "crimson" in contemporary references, but an advertisement of 1768, cited by Nightingale (p. xxvi), speaks of "Mazareen and Pompadour Sets for Deserts".

[2] *Cheyne Book*, No. 52, Plate 21.

is probable that the ground colour was copied from Meissen rather than from the *jaune jonquille* of Sèvres. But Meissen styles were rarely used in this period, though another exception is found in the style of painting in black washed over with green, represented by a group of pieces in the Schreiber Collection, including a plate (No. 204) with a view of Battersea Church, and the charming sets of heart- and fan-shaped toilet-boxes. A great stand with this decoration, at the British Museum, is also a noteworthy piece.

A famous service of later Chelsea porcelain was given in 1763 by George III. and Queen Charlotte to the latter's brother, the Duke of Mecklenburg-Strelitz. This service was mentioned by Horace Walpole in a letter of March 4, 1763, ". . . I saw yesterday a magnificent service of Chelsea China, which the King and Queen are sending to the Duke of Mecklenburg. There are dishes and plates without number, an épergne, candlesticks, salt-sellers, sauce-boats, tea and coffee equipages, in short, it is complete, and costs twelve hundred pounds! I cannot boast of our taste; the forms are neither new, beautiful, nor various. Yet Sprimont the manufacturer is a Frenchman. It seems their taste will not bear transplanting." The Schreiber collection includes a specimen of this service in a pair of branch candelabra (No. 210), sold as damaged by the steward of the ducal household. A plate with a similar pattern (Schr. No. 211: Plate 14A) is probably part of the service advertised in 1763 and 1764[1] as "the same as the Royal Pattern which was sold for 1150 Pounds".

A favourite decoration in this period took the form of an imbricated scale pattern (sometimes applied in gilding over the coloured grounds) resembling peacock's feathers, as on a plate and a cup and saucer in the Allen Collection (Nos. 70 and 93: Plate 19 A), and the fine chocolate-cup and saucer in the Schreiber

[1] Nightingale, pp. xxiv and xxv.

Collection (No. 218). The cups of "artichoke pattern" of the 1770 Catalogue were probably of a similar pattern moulded in slight relief, which is often seen. This moulded scale pattern is seen on the plate at South Kensington (No. C 669—1925) figured in Plate 18 B, which also shows the characteristic flowers of the gold-anchor period. It is interesting to note that this plate, though of the later body and glaze and decorated in the later style, bears a *red*-anchor mark. A singular style, totally different in effect from anything in English porcelain of the time, is seen in the pieces painted with crowded flowers on an entirely gilt ground. A covered bowl and stand at the British Museum is an example (II. 95); whilst a plate at South Kensington (No. 2948—1901: Plate 14 B) is a rare instance of flowers by the same hand on a ground left white.

Far Eastern models were seldom copied in this period, but an exception is found in the copies of the "brocaded" Japanese porcelain made at Arita and so largely exported from Imari. These greatly surpass in beauty their dull originals. The brocaded design is common to earlier and later periods, and two specimens in Mr. Herbert Allen's collection (Nos. 86 and 87: Plate 9 B) are of red-anchor paste: similar plates are sometimes marked with the anchor in underglaze blue, like the blue-and-white plates already mentioned. The soft tone of blue is similar on all these. But two examples in the Schreiber Collection (No. 221), with a stronger blue, have the gold anchor, and this is more usually found. The pattern was doubtless continued at Derby in the "Chelsea-Derby" period.

In general, the painting of later Chelsea porcelain, though more extravagant than in the preceding period, is not less accomplished, and the same hands may sometimes be recognised. The so-called exotic birds [1] which frequently appear were soon to become a characteristic feature of the more ambitious English

[1] The *Fantasievögel*, invented at Meissen.

porcelain. One bird-painter of great ability is proved to be no other than the artist of the fable-subjects of the earlier pieces by the occurrence of these subjects, treated with somewhat greater assurance than before, on a large gold-anchor-marked tureen in the Allen Collection (No. 61), while its fellow (No. 63) is painted with the very distinctive birds (including one in red monochrome) often seen on pieces marked with the gold anchor. The same touch may be recognised in the handling of trees and ground. This painter's work is seen again on two beautiful flower-holders in Mr. Allen's collection (No. 53) and on a pear-shaped vase in the Schreiber Collection (No. 220). Another style of exotic birds (Plate 20 B: V. & A.M. No. 2945—1901) shows the bold touch of a painter [1] who subsequently joined the Worcester factory,[2] and associated with these are the no less sumptuously rendered fruit (again inspired by Meissen), which became, like the birds, a favourite subject for porcelain painting. They are rendered with the most magnificent effect in the set of dishes in the Thomson Bequest (Nos. 524 to 527—1902), in which the fruit painting is combined with the finest mazarine blue and the richest gilding. The dusky richness of colour of these dishes represents perhaps the highest pitch of splendour ever reached in English porcelain. More naturalistic bird-painting is seen on the charming plate from Mr. Bunford's collection figured in Plate 18 A and on a plate with "peacock's eye" ground and beautiful gilding in Mr. Allen's collection (No. 93: Plate 20 A); whilst the birds in crimson monochrome, represented by a bowl and stand in the British Museum (Barwell Bequest), should be mentioned here.

Sèvres porcelain was the medium through which were derived the delightful *chinoiseries* on the claret-

[1] Earlier work perhaps by his hand is mentioned on p. 33.

[2] See p. 170 for his Worcester work. His style was closely copied in the nineteenth century at Derby. There is a dish in this manner at South Kensington, with the red Crown-Derby mark.

ground tea-service in the Thomson Bequest (Plate 17A). These were described in the catalogue quoted above as "from the design of *Watteau*", but Watteau actually did little work in this style, which is more justly ascribed to Pillement. The *chinoiserie* is an interesting phenomenon. As porcelain-decoration it may be traced to J. G. Herold, and Meissen examples can be dated as early as 1725. The name "Chippendale Chinese" sometimes given to these figures records the phase when its vogue spread to English furniture. Two hands may be recognised in these Chinese figures on Chelsea porcelain. One of these, the painter of the tea-service just mentioned, perhaps went to Worcester.[1] Another, who painted larger figures, was perhaps an "outside decorator", since the fine octagonal vases with his work[2] seem rarely to be marked, though a set of three apparently from his hand, formerly in Lt.-Col. Croft-Lyons' collection,[3] has the gold-anchor mark. Two other vases with this painting, in the Barwell Bequest at the British Museum, have an unusually light-blue ground. They also are unmarked. This style is sometimes attributed, I think wrongly, to John Donaldson (1737–1801), a miniature-painter who is traditionally said to have worked at the factory. A charmingly direct style of figure-painting is seen in some other subjects, such as that after Teniers on the vase with turquoise-ground figured in Plate 17B (V. & A.M. No. 477—1902). The "Watteau subjects" by this hand on a fine vase in the British Museum (Barwell Bequest) have also been ascribed to Donaldson, but this style is seen on toys which are not likely to have been painted by him, and it is very unlike his signed work on Worcester porcelain.[4]

[1] See p. 176.
[2] Such as that at South Kensington (No. C 336—1926), or that in Mr. Hutton's collection (*Cheyne Book*, No. 83, Plate 24).
[3] King, *Chelsea Porcelain*, Plate 54.
[4] See p. 176.

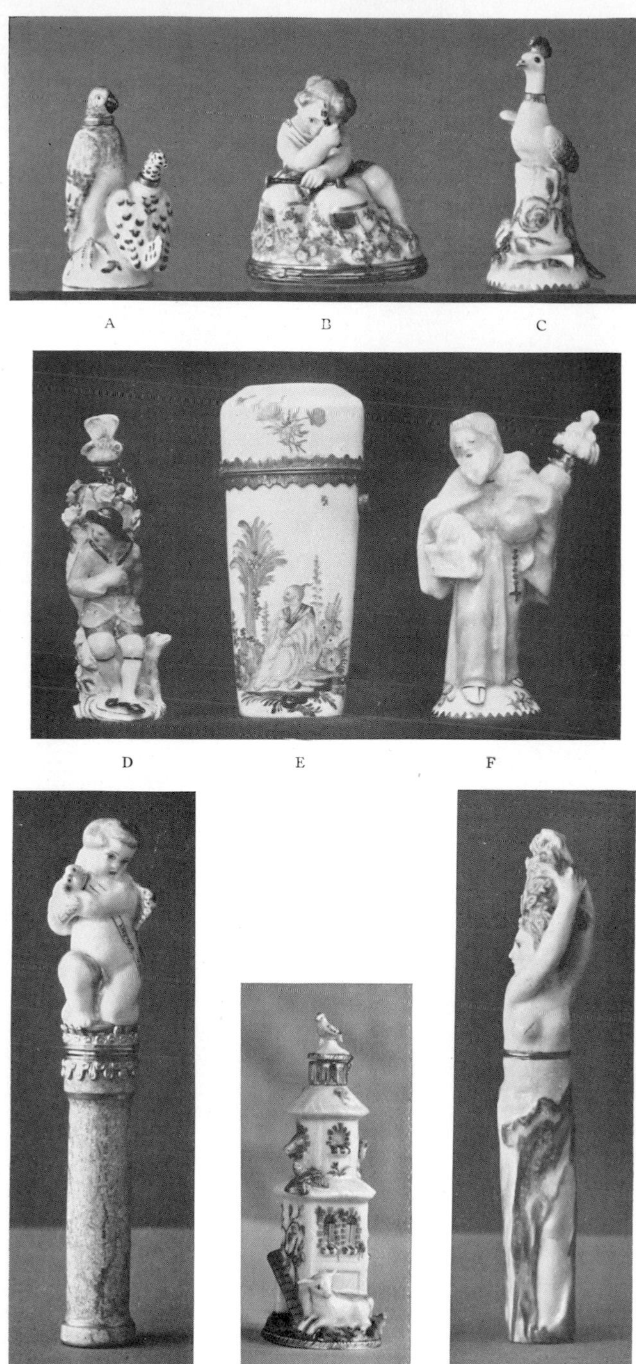

A B C

D E F

G H I

About 1750–60.
H is in *Mr. A. H. S. Bunford's Collection*; D, E and F in the *British Museum*; the others in the *Schreiber Collection*. See p. 52.

A

B

C

D E F

G H I

About 1755–65.

D, E and F are in *Lord and Lady Fisher's Collection*; A, B, C, G and I in the *Schreiber Collection*; and H is in the *V. and A. Museum*.

See pp. 51 to 53.

Donaldson is far more likely to have been the painter of some of the elaborate figure-subjects in the style of Boucher and Rubens, and the naturalistic birds after Hondekoeter, which decorate the imposing vases in the Sèvres manner made in this period. These are commonly modelled in the most riotous *rococo* style, but the naturalistic painting in panels reserved on the coloured grounds is more remarkable for its accomplishment than for its vitality or fitness as porcelain decoration. The classics of this style are of course the seven "Dudley Vases" said to have been made for presentation by George III. to Lady Liverpool, subsequently in the possession of Lord Dudley and now in Lord Bearsted's collection.[1] Most of these pieces were evidently made to order for presentation, and could never have been articles of commerce. Two such vases in the British Museum with mazarine-blue ground (No. II. 28) are recorded as "made in the year 1762, under the direction of Mr. Sprimont". The anonymous donor is supposed to have been a Dr. George Garnier, who presented to the Foundling Hospital at about the same time a somewhat similar vase with a subject after Boucher: its companion was in the possession of Lord Chesterfield. Both are illustrated in M. L. Solon, *Old English Porcelain*, Nos. 21 and 22. In the British Museum, too, are a great vase and stand, and a large covered jar with a figure of Diana (Nos. II. 27 and 29), which represent this elaborate manner at its best and most tasteful; a group of fantastically modelled vases in this style is also in the Jones Collection at South Kensington.[2] On one of these last is a careful landscape which is apparently an early work by Zachariah Boreman, who afterwards created the broader style so familiar on Derby porcelain. Askew, who also went to Derby, was probably the painter of figure-subjects on some of these vases.

[1] Three of them are illustrated in King, Plates 57 and 58.

[2] Nos. 172 and 172 A.

Their styles were continued into the Chelsea-Derby period, when classical symmetry began to replace the delicious caprice of the *rococo*,[1] and a further account of the work of these painters will be found on a later page.

If these great vases represent Sprimont's most ambitious performances, the unique and tiny objects for long known as "Chelsea toys" are more rightly regarded as his best and most original work. They were, and are, among the most valued of all Chelsea productions. These scent-bottles, *bonbonnières*, needle-cases, thimbles, seals, knife-handles, miniature figures and the like were for long mistaken for Sèvres productions, but this can only have been in England! They seem to have been produced at all times during Sprimont's management, and in the weekly accounts of the work done at Chelsea in the first years of Duesbury's control [2] scent-bottles form a large proportion of the objects mentioned. They were even much exported to the Continent: one specimen in the Schreiber Collection was bought at Granada, and an advertisement of 1756 includes "Chelsea China Knives and Forks" and "Smelling Bottles" in the sale of the "intire stock of Laumas and Rolyat, late of Lisbon". A reference to "flacons de sel d'Angleterre" occurs in Beaumarchais' *Mariage de Figaro* [3] and Chelsea scent-bottles may have been meant. A sale devoted solely to these objects was advertised in 1754, "By Order of the Proprietors of the Chelsea Porcelain Manufactory", as follows: ". . . All the entire stock of Porcelain Toys . . . consisting of Snuff-boxes, Smelling Bottles,

[1] It has been remarked by Mr. William King that the Louis Seize style made its appearance some years before the death of Louis XV; and three stately vases in Mr. Herbert Allen's collection (Nos. 47 and 48, Plate 40 B), obviously made in imitation of Sèvres porcelain, may be regarded as Chelsea from the quality of their claret ground, though the symmetry of their forms decidedly suggests the later period.

[2] See p. 98.

[3] Quoted by Max Sauerlandt in the *Kunstsammlerjahrbuch* for 1924–25, in an essay on "Chelsea Toys", which is an admirable study of eighteenth-century sentiment as well as a penetrating tribute to Sprimont's genius.

Etwees and Trinkets for Watches (mounted in gold and unmounted) in various beautiful shapes, of an elegant design and curiously painted in enamel. . . . A large parcel of Porcelain Hafts for table and Dessert Knives and Forks." But we have good reason to believe that the toys had been made for some time before this date.

Though some of these toys were perhaps inspired by Kaendler, most of them show the characteristic English sentiment of the time, surprising in the work of a Frenchman. That the delicious mottoes in misspelt French were copied from script, presumably Sprimont's own, is proved by such mistakes as L'ESPERANU for L'ESPERANCE.[1] Such an error would be unlikely to occur in copying from another model bearing the inscription in capitals, but is easy to understand if the legend were provided for the English painter in the form of a manuscript copy. Moreover, no earlier versions have ever been found for the majority of the toys.

The Schreiber Collection is rich in toys of the finest quality. The patch-box in the form of a woman's head (No. 231: Plate 24 A), and the even finer man's head (No. 274), the *bonbonnière* with a lady caressing a dog (No. 271), and the charmingly indefinite group of a rabbit with its young (No. 229) may be specially mentioned. All these, and many others, have lids of enamel-painting on copper, presumably made at the neighbouring Battersea factory, and not later in date than 1756.[2] Some of the models are found also entirely in Battersea enamel, as, for instance, the scent-bottles in the form of a *Boy as a gardener* (No. 279: Plate 24 I). Many Kaendlerish small figures represent Cupid in various employments. Among the tiny figures mounted as seals (Plate 24 B) he is seen holding

[1] JE VOUS COFFRE (for L'OFFRE) and JE VOUS CHARMEIAY are similar errors.

[2] The Battersea enamel factory is believed to have come to an end in this year.

a heart in each hand; the *bonbonnière* (No. 270: Plate 23 B) in the form of a winsome Cupid playing upon a pair of kettledrums in the form of a woman's breasts, with the inscription POUR LES CAVALIERS DE CITHERE; Cupid with a lady, standing beside a clock (No. 242) inscribed L'HEURE DU BERGER FIDELLE, and No. 243, Cupid at a furnace distilling a potion (MON FEU DURERA TOUJOURS) are typical of these. Soft colouring and a purposeful indefiniteness mark such models as the *étui* with *Daphne turning into a laurel* (No. 227: Plate 23 I), and that with Cupid and a pair of doves on a column (No. 266: Plate 23 G), inscribed IMITEZ NOUS. The same quality distinguishes a fine *bonbonnière* in the Museum collection at South Kensington (No. C 1332—1924: Plate 24 H), in the form of a fantastic crouching camel, with panniers containing hay and lambs over its back. Some beautiful painting distinguishes the *rococo* scent-bottle (Schr. No. 234: Plate 24 C), and an *étui* in the British Museum (Plate 23 E). A charming fancy of Sprimont's took the form of a group of nautical instruments, a set of hunting implements (inscribed [LA] CHAS[SE] DES BELLES), or a table laid for a meal. The inscriptions with their almost invariably amorous suggestions are a study in themselves: Cupid triumphant, with a net or holding a bag of hearts (AUCUN NE S'ECHAPERAS or AQUIS PAR MON COURAGE), holding up a globe (JE SOUTIENS LE MONDE), or in a lawyer's wig (JE PLAIS POUR MA BELLE); the boy trying to rouse a pig (PEINE PERDU) or Europa garlanding the bull (TROMPERIE D'AMOUR); the cat (JE BRILLE DANS L'OBSCURITE) and the toy-dog (CHIEN SAVANT). JE VIS EN ESPERANCE is significantly written on a scent-bottle with a boy snaring birds (Plate 24 G). But the parrot is DISCRET EN AMOUR; the soldier, MUNI POUR VOUS RESISTER; and among the exquisite fruits and bunches of flowers we find POINT DE ROSES SANS EPINES. A snuff-box with the British lion devouring the Gallic cock, with the inscription MALGRE TA

FIERTE TU PERIS (B.M. No. II. 165), is a rare instance of a political reference, and it reveals Sprimont the Huguenot as no lover of his native France. Many of these can be seen in the British Museum as well as in the Schreiber Collection, and a complete repertory is contained in Mr. Bryant's monograph on these very lovable things. Of the toy figures the delightful gardeners may be mentioned. One of these and two other charming specimens from Lord and Lady Fisher's collection arc figured in Plate 24 D, E & F. The little man with a wheelbarrow is represented at South Kensington (No. C 1286—1919), where there is also a specimen, in the form of strawberries and leaves, of the "matchless knives and forks of the Chelsea china" advertised in 1759.

CHAPTER III

BOW

THE materials for a history of Bow china are indeed of the scantiest. Bow (properly Stratford-le-Bow) is in east London; and the factory may be said to have been founded in 1744 when a patent [1] for the manufacture of porcelain was taken out by Edward Heylyn, a copper and mineral merchant,[2] and Thomas Frye (1710–1762), an artist best known as a mezzotint engraver.[3] Under this patent a clay ". . . the produce of the Chirokee nation in America,[4] called by the natives unaker", was to be mixed with a frit made of "pott ash, fern ash, pearl ash, kelp, or any other vegetable lixiviall salt", and "sands, flints, pebbles or any other stones of the vitrifying kind". Mr. William Burton has asserted,[5] on technical grounds, that a paste so made would lack plasticity and that little porcelain could have been made under this patent. It is likely, however, that the specification was deliberately vague or even

[1] Jewitt, vol. i, p. 112.

[2] See Pountney, *Old Bristol Potteries*, pp. 195-200, for details of his family history. See also p. 140 for a possible connection with Lowdin's Bristol factory.

[3] He studied engraving under James Brooks, and his works in mezzotint include his own portrait, of which there is an impression in the Schreiber Collection (No. 1814); he also painted in oils, and a portrait of Jeremy Bentham by him is in the National Portrait Gallery.

[4] In 1745 William Cookworthy of Plymouth mentioned the discovery of this china-clay. Both Heylyn and Cookworthy had Bristol connections, and the introduction of this American clay at Bow may have been due to Cookworthy's report of it. See pp. 139 and 219.

[5] *English Porcelain*, p. 59.

inaccurate,[1] and doubtless modifications in composition would have been quickly adopted when the original formula was found to be unworkable. No specimens of this earliest Bow china can be quite certainly identified, but that porcelain was actually made at Bow before the introduction of the characteristic bone-ash paste I shall show presently.

A second patent was taken out by Frye alone in 1748. The doubtless intentionally vague specification mentions a material called "Virgin Earth", to be produced by calcining "all animal substances, all Fossils of the Calcarious kind such as Chalk, Lime Stone, etc." Bone is the only animal substance which yields by calcining a white, abundant and insoluble material such as Frye described, and the phosphoric acid in the paste, due to this ingredient, has for long been recognised as a characteristic of all but the earliest Bow porcelain. It was suggested by Professor Church that Frye became acquainted with the whiteness of calcined bones through his knowledge of the bone-black used by engravers.[2]

Much of the information we have about the factory, and it is little enough, has been obtained from a collection of memorandum and account books and other papers left by John Bowcocke, clerk to the factory,[3] who died in 1765. They relate to a period beginning in 1750 when two merchants, Weatherby and John Crowther, were partners in the ownership. The manufacture was of some size, and the value of china sold in 1753, 1754 and 1755 exceeded £10,000 in each year. Weatherby died in 1762 and John Crowther became bankrupt in the following year. Frye remained manager of the works until 1759, three years before his death. In his epitaph he is described as "the inventor

[1] See Church, *English Porcelain*, p. 35.

[2] But oyster-shells and burnt bones were given in a porcelain recipe published in Germany in 1649. See E. Zimmermann, *Erfindung . . . des Meissner Porzellan*, p. 37.

[3] Extracts from these were first published by Chaffers (3rd edition) in 1870. Some of them are preserved at the British Museum, but others formerly in the possession of Lady Charlotte Schreiber seem to have been lost.

and first manufacturer of porcelain in England". He was in part the inventor of the bone-porcelain which was later to win universal adoption in England, and the pious tribute may well be allowed to stand.

It was stated in the Catalogue of the Jermyn Street Collection,[1] issued in 1855, that when the Bow factory was discontinued all the moulds and models were purchased and removed to the Derby works. No date was given for the event, and no authority was quoted for the statement, which has often been repeated. In Chaffers[2] (3rd edition, 1870, page 691) "1775 or 1776" is given, without any authority or reference, as the date of the purchase, but in the recollections of Samuel Keys, a Derby workman, reported in the same work (page 595), the purchase or part-purchase of Bow models is again mentioned. It has been suggested,[3] with some probability, that after Crowther's bankruptcy in 1763 the factory was continued with the aid of loans from William Duesbury of Derby, who similarly assisted the Kentish Town enameller Giles.[4] This connection would explain the surprising fact that Craft, a Bow hand, took his bowl (now in the British Museum) to Giles for its enamel firing.

This curious fact and the circumstance that in Bowcocke's papers mention is made of Bow porcelain enamelled by "Richard Dyer, at Mr. Bolton's, enameler near the Church, Lambeth", raises a doubt as to how much of the china was enamelled outside the factory. Bowcocke in his memoranda speaks of "bisket ware made at New Canton", as if the glazing and enamelling was done elsewhere. Lambeth, too, is brought into the question by some references to the employment in a china factory of John Bacon, R.A. (1740–99). In Alan Cunningham's *Lives of the Most Eminent British Painters, Sculptors and Architects* (1830), vol. iii, p. 201,

[1] London Museum of Practical Geology.
[2] *Marks and Monograms.*
[3] F. Hurlbutt, *Bow Porcelain*, p. 20.
[4] Jewitt, vol. i, pp. 214-218.

A B C

D

A and B, about 1745–50; C and D, about 1750–55.
(*Schreiber and V. and A. Museum Collections.*)
See pp. 60, 62, 64, 72.

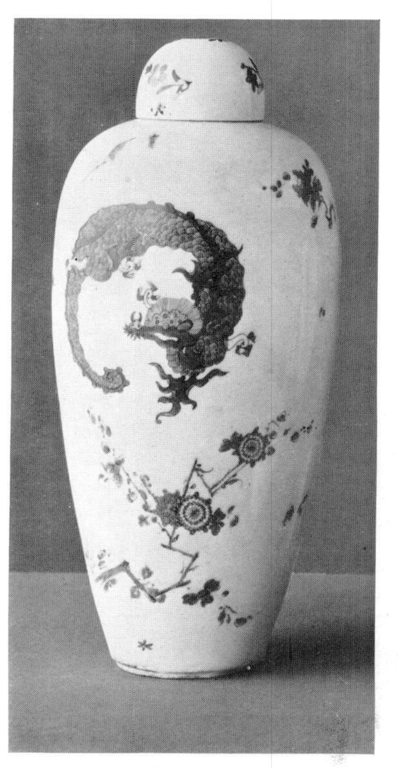

A

B

C

"Kakiemon" patterns. About 1755. (*V. and A. Museum and Schreiber Collections.*)

See p. 7[illegible]

A B

C

About 1755.
A and B are painted in *famille rose* style.
C is painted with "Bow flowers", and marked with a *B* in blue.
(*V. and A. Museum Collections.*)
See p. 71.

A B C

D

About 1755.

A, B and C are in the *Schreiber Collection*. D is in the *V. and A. Museum*.

See pp. 70, 71.

Bacon is stated to have been apprenticed in 1755 at the age of fourteen, "to one Crispe of Bow Churchyard, an eminent maker of porcelain, who taught him the art of modelling the deer and holly tree, the bird and the bush, the shepherd and shepherdess, and birds and beasts of every kind such as are yet made for show or for use in our manufactories. That these early attempts contained the rudiments of his future excellence has been asserted by some and denied by others. . . . It ought to be mentioned that he was frequently employed in painting on plates and dishes: these were probably a repetition of his models with the addition of the duck in the pond, the angler and his rod, and the hunter with his hounds." This deliciously padded passage is probably based on R. Cecil's *Memoirs of John Bacon* (1801), where it is further stated that Mr. Crispe had a manufactory of china at Lambeth at which Bacon occasionally assisted. Bacon is also known to have worked for Coade's "Artificial-Stone Works" at Narrow Wall in Pedlar's Acre, Lambeth,[1] and Jewitt states that in addition to purchasing the Bow factory, Duesbury also "owned the pottery at Pedlar's Acre at Lambeth, the rents of which he assigned in 1781".[2] This last may merely refer to Coade's, but it may, on the other hand, indicate the site of the presumed Bow branch. Promised excavations in Lambeth may throw light on this obscure matter. Crispe's Lambeth branch may turn out to be no other than one of the painting establishments of Richard Dyer; or it may, on the other hand, prove to be Coade's Artificial-Stone Works.

It is clear that the factory output largely consisted of table-ware. *The Case of the Undertaker of the Chelsea Manufacture*[3] mentioned that "the chief endeavours at Bow have been towards making a more ordinary sort of ware for common uses", and this is borne out by the

[1] Jewitt, vol. i, p. 139. [2] Vol. ii, p. 74.
[3] See p. 19.

advertisements. "All Sorts of China" were offered in advertisements in Birmingham and Derby newspapers in 1753. Public sales were announced in 1757 and 1758, but the catalogues of these do not seem to have survived. The earlier announcement mentioned "Epargnes, Branch Candlesticks, Services for Deserts, etc. etc. exquisitely painted in enamel and Blue and White. Also a large assortment of the most useful China in Lots, for the Use of Gentlemen's Kitchens, Private Families, Taverns, etc.". At a later sale were offered "beautiful Groups of Figures", essence and perfume pots, jars, beakers, bottles, "Services of Dishes, Plates, Sauce-boats, compleat Tea and Coffee Equipages, a large Assortment of fine Enamel and fine partridge Sets which are most beautifully painted by several of the finest Masters from Dresden". This advertiser's reference to painters "from Dresden" is not to be accepted literally. In 1753 the factory had advertised in Birmingham for enamellers and "Painters in the Blue and White Potting Way"; and for a "Person who can model small figures in Clay neatly". We know from the advertisements of 1753 that the firm had a retail shop in Cornhill, near the Royal Exchange. This was closed after Crowther's bankruptcy, in 1764. Later, from 1770 to 1775, the warehouse was in St. Paul's Churchyard.

THE IDENTIFICATION OF THE BOW CHINA DEPENDS (apart from the evidence of chemical analysis[1]) upon the following documents:

(i.) The papers of John Bowcocke mentioned above, relating to the period between 1750 and 1758.

(ii.) A bowl in the British Museum presented in 1790 and accompanied by a note stating that it was made at Bow in 1760 and painted by Thomas Craft.[2] In the course of a wordy account, obviously that of an

[1] This cannot by itself be conclusive, as bone-ash was also used at Lowestoft, and at a rather later date at Chelsea.

[2] Hobson, *Catalogue*, No. I. 62.

old man and not very trustworthy, Craft states that about three hundred persons including ninety painters were at one time employed at the factory.

(iii.) Certain inkstands dated 1750 and 1751 and inscribed *Made at New Canton*. Bowcocke spoke of the factory by this name, and Craft described the factory as modelled on one "at Canton".

(iv.) Two blue-and-white plates in the British Museum[1] dated 1770 and inscribed *Robert Crowther*, presumed to be the name of a relative of the Bow proprietor.

(v.) Fragments of porcelain and wasters found on the site of the works in 1868[2] and 1922.[3] Several pieces from the earlier find are at South Kensington.

As the earliest of the Bow porcelain did not yet contain bones and was unmarked, its identification is very much of the nature of guess-work. Pastes would vary much in this experimental stage. We know as little of the earliest Derby china, and the doubtful class will probably always be disputed by the partisans of the two factories. Chelsea may be excluded as of fairly well-established character. Certain slight indications point to a Bow origin for a well-defined class marked by an exceptionally thick greenish-toned glaze, made opaque with minute bubbles, which obscures the modelling of the figures: a pair of cows and a pheasant in the Museum Collection at South Kensington[4] may be taken as typical. A clumsy applied flower, like a single, formal rose, is often found on the bases. Mr. Wallace Elliot has a pair of bagpipers so smothered in this glaze

[1] *Catalogue*, No. I. 36.

[2] Described in Jewitt, vol. i, 203-206 (reprinted from *The Art Journal* of 1869), and in Chaffers, *op. cit.*, pp. 694-699.

[3] See an article by Aubrey J. Toppin in *The Burlington Magazine*, vol. xl (1922), p. 224.

[4] I need offer no apology for drawing my examples in this section almost wholly from the collections at South Kensington. The wonderful series in the Schreiber Collection has in recent years been enriched by the splendid gift of Mr. Edmund F. Broderip, and no type of any importance is unrepresented there.

that they might be "snow-men":[1] they have a decidedly Dutch look (though I have found no actual prototype), and Dutch influences, as we shall see, were not unknown at Bow. To this class, but showing a marked improvement in quality, belongs the delightfully modelled recumbent *Lion* of which there is an example in the Schreiber Collection (No. 8: Plate 25 A). This has still the greenish glaze, but is much cleaner in finish. There are others of the same family.

A figure of *Kitty Clive* as the Fine Lady in Garrick's farce *Lethe*, in the Schreiber Collection at South Kensington (No. 1 A), is an important document for the identification of the earliest Bow. This figure has been analysed and proved non-phosphatic and therefore is not likely to have been made after the date of the second patent (1748). But her companion, *Henry Woodward* as the Fine Gentleman (No. 1),[2] and *James Quin* as Falstaff (No. 2), have both been proved to have a phosphatic paste. It must be concluded that earlier and later versions of these figures were made before and after the second patent. We know that Mrs. Clive and Mr. Woodward appeared in *Lethe* as early as 1740; Quin was appearing as Falstaff even before this, and it is likely that these figures would have retained their popularity over a long period. Mrs. Clive even appeared as the Fine Lady in her farewell performance in 1769.[3] The three models are inseparable in style and in the treatment of the costumes (the applied bits of clay are noteworthy), so that the Schreiber *Kitty Clive* becomes an important early example of Bow porcelain, assuming, of course, that a Bow origin may be ascribed to any of them. The fact that two of them have a phosphatic paste should be

[1] Mr. Bernard Rackham tells me that this term was actually used long ago to describe the technique of some ancient Cyprian figurines.

[2] Apparently adapted from an undated engraving after Hayman by James MacArdell, who was like Thomas Frye, a pupil of James Brooks.

[3] See the *Schreiber Catalogue* (1928), vol. i (Porcelain), No. 1, for a fuller discussion of the date of these figures.

almost conclusive, but Nightingale and others have strongly contended that all three are Chelsea figures. They were mentioned by J. T. Smith, in *A Book for a Rainy Day* (1845),[1] in describing a visit to Hampton Court in 1829, as Chelsea figures; but the same author elsewhere [2] mentions *Quin* as a Bow model. White figures of *Woodward* and *Kitty Clive* were offered as Chelsea at a sale in 1767 of the property of Thomas Turner, a china-dealer who had employed Duesbury as an enameller.[3] But as the pieces would have been without marks in the paste, and the Bow factory was in disrepute whilst that of Chelsea was at the height of its fame, it is probable that the name of the latter would have been unscrupulously used whenever possible. The surviving specimens of these models, moreover, bear no resemblance whatever to admitted Chelsea porcelain. Examples of the pair in Mr. E. S. McEuen's collection are painted with small sprigs of flowers, obviously by the same hand as those on two other specimens in the Schreiber Collection—the *Charity* (No. 31) and the large figures of *Boys with Baskets* (No. 32), and on the *Lovers with a Birdcage* also at South Kensington (No. C 1320—1924: Plate 29 B). All these have a phosphatic paste, and are to be attributed to Bow on other grounds, as I shall presently show.

THE FACT THAT DUESBURY PAINTED "BOGH" AS WELL as other makes of china suggests the need for caution in arguing from similarity of painting. But I think we may more probably detect Duesbury's hand in the painting of two other well-known early Bow models, of a class which is sometimes marked with the sign for Mercury, incised.[4] These are the *Man and Woman in Turkish Costume* (Schreiber No. 33). The male model is one frequently repeated in later Bow porcelain,[5] but

[1] Pp. 266-267. [2] *Nollekens and his Times* (1829), vol. i, p. 191.

[3] See p. 14, footnote.

[4] See Appendix, p. 260, for this "planet-mark".

[5] There is a specimen marked with an anchor and dagger in the Schreiber Collection (No. 87).

analysis has shown this early specimen to contain only a trace of phosphoric acid. Another piece with the same mark, a sweetmeat dish in the form of conjoined shells, also at South Kensington, shows the same analysis, and we may reasonably assume that these pieces were made at Bow of a paste in which the new ingredient was only tentatively used, about the time of the second patent or shortly after. Now the painting on the *Turk* and his companion, which includes a smudgy use of bright green and brown and some rather crude pink and green flowers, is obviously by the same hand as a *Lady with a Basket*, of non-phosphatic paste, which for various reasons may be regarded as a Derby production.[1] This painting was therefore either that of a migrant workman, or done in William Duesbury's London shop.[2] The same hand may not uncommonly be detected on other porcelain of this time (a charming teapot in the form of overlapping leaves, No. 36 in the Schreiber Collection: Plate 25 B, is another instance), and we may, I think, provisionally regard this work as Duesbury's.

ANOTHER CLASS OF EARLY BOW FIGURES WHICH WE MAY ascribe to a period shortly after 1750 has been proved phosphatic by chemical analysis,[3] and is brought together by a distinctive manner of modelling the heads, in a style which foreshadows the best Bow figures of the following decade. A damaged figure of a woman, in plain white, at South Kensington,[4] came from the Jermyn Street Collection in company with many wasters and fragments from the Bow factory site, and may itself be a waster. There is no record, however,

[1] See p. 86.

[2] The published Duesbury work-book covers the period 1751–53; but it is probable that he was at work as an enameller before this.

[3] We may, I think, safely assume that once bone-ash was established as an ingredient in Bow china, it would never be abandoned. This is proved by the firm adoption successively at Chelsea (1758), Derby (1770), and eventually throughout England of a bone-porcelain body. See also Appendix B.

[4] No. 2882—1901.

of the provenance of this figure, which shows the characteristic, somewhat receding chin and heavily marked eyelids of this class. The charming *Lovers with a Birdcage* (C 1320—1924: Plate 29 B)[1] and the group allegorical of *Charity* in the Schreiber Collection, already mentioned for their painting of small sprigs, are also good examples of this modelling. The *Boys with Baskets* (Schr. No. 32), which have similar painting and the same rather dull white glaze, are of the same model as certain pieces of Delft earthenware, a circumstance not uncommon in Bow porcelain. To this group belong also the delightful *Muses*, represented at South Kensington by the *Polyhymnia* and *Erato*, inscribed "Polimnie" and "Eraton for the Love", suggesting a French repairer.[2] The rare group of a *Mother and Children* from the London Museum, figured in Plate 29, is also apparently early.

Similar to the very early *Kitty Clive* in paste and glaze (which is of a somewhat dirty or brownish cream-colour) are a number of white figures of lions, pug-dogs and the like, and these show a further link in the curious *impressed* sprigs of flowers sometimes found on the bases. The colour was doubtless improved as experience was gained, and a very pleasing, slightly greenish-toned material is characteristic of much of the early useful ware. This includes the distinctive series of pieces with decoration of sprays of plum-blossom in applied relief,[3] copied from Fukien porcelain: many wasters with this decoration were found on the factory site. Examples of these wasters, and many fine pieces

[1] Analysed by Dr. H. J. Plenderleith with the following result:

Silica	47·8
Oxide of lead . . .	0·5
Alumina	8·1
Lime	24·6
Phosphoric acid . . .	17·6
	98·6

[2] Perhaps "Mr. Tebo" or someone from Mennecy. See pp. 66 and 70.

[3] Doubtless the "sprigged" patterns of Bowcocke's notes. "Sprigging" is the Staffordshire name for the process of applying these reliefs.

in the same style, are in the collection at South Kensington (Plate 25c). A pair of sauce-boats moulded with festoons (Schr. No. 35) are of similar material: formerly believed to be Bristol (from an error in W. Moore Binns' book *The First Century of English Porcelain*, where a marked specimen was said to exist), they have been analysed and proved phosphatic. A sauce-boat and a vase at South Kensington,[1] marked with an incised CT and R respectively, both reveal on analysis a highly phosphatic body; both are linked with a vase in the Schreiber Collection (No. 38) by some rather crude, stringy painting with leaves outlined in brown, and we may regard this style as one of the earliest of those seen on the useful wares. The R mark identifies as Bow some vases painted in Chinese style in red and blue, of which there are examples at South Kensington (Nos. 967 and 968—1924). The inkstands inscribed *New Canton* (those at the British Museum and South Kensington are dated 1750 and 1751 respectively) show that enamelled porcelain of very fine quality was made at Bow, even in this early period: they are of a fine ivory-like material, painted in clear enamels of the *famille rose*.

THE FORM OF THE ANALYSED SAUCE-BOAT JUST mentioned is typical of Bow; it is repeated in the blue-and-white specimen figured in Plate 31, which has an incised planet-mark. A similar mark is found on the sweetmeat dish also mentioned above, and both are painted in an especially bright blue. The distinctive colour of these two specimens helps us to identify other early Bow blue-and-white. The painting is distinguished by a certain fantastic quality, and a script *G* of varying form is sufficiently common to be a useful guide. A white shell-salt in Dr. Bellamy Gardner's collection, incised 1750,[2] provides us with

[1] Nos. C 845—1920 and C 1246—1924.

[2] There is also the *Edward Vernon 1752* blue-painted inkstand in the Willett Collection.

a date. The form of these salt-cellars and sweetmeat dishes suggests that they were moulded from actual specimens, and the notion was probably taken from place to place by a repairer, perhaps the "Mr. Tebo"[1] to be mentioned presently. The larger Bow shells often have a transverse ribbing underneath, not found on those made elsewhere: a powdered-blue dish in the Schreiber Collection (No. 25) also shows this feature.

THE FINE PRODUCTIONS OF THE SUCCEEDING PERIOD, dating from about 1752 to 1760, include some of the most charming porcelain ever made in England. The paste was of a warm creamy-yellow tone, often showing brighter flecks, by transmitted light. These flecks are due to "tearings" which are sometimes visible on the surface, resembling the parting of uncooked dough, or of dry non-plastic clay. The glaze is rather waxen-looking, so soft as to be easily scratched, but of an ivory tone and smoothness. The pure and rich enamel colours used include a very distinctive opaque blue, a soft rose-pink and a bright translucent green. The clean strength of the colours and their juxtaposition in bold discords give the best Bow china much of its charm. The gilding in this as in other periods of the factory was not of high quality technically, but has the soft and rather dull appearance that is so much pleasanter than the brassy gilding of modern times. In this period it was used very sparingly with good effect.

MANY ATTRACTIVE FIGURES WERE MADE, MOST OF them closely copied from Meissen models,[2] but with a

[1] Plymouth specimens, such as that figured in Plate 87, often bear his mark.

[2] Models from other factories were occasionally copied: the *Gallant* and his companion holding a fan at South Kensington (Nos. C 654 and 655—1925) are after Frankenthal originals (compare F. H. Hofmann, *Frankenthaler Porzellan*, Nos. 210 and 211), and this circumstance doubtless accounts for their unusual colouring, which includes a dull green. Two charming white figures in the same collection, of a fiddler and his companion (Nos. C 726 and 727—1925), are of a model known to occur in Höchst faïence (compare *Schriften des Historischen Museums Frankfurt-am-Main*, i, Plate 28, p. 84).

remarkable vivacity and delicacy of execution. Bases for the figures were at first of simple mounded or rectangular form, but latterly a characteristic four-footed pedestal was invented, its scroll-work outlined in the strong crimson purple enamel which is quite peculiar to Bow. A hole at the back of many of the figures was formerly believed to be intended for a metal mount, and a mark of Bow manufacture, but like the holes commonly found in the bases this was nothing but a vent for the escape of enclosed air during the firing process. It occurs in porcelain from other factories. Many of the models bear an impressed mark, T or T°, which is found at a later period on Worcester, Plymouth and Bristol porcelain.[1] This was formerly regarded as the mark of a modeller employed by Josiah Wedgwood in 1775, called "Mr. Tebo" in his correspondence.[2] He was probably a Frenchman who altered his name Thibaud to its phonetic form in English spelling.[3] Whilst there is in fact no evidence to connect this Tebo with the person who used the mark in question, the incompetence as a modeller [4] of the "Mr. Tebo" so scathingly referred to by Wedgwood is not inconsistent with a high degree of skill as a "repairer", such as is shown in some of the Bow and Bristol pieces with this mark.[5] It should be emphasised again that marks of this kind on finished pieces are those of "repairers" and not of modellers. An impressed B found on a pair of figures

[1] See pp. 174, 227, and 260.

[2] *Letters of Wedgwood*, ii, pp. 119, 121, 130; *Owen*, p. 242. For a discussion of this question see *The Burlington Magazine*, vol. xxv (1914), p. 108. Owen seems to have made the suggestion that *T°* stood for Tebo.

[3] Such anglicising occurs also in the spelling "Busha" for Boucher, quoted on p. 101.

[4] This incompetence would be quite consistent with my suggestion that "Mr. Tebo" was the inventor of shell-salts. The notion would have appealed to a "repairer" with limited powers of invention.

[5] It is not always accepted that the mark is that of a "repairer" or any other workman, and it has even been suggested (F. Rathbone, *Old Wedgwood*, 1898, p. 16) that the letters indicate "top of oven"; the mark TBO on certain pieces of Wedgwood's ware is definitely stated to mean "top of biscuit oven".

of *A Man and Woman carrying dishes*, usually known as the *Cooks* (Schr. No. 46) was formerly regarded as the mark of John Bacon. These figures, which rank amongst the very best produced at Bow, may well be the "Cooks" mentioned in a memorandum of Bowcocke's of 1756, when sixteen of them were ordered by a dealer named Fogg. Bacon was only sixteen years old at this date, and it is unlikely that he was then responsible for such figures as these, either as repairer or modeller. The fine *Flora* [1] (from the antique statue at the Farnese Palace at Rome) is traditionally associated with Bacon, and is much more likely to be the work of an apprentice-sculptor such as he was about this time. The untrustworthy J. T. Smith, in his *Nollekens and his Times*, declared that Moser, afterwards Keeper of the Royal Academy, also modelled for Bow porcelain.

The Bow figures continue to show a fairly close sequence in the modelling of the heads, in a style differing much from those of other factories. This is a useful criterion. The head of the little boy in the early *Charity* already mentioned is almost identical with that of another *Boy seated on a mound* (Schr. No. 49), and is similar, again, to that of the characteristically coloured *Boy and Girl selling Fish* (Schr. No. 51). This feature almost identifies many Bow figures of about 1755. Rather later models show increasingly delicate rendering of the features, as in the group figured in Plate 32, though these are still recognisably akin to those in the earlier style. Among the models closely copied from Meissen, but nevertheless among the best English figures, may be mentioned the delightful *Pierrot* in yellow, and the lively *Harlequin* and *Columbine* (Bowcocke speaks of "Harliquin" and "Pero"); the *Negro* and *Negress*; the *Woman in Turkish Costume holding a shell*, and the *Gallant kissing his hand*. All of these are represented in the Schreiber Collection. A

[1] No. 533—1868 at South Kensington.

Boy holding a bunch of grapes is represented at South Kensington [1] in two copies, differing slightly in colour. One is marked with a script D and so has been thought to be an early Derby figure, but analysis has revealed a bone-ash paste. And the other is marked A F! [2] The *Waterman wearing Doggett's badge*, in the British Museum No. II. 3, is often thought to be Chelsea, but is proved as Bow by the colouring of a characteristic Bow base on a specimen in the Willett Collection at Brighton.[3]

In the Museum collection at South Kensington is a case filled with figures of the finest quality, most of them part of Mr. Broderip's magnificent gift. The delicious poise and balance of the modelling and the directness and simplicity of the colouring of their smooth ivory surface could not be better studied than in the *Apollo*, the *Air* (from a set of *Elements*), the *Bagpiper* (Plate 30) and the *Sportsman* and his companion (C 323 and 324—1926). The last-named have a rare mark in an incised *W* on the upper surface of the base. Another pair of models, rather similar to the last (Nos. C 1316 and 1317—1924) but apparently later (about 1760), shows the more delicate modelling of heads of the later figures of this period; the male figure has a curious impressed mark like a ladder.[4] One of these pairs is presumably the "sporters" mentioned by Bowcocke. The group figured in Plate 30 is of about the same date as the last-mentioned pair, and has the *T°* mark.

The most ambitious Bow figures were the famous *General Wolfe* and *Marquis of Granby*, large models over a foot high, represented both at the British Museum and in the Schreiber Collection.[5] These

[1] In the Museum collection, Nos. C. 1314 and 1315—1924.

[2] See Appendix, p. 260, Nos. 8 and 9, for both these marks.

[3] The British Museum specimen has lately been tested and found to have a phosphatic paste. See *British Museum Quarterly*, vol. ii, No. 1, p. 31. But Chelsea versions may also have been made.

[4] Appendix, p. 260, No. 10.

[5] Schr. No. 54 & A, and B.M. No. I. 19.

were probably made to celebrate victories over the French in 1759 at Quebec and Minden, battles in which these generals were engaged. They seem to have been modelled after engravings by Richard Houston,[1] who was, like Frye, a pupil of James Brooks. Fragments identical with parts of these figures were found on the site of the works,[2] and the distinctive opaque "Bow blue", used on the uniforms, is thus confirmed as of Bow origin.

Two charming figures of a "Fluter and Companion" at the British Museum (I. 23) also belong to the latter part of this middle period.[3] Sketches slightly resembling them, with this title and the prices "3s. and 4s. 6d." are among the Bowcocke papers. Like other drawings included in the papers they are apparently the work of a child or amateur, and not in the least likely to be designs for the figures.

Figures of birds and animals follow the Meissen and Chelsea fashion. But most of the Bow birds are wholly fanciful in their clear, bold colouring. The beautiful plumage of the *Tawny Owls* in the Schreiber Collection (No. 61), for example, is rendered by a pure convention, appropriate to brushwork; and the applied leaves, here and on many other pieces belonging to this period, are enamelled in the characteristic Bow rich emerald-green, with an admirable disregard of natural appearance. On the other hand, the tureens in the form of sitting *Partridges* are decidedly closer to nature than those made at Chelsea. A note in Bowcocke's papers reads "to buy a partridge alive or dead" and it is perhaps not fanciful to see in this a reference to the exactness in the rendering of these. The dishes on

[1] The engraving used for *Wolfe* is based on a sketch by Captain Hervey Smyth (discussed in *The Century Magazine*, New Series, xxxiii, p. 327). The portrait of Granby, published in 1760, was engraved after a painting by Sir Joshua Reynolds, and shows the General bare-headed—a record of an incident in the battle of Minden.

[2] *The Burlington Magazine*, vol. xl (1922), p. 224, Plate K.

[3] A pair in the Schreiber Collection (No. 83), representing *Spring* and *Winter*, are of the same model slightly altered.

which these tureens stand are quite different from those with the Chelsea partridges, though a fragment from one of the latter was found on the Bow site.[1] The *Cock* and *Hen* (Schr. No. 60), figured in Plate 28, are typical in modelling of the birds made at Bow.

We may associate with the figures some fine decorative pieces. The frilled *rococo* vases (Plate 28), sometimes with applied masks, seem to have been a favourite with "Mr. Tebo"; we find them with his mark also at Bristol and Worcester. One may, I think, assume that models of this kind would have been the inventions of repairers, like the shell-salts previously mentioned. There are good specimens in both collections at South Kensington. The similar flower-holders in the form of cornucopias, and such things as a four-sided pedestal in the Schreiber Collection (Nos. 71 and 72), with their clean ivory-like glaze and rich colours, rank among the best work of the factory. A pot-pourri vase (Schr. No. 68) marked T°, of bronze or silver form, with gadroonings picked out in that characteristic and delightful Bow crimson which Mr. William Burton found "barely tolerable", has on the lid a figure of a seated bagpiper identical with one found in Delft, but ultimately to be traced to a bronze by Giovanni Bologna.

A REMARKABLY SOFT AND DELICATE STYLE OF FLOWER painting is quite peculiar to Bow amongst the English factories, though so like that on some Mennecy porcelain as to suggest a migrant Frenchman.[2] Two vases mounted in *ormoulu* in the Schreiber Collection (No. 73) are painted by this hand, and a mug in Mr. Broderip's gift is inscribed in crimson *William Taylor 1759* (C 943—1924).[3] The vase painted with these

[1] See p. 33.

[2] A vase in the V. & A.M. (No. C 334—1909) is a Mennecy piece showing this resemblance in a marked degree. A Mennecy figure of a boy with a shell, in the same collection (No. C 1324—1919) shows a kinship in modelling as well as in flower-painting.

[3] A William Taylor was employed as a painter at Derby, but more than thirty years later. Another was apprenticed at Worcester in 1763.

flowers figured in Plate 27 C is marked with a *B* in underglaze blue, which some would regard as a Bow factory mark. But as other letters, as well as numerals, occur at least as frequently it is probably no more than a workman's mark. An octagonal plate (No. C 652—1925: Plate 28 D) in the same case also shows the Bow flowers at their best.

Much Bow "useful" ware was painted in a rather summary style copied from the Chinese *famille rose* (Plate 27 A & B). This painting is distinguished by clean fresh colouring, and is proved as Bow not only by paste and glaze, but by certain peculiarities of form. An inkstand so painted (V. & A.M. No. 2865—1901) is of nearly the same shape as those inscribed *New Canton*. Mr. Wallace Elliot has a document for this style in a large tureen, with applied sprigs of *prunus* and painted in *famille rose* style, which is dated 1753. Many plates with this decoration are of the favourite Bow octagonal form with a rather deep well having thick walls rounded towards a hollowed base which is without the usual triangular foot-ring. This form is not, I believe, found on other English china, but is common in Chinese "export porcelain" and is seen also in Delft pottery. This is perhaps another instance of the Dutch influence we have previously met. A plate in the British Museum, of this form, is inscribed *P TB DARBY* in incised script letters. It is painted in *famille rose* style, has been proved phosphatic, and was almost certainly made at Bow.

Amongst other typical Bow shapes of this and the earlier period I may mention here the cup or cylindrical mug with a loop handle that joins the body almost horizontally at top and bottom, instead of, as usual, descending to join it below at a more or less acute angle.[1] Another type of mug with nearly cylindrical body slightly spreading to the base was made at several

[1] A mug at South Kensington (No. C 438—1924) is an example, proved as Bow by its style of *famille rose* painting.

factories, but the heart-shaped lower termination of the handle helps to distinguish those made at Bow.

The so-called Kakiemon designs, mainly in red, blue and gold, must have been even more popular here than at Chelsea, and, as we have seen, Bow specialised in "useful wares". We meet the "parteridge octogon plates" in Bowcocke's papers (1756) as well as in the advertisements. There is a whole shelf of pieces painted in this style—shell-salts, plates, cups and saucers—in Mr. Broderip's gift at South Kensington. To distinguish Bow, Chelsea and Worcester "Kakiemons" by painting alone is a simple matter, once the differences have been observed. Bow partridge patterns tend to a rather careless freedom, soft and rich in total effect. The garrulous Craft spoke of his bowl as painted in "what we used to call the old Japan Taste, a taste much esteemed by the then Duke of Argyle"; but the colouring alone recalls the Japanese designs. The garlanded flowers of the bowl appear also with phoenixes on a plate in the Schreiber Collection (No. 75), which we may attribute to Craft's hand. Another class closely imitating the Kakiemons has the "banded hedge", the bursting pomegranates and other motives of the Japanese porcelain executed with great fineness and delicacy. A cup and saucer in the Schreiber Collection (Plate 26 B) is a good example; a mug (Schr. No. 79) figured in Plate 26 C shows a delightfully rendered piece of heraldry boldly combined with Japanese motives, the whole surmounted by a typical Bow figure of a pug dog. Such combinations of motives are entirely characteristic of the factory. A beautiful (but damaged) square dish in South Kensington (No. 2909—1901) has Chinese plum-blossom in relief, finely painted Meissen flowers in colours, and a red Kakiemon border. Another fine Kakiemon piece, figured in Plate 26 A, is a vase bequeathed to the Victoria and Albert Museum by the late Lieut.-Colonel G. B. Croft Lyons. It is of an elongated egg-

A

B

About 1750–55.
(*London and V. and A. Museums.*)
See pp. 61, 63.

A

About 1750–55. (*V. and A. Museum.*)
See p. 68.

B

About 1760. (*Schreiber Collection.*)
See p. 67.

C

About 1765. (*London Museum.*)
See p. 78

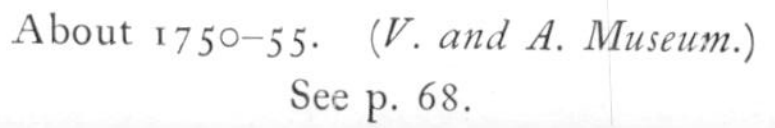

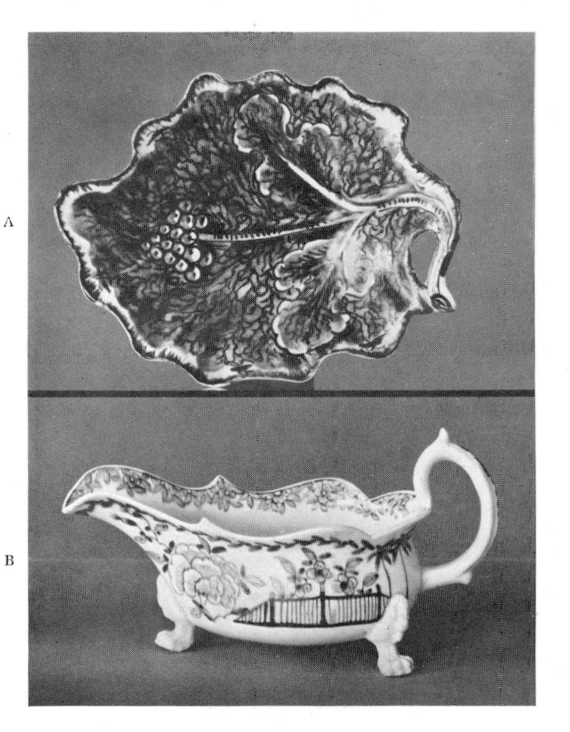

A

B

C

Blue-and-white porcelain. About 1755–65.

A and C are marked with simulated Chinese characters; B with a planet-mark incised, and G in blue.

(V. and A. Museum and Schreiber Collections.) See pp. 64, 76, 77.

A

B

Transfer-printed wares. About 1750–55.
(*Dr. S. W. Woodhouse's and V. and A. Museum Collections.*)
See p. 74.

shape which is almost peculiar to Bow among the English factories, and the form serves to confirm as Bow a class with Chinese subjects faintly printed in outline and enamelled over in colours. A characteristic Bow freshness of colour is the only merit in these. There are several examples in both rooms at South Kensington.

Printed decoration seems to have been used at Bow quite early in this period, but no document is available to give a precise date for its introduction.[1] A print in brick-red on a plate in the Schreiber Collection (No. 111) with the subject of Æneas and Anchises strongly recalls those attributable to Simon-François Ravenet at Battersea.[2] A long, fluent line and a distinctive use of cross-hatching mark the work of Ravenet. Similar qualities are seen in the engraving copied from one by J. P. Le Bas after Chardin entitled *Le Négligé, ou La Toilette de Matin*, of which examples are known on unquestionable Bow porcelain. Rouquet, the French traveller whom I have quoted before, reported a china-factory at Battersea[3] where decoration was carried out by a kind of printing. It is not impossible that the china seen by Rouquet had been brought to the factory from Chelsea or Bow to receive its decoration by printing. But the process is not a difficult one, and it is hard to understand why Thomas Frye, an engraver, should not have carried out printed decoration at Bow and even engraved plates himself.

[1] Bowcocke wrote in 1756 of "printed teas", but it would be rash to assume that this is a reference to printed wares as we understand the word. His notes were of course never intended to be understood by others, and the tantalisingly brief descriptions can but seldom be identified with existing pieces. The "fine landskip pattern", "image pattern", "Newark pattern", and "Dresden sprig" leave us altogether in doubt as to the particular designs in question. And "Paris Cries", "Dutch Dancers", " Nuns and Fryers", "Fostinas", "Swan", and "Woman with Chicken", etc., are models well-known also in porcelain from other factories, and we are thus not helped in the task of identifying those from Bow.

[2] See *Catalogue of the Schreiber Collection*, vol. iii, p. 7.

[3] *Op. cit.*, p. 143. I have discussed this passage and the probably mythical china-factory on p. 252.

The absence of any trace of his personal style in the Bow decoration (charming though it is) suggests that as far as porcelain manufacture was concerned he was a technician only. And I have already suggested that much of the Bow china may have been decorated elsewhere.

But if Bow porcelain was printed at Battersea then the old legend that Hancock worked there may have some foundation after all. The common belief in Hancock-at-Battersea was shown by Mr. Rackham [1] to be based entirely (so far as actual evidence is concerned) upon the mistaken attribution to Battersea of a Staffordshire enamel. The evidence of Hancock's work at or for Bow exists in the form of a signed print on an unmistakable Bow plate at the British Museum (No. I. 65).[2] There are other Hancock prints on porcelain attributed to Bow, but the ascription either to the factory or the engraver has usually been open to question. Here there can be no doubt: the specimen shows all the characteristics of Bow porcelain of 1750–55. The partings in the paste, the bright flecks and warm cream-colour by transmitted light, and the soft glaze, no less than the Kakiemon border naïvely combined with a brick-red transfer-print, speak clearly of a Bow origin. I think we may confidently assign this plate to a date considerably before 1757, the year of the earliest dated Hancock prints on Worcester porcelain. If the primitive style of engraving on the early Bristol china to be described on a later page [3] is by Hancock (though I do not consider this to be proved), we must conjecture an interval spent in London by the engraver, or that he sold some plates to the Bow or Battersea proprietors, neither alternative being impossible, of course.

[1] In *The Burlington Magazine*, vol. xxvi (1915), p. 155: the assertion that he learnt mezzotint engraving from Thomas Frye and line-engraving from Ravenet is based on nothing better than surmise.

[2] This evidence has been for long overlooked: the latest historian of the Battersea factory, who was much concerned with the matter, does not mention it.

[3] See p. 145.

But printing on Bow china was never well-established as a mode of decoration. The Bow glaze was evidently too soft and fusible, and prints, especially those in the purplish or brownish black which was favoured, were apt to be blurred or fuzzy. The beautiful warm brick-red of many of the prints seems to have made for success, and such examples as those figured in Plate 32 are surpassed by none in delicacy of line and charm of effect. The groups of sheep and poultry and the Italian landscapes (Schr. Nos. 113 and 114) should also be noted as typical Bow prints quite different in effect from those of other factories. The naïve mixture of motives so characteristic of Bow is well seen again in a teapot in the Schreiber Collection (No. 110), printed with a portrait of Frederick the Great, and having a twig handle with brilliant green leaves attached, and a spout painted with flowers in Chinese style! The portraits of Frederick the Great, common on English porcelain of this time, commemorate his successes in the Seven Years' War and his convention with England in 1756 against France and her allies. There is no evidence that printing in blue was ever done at Bow,[1] and pieces with this decoration and a bone-ash paste must be presumed to be of either Liverpool or Lowestoft manufacture.

Porcelain painted in blue undoubtedly formed a large part of the Bow productions in this period and later, but its identification continues to be the subject of dispute. The classification of some specimens as between Bow, Lowestoft and Liverpool is still a little uncertain. I shall, however, describe some characteristics which identify certain well-defined types. The earliest specimens attributed to the factory, painted in very bright blue, have already been mentioned. An apparently later specimen, a dish of the familiar type in the form of a leaf painted with vines and grapes

[1] No fragments with blue-printing seem ever to have been found on the factory site.

(Plate 31), and bearing a common and distinctively written mark of four simulated Chinese characters,[1] has been analysed[2] and found to contain phosphoric acid; and fragments were found on the site of the factory[3] with part of the design of a Chinaman with a staff and a boy attendant, seen on a sauce-boat, a large dish and a plate in the Museum collection at South Kensington (Nos. C 566—1924, C 51—1916 and C 491—1924). The characteristics of these, together with the marks on the leaf dish, supply evidence for the attribution to Bow of certain other specimens of blue-and-white. Letters and numerals in blue on the base (not on the foot-ring as in Lowestoft) are common on Bow blue-and-white; the B which sometimes occurs is more likely to be a workman's mark than to stand for Bow. A mark resembling T and F[4] conjoined was for long believed to be a Bow mark, standing for Thomas Frye; but the oviform vases so marked are now known to be of Worcester porcelain. This mark is an imperfect copy of the Chinese character *yü* (jade), commonly found on Chinese blue-and-white. Another form of the same letters is, however, sometimes seen on Bow porcelain,[5] but is easily distinguished from the Worcester mark.

Amongst the later Bow blue-and-white are certain much-disputed dishes and plates with Chinese subjects painted in panels reserved on a powdered-blue ground.[6] The Bow glaze and strong blue are usually sufficient proof of the origin of these.[7] And two plates with this

[1] See Appendix, p. 260, No. 16.

[2] *Analysed Specimens*, No. 13.

[3] *The Burlington Magazine*, vol. xl (1922) p. 229, Plate F.

[4] See p. 156, and Appendix, p. 264, No. 5.

[5] As on an early blue-and-white bowl at South Kensington (No. C 538—1924). See Appendix, p. 260, No. 11.

[6] These have also been attributed to Lowestoft (Spelman, *Lowestoft Porcelain*, Plate 25) and to Worcester and Caughley (Hobson, *Worcester Porcelain*, pp. 58, 189). See pp. 134, 156 and 187.

[7] Bow coloured enamels, including a "stale-mustard" yellow and a slaty blue, on a powdered-blue plate in Mr. Herbert Allen's collection (No. 24), prove this specimen to belong to the factory.

decoration in the Schreiber Collection (Plate 31) bear marks not dissimilar to those on the analysed dish and are also of the distinctive Bow shape, a form found also in the *Robert Crowther* plate, dated 1770, in the British Museum.[1] A punch bowl in the Schreiber Collection (No. 29), painted in blue with masonic emblems, is noteworthy for the date it bears (1768). Apart from the evidence of style, the Bow blue-and-white may usually be distinguished from the similar ware made at Lowestoft (which also contained bone-ash) by the quality of its glaze. An unusual quantity of lead was apparently used, giving a markedly yellowish tone to the enamel-painted pieces, and rendering it liable to decomposition especially at the foot. The faint iridescence of surface, also due to excess of lead, is more marked on Bow than on any other English china. A liability to blackish specks is also noticeable in the commoner wares. The blue-painted pieces rarely have the ivory colour of the others, and one may suppose that the glaze for these was deliberately "blued" with a minute quantity of cobalt, or the blue-colour used for the painting has perhaps "flown" in the kiln. At Bow the colour was always inclined to run, from the softness of the glaze. A common feature of Bow bowls is the trace of the second firing in spur marks on the *rims*.

The later productions of the factory show a great falling-away from the standard of originality and charm previously reached. The porcelain itself was no longer of fine quality; the paste was often nearly opaque, showing a dusky brownish translucency, and the uneven-surfaced glaze, now much disfigured by black specks, was strongly tinged with blue, apparently to counteract the former yellowish or ivory tone, which was evidently regarded as a shortcoming. For the greater part, the designs and styles were frankly imitated from those of contemporary "gold anchor" Chelsea. In this, Bow was perhaps aided by the

[1] See pp. 59 and 71.

migration of Chelsea workmen: Mason [1] stated that he worked at Bow when the other factory was closed on account of Sprimont's illness. Figures were as a rule clumsily modelled, the costumes extravagantly but crudely decorated with diaper-patterns in colours dull and lifeless in comparison with those of the earlier period: the beautiful opaque blue enamel was replaced by a dark translucent blue, and muddy pink and watery green colours were much employed. The Schreiber Collection is again representative. The *Dancing Peasants* (No. 90), and the well-dressed *Gardener*, symbolical of Autumn (No. 85) are perhaps the best modelled of the later figures. The last-named is adapted from the famous Chelsea gardener in the gold-anchor *Autumn* (as in the Schreiber Collection, No. 198). Though poor in material and colour, in my opinion he surpasses the Chelsea figure as a piece of porcelain-modelling. The *Man in Turkish Costume* (No. 87) is interesting as a version of a model made in the earlier periods. The droll *Dancing Girl*, adapted from a Meissen model, figured in Plate 30, is typical and charming in its Bow-ish way: it shows the Bow version of the "gold-anchor style". The four-footed pedestal of this figure belongs to a rather earlier phase, and was now often replaced by a moulded base decorated with *rococo* scroll-work (again in imitation of Chelsea), as in the *Bishop* in the Schreiber Collection (No. 91), the Candlestick with a *Woman holding a Boy* (No. 93) and the Red Indian woman emblematic of *America* (No. 86). The last-named was inspired by the Greco-Roman statue in the Louvre, Paris, known as *Diane Chasseresse*; a similar model was used at Plymouth and Bristol. The heads of many of these late Bow figures are quite distinctive: the *Drummers* (Schr. No. 84), as well as the *Dancing Peasants* mentioned above and the *Girl* figured in Plate 32, should be noticed as typical.

The "exotic birds" of Chelsea were also copied, as

[1] See p. 30.

on the panels of a plate in the Schreiber Collection (No. 105), on which the ground colour is probably intended to imitate the "mazarine" blue: the fantastic and ugly large *rococo* vases are also painted with birds in this style, in panels on a powdered-blue ground. Worcester scale-blue was copied, and a specimen of this kind in Mr. Wallace Elliot's collection has the square-mark of the Worcester factory as well as the Bow anchor and dagger in red. The "dishevelled birds", best known on Worcester porcelain, are seen on a late Bow plate in the Schreiber Collection (No. 107). The occurrence of painting by this hand on porcelain from several factories suggests the work of an outside decorator.[1] The "Watteau figures" of Chelsea were imitated on a "frill vase" in the Herbert Allen Collection (No. 11), and on a fine tureen at South Kensington (No. C 307—1927), the stand for which is figured in Plate 33. This piece proves the survival of something of the old Bow *naïveté* even at this date. The figure-painting is of great charm and simplicity. The painting of flowers and fruit (as on Schr. Nos. 76 and 103: Plate 33), though obviously inspired by the rival London factory, is often very successful in its bold drawing and full-toned colour. A Chelsea plate in the Museum collection at South Kensington (No. 2943—1901) is painted with fruit apparently by the same hand as these Bow pieces: we may wonder whether this is perhaps the work of the migrant painter Mason. This plate should be compared with a fine mug in the Schreiber Collection (No. 102), from which a mark (presumably a dagger) has been ground away to leave an anchor only. A previous owner evidently felt that it was worthy to be regarded as Chelsea! The scale-blue of the Worcester factory was also copied on a plate in the British Museum (No. I. 40).

Some painting in red-brown, green and purple of lake-scenes with trees and foliage, as on a pair of dishes

[1] I have discussed this question on p. 171.

in the Schreiber Collection (No. 104) and on a mug in the Museum collection at South Kensington (No. 3272—1853: Plate 34), forms a noteworthy exception to the general rule of incompetence in this period: a limited palette and sensitive handling give these pieces a charm rare enough in this period of Bow china.

Many pieces attributable to Bow in its last period are marked with an anchor and a dagger, in red or brown, often accompanied by letters, dots or symbols in underglaze blue. The anchor may have been first used by a migrant Chelsea workman. A pair of dishes at South Kensington moulded with fruit and painted with flowers in unmistakable Bow style are marked with an anchor only; but the curious discoloration of the glaze makes it almost certain that the anchor is a later addition unskilfully refired. The dagger of the late Bow mark is sometimes said to have been drawn from the arms of the city of London. It is found also in underglaze blue, sometimes with the red dagger as well. The letter I and an A of archaic form[1] in underglaze blue are common. These are doubtless workmen's marks, and the cursive B in blue, also found, is no more likely to stand for Bow than the similar letter sometimes found on earlier pieces, as already mentioned. The recurrence of a rather clumsy crescent has led to the mistaken attribution to Worcester of figures with this mark. Analysis has, however, proved a crescent-marked figure to contain bone-ash, whilst a similar test has shown that the few figures believed to have been made at Worcester contain magnesia due to soapstone, the characteristic Worcester ingredient.[2] Moreover, the blue crescent occurs on figures in combination with the red anchor and dagger.

[1] See Appendix, p. 261, No. 24. Erroneously stated by Chaffers to be a Longton Hall mark.

[2] See p. 175.

A

B

About 1760–65. A has the anchor-and-dagger mark.
(*Schreiber and V. and A. Museum Collections.*)
See p. 79.

A

B

About 1760–65. Anchor-and-dagger marks.
(*Schreiber and V. and A. Museum Collections.*)
See p. 80.

CHAPTER IV

DERBY

ACCORDING to a vague tradition preserved by the older workmen at the factory, porcelain was made at Derby as early as 1745. William Locker, clerk to the factory towards the end of its existence, reported a statement by Samuel Keys, a workman who had been apprenticed in 1785, to the effect that a foreigner in poor circumstances, living in Lodge Lane, had "about 1745" modelled "small articles in china, such as birds, cats, dogs, sheep and small ornamental toys", and fired them at a kiln in the neighbourhood, belonging to Woodward, a pipe-maker.[1] Mr. F. Williamson has recently shown[2] that the only pipe-maker's kiln that could be in question was built as late as 1795, and that this part of the tradition at least must be mistaken.

That porcelain was in fact made in Derby as early as 1750 is proved by certain white porcelain cream-jugs, decorated with strawberries and leaves in applied relief. One of these, in the possession of Mr. Egerton Leigh, is inscribed under the base with the word *Derby*[3] incised; another, in the Victoria and Albert Museum (C 629—1920), has the inscription *D 1750*; a third, in the British Museum, is marked with the initial *D* alone.

[1] Quoted by Chaffers, *op. cit.*, 13th edition (1912), p. 818.
[2] *The Connoisseur*, vol. lxxvii (1927), p. 228.
[3] This jug is erroneously stated by Chaffers (*op. cit.*, p. 829) to be painted. The jug is reproduced in an article by W. B. Honey, Bernard Rackham and Herbert Read in *The Burlington Magazine*, vol. xlix (1926), p. 292, where the question of the earliest Derby china is fully discussed.

All are of porcelain of poor quality; they bear little or no resemblance to other existing specimens, and are thus useless as a means of identifying the remainder of the earliest Derby productions that may be presumed to survive.

From entries in the work-books of William Duesbury, relating to his employment in London as an enameller,[1] we know that figures were in fact made at Derby soon after 1750. Frequent entries for dates between 1751 and 1753 mention "Darbey" and "Darbishire figars" of dancers, "sesons" and the like. No dated specimen or evidence directly concerning an actual porcelain factory at Derby is available for dates between 1750 and 1756, unless we admit as proof an entry dated June 1754, in the register of a Derby church, recording the marriage of William Whitehall, "labourer at the China House".[2] A workman of the same name was a fireman at the Nottingham Road China-Works eighteen years later. For 1756, however, we have an important document in the famous draft agreement published by Jewitt.[3] This was never executed, though dated as for January 1, 1756. "John Heath of Derby . . . Gentleman . . . Andrew Planché of the same place, China Maker . . . and Wm. Duesbury of Longton, Enamellor", were named as partners "in the Art of making English China". Heath, a Derby banker, was to find a thousand pounds and take a third share of the profits. He was already the proprietor of a pottery at Cockpit Hill in the town of Derby. Duesbury had in 1755 made an arrangement with his father, a currier of Cannock, by which he agreed to support him for the rest of his life in return for the transference of his possessions. It seems highly

[1] Described and published in part by W. Bemrose, *Bow, Chelsea and Derby Porcelain*, 1898, pp. 7-17.

[2] See an article by F. Williamson in the *Museums Journal*, vol. xxii, p. 141. No earlier entry of this kind can be quoted, as occupations began to be entered in the registers only in 1754.

[3] Vol. ii, p. 64.

probable that this arrangement was made to provide the younger Duesbury with capital with which to start a china-factory. Of Andrew Planché little is known. He is said to have been in Saxony and "there learnt the art of making porcelain in Dresden", but this family tradition would merely imply that he had been abroad and there acquired some knowledge of china-making. He is generally assumed to have been the "foreigner" referred to by Keys though he would have been only seventeen years old at the date given (1745). He was apparently living in Derby in 1751, as in that year he had a son baptized at St. Alkmund's Church.[1] It is likely enough that the figures enamelled by Duesbury in London were the work of Planché, and were fired if not made at Heath's pottery.

No place is named in the 1756 agreement, and Nightingale, excited by his rediscovery of Longton Hall, rather perversely assumed that it related to that factory. It is almost certain, however, that it referred to the establishment of new works in Nottingham Road for a manufacture that had grown too large or ambitious for the Cockpit Hill Pottery. The actual date of the foundation of these new works may be inferred from a later document, which records the transfer of the premises to William Duesbury alone on the bankruptcy of John Heath, and refers to an earlier conveyance of April 19, 1756. We hear no more of Planché in connection with Derby porcelain. He was presumably still living in Derby in 1756, since he had an illegitimate son baptized there in March of that year and a lawful son four months later, but we can scarcely accept the suggestion of Bemrose and others that the low moral standard implied by this led to his exclusion from the partnership. He is said to have been living in Bath at the "ripe age of 76 in 1804 and died soon afterwards".[2]

The first undoubted contemporary reference to

[1] Jewitt, vol. ii, p. 65. [2] *Ibid.*

Derby porcelain is contained in announcements in the *Public Advertiser* of December 1756 of an auction sale to be held in London "by order of the Proprietors of the DERBY PORCELAIN Manufactory", offering "A Curious Collection of fine *Figures*, *Jars*, *Sauceboats*, *Services for Deserts*, and Great *Variety* of other useful and ornamental Porcelain, after the finest Dresden models". In May 1757 an advertisement in the same paper announced ". . . the largest variety of the Derby or second Dresden", and a paragraph also spoke of "the Perfection the Derby figures in particular are arrived to". In 1758 another advertisement announced the sale of "great Variety of Figures, the nearest the Dresden. . . . As with great Care and Expence, this Factory is allow'd by all Judges to exceed any Thing of the kind made in England, and the great demand there is for them, has encouraged the Proprietors to enlarge their Manufactory, and have engaged double the Number of Hands they used to employ". This date marked the cessation of the advertisements of Longton Hall porcelain, and it has therefore been supposed that the workmen from Longton were about this time transferred to Derby.[1] In 1770 the Chelsea factory was bought, and for fourteen years carried on in combination with that at Derby. It is commonly said that about 1776 the Bow works were also purchased, and I have already discussed the evidence for this under the heading of Bow.[2]

So LITTLE IS KNOWN AT PRESENT OF THE VERY earliest Derby porcelain, contemporary with or a little later than the dated cream-jugs, that it is little better than guesswork to attempt to identify them. A process of elimination and the common feature of a band at the foot bare of glaze have led to the identification of the almost mythical Planché figures with a group loosely named "the dry-edge class", represented by a pair of *Goats* in the Schreiber Collection (No. 307) and

[1] See p. 119. [2] See p. 56.

several other pieces at South Kensington.[1] The "dry-edge" is perhaps no more than the evidence of timidity or a lack of skill on the part of the workman dipping the piece in the glaze, such as might occur anywhere. But in point of fact the peculiar *appearance* of shrinkage is rarely found on pieces more certainly attributable to other factories. Another peculiarity seen on a number of these pieces (including the *Lady with a Basket* to be mentioned presently) is a *funnel*-shaped hole in the base, different from the straight-sided hole of the Bow figures.[2] Moreover there is a decidedly un-English look about Mr. Herbert Allen's white *Boys milking a Goat* (No. 2) and his *Florentine Boars* (No. 1) that suggests the work of a "foreigner"; and they do not resemble anything we know as Chelsea. Similarly, a fine little series of Chinese groups was for long assigned to Chelsea, but cannot be linked with any other ascertained productions of that factory. These are represented at South Kensington by the *Chinaman and Boy* (Schreiber Collection No. 284 : Plate 35 A) and at the British Museum by the two other groups, a man and woman, and a lady and child (Nos. II. 4 and 5). Coloured versions exist but do not throw any light on their place of origin. All are most beautifully modelled and of milky-white porcelain with a "solid" glaze suggesting the use of more than the usual small quantity of tin-oxide. The "dry-edge" is apparent on most of them, and a variety of the funnel-shaped hole is seen on their bases: in this case it proceeds from a countersunk circle. The funnel-shaped hole appears on a pair of white figures of *Bagpipers* in Mr. Wallace Elliot's collection[3] of a model often found in Bow. The glaze and the treatment of the ribbons suggest that these are early Derby specimens.

The figures of *Cows* and *Pheasants* which I have

[1] See *The Burlington Magazine, loc. cit.*

[2] The form of the hole recalls the conical head and top of the shank of a wood-screw.

[3] Figured in *The Connoisseur*, vol. lxxix (Sept. 1927), p. 7.

ascribed to the earliest period of Bow[1] may almost equally well be claimed for Derby. They would, of course, be much earlier than the pieces just mentioned. They temptingly agree with Keys' description. All are non-phosphatic, so chemical analysis does not help. But since non-phosphatic Bow must be before 1750 (nearer to 1745 in fact) and we have no real evidence that Derby began before 1750, any pieces in a style suggesting the earlier date are more probably Bow, and any that are to be dated after 1750 must be either Chelsea or Derby. There are few opportunities, however, for applying this criterion: the specimens in question are usually quite primitive in character.

Against the ascription of most of these pieces to Derby is the important argument resting upon the absence of a link with the later and better-proved productions of the factory. One specimen of this "dry-edge" class, the *Lady with a Basket*, at South Kensington (Schr. No. 286: Plate 35) is from the same model and perhaps from the same mould as a rather later *Lady playing a lute*, also in the Museum collection (No. C 679—1925), which can be shown with fair probability to be Derby. I have already mentioned the former of these two figures in connection with certain Bow pieces,[2] apparently painted by the same hand. The *Lady* is, however, of a non-phosphatic paste, and we may provisionally regard her as one of the earliest Derby figures, made soon after 1750. A solidly milk-white glaze is a feature, but it is scarcely distinctive enough to identify others of a like origin. A figure of a *Dancing Man* at South Kensington (No. C 312—1916) in plain white, with rather dirty white but somewhat opaque glaze, has the funnel-shaped hole in the base, mentioned above, and is of the same model as a coloured figure in Mr. A. H. S. Bunford's collection bearing the incised mark *N318* and quite certainly Derby.[3] The white group

[1] See p. 59. [2] See p. 62.
[3] No. 318 in the Derby price-list is *Pair of Dancing Figures*.

of *Pluto and Cerberus* (Plate 35), for long ascribed to Bow, has been proved non-phosphatic and is most probably a Derby piece: it was probably intended for *Earth* in a set of *Elements*.[1] A "dry-edge" and a similar rather dirty-coloured and opaque glaze distinguishes two interesting pieces that bear a curious mark resembling a Y within a triangle enclosed by a circle. A *Dancing Youth* at South Kensington (No. C 540—1921)[2] and a defective group of a dog barking at a cat in a tree, belonging to Mr. F. E. Sidney, both bear this mark. The painting on the first-named bears a slight resemblance to the pale-coloured family of Derby figures ascribed below to the period about 1755; but a smeared unpleasant surface-quality distinguishes it, and we may conjecturally regard these pieces as coloured specimens of the "Planché period".

It may be argued that a resemblance in model is of little account where one factory so commonly moulded its figures from those of another; and that Planché may well have removed his stock of moulds on his exclusion from the new partnership. But links of some kind between later and earlier are generally to be found in the work of a factory with an unbroken tradition. It was in fact by this means that the Derby pieces of the period from about 1755 to 1770 were eventually identified. These had remained for many years unrecognised amongst the Bow and unmarked Chelsea until Mr. Bernard Rackham found a clue in their similarity in certain respects to later and well-authenticated Derby porcelain. An almost constant feature of the figures is the presence on the base (which is commonly flat) of three or four dark unglazed patches left by the pads of clay upon which the pieces rested during their second or glaze firing. These patches do occur also, but much more rarely, on pieces known to

[1] Mr. Wallace Elliot has others from the same set (figured in *The Connoisseur*, vol. lxxix (Sept. 1927), p. 7). See p. 229 for a connection with the Bristol *Elements*, which resemble these and were the work of a Derby modeller.

[2] Illustrated in *The Burlington Magazine*, *loc. cit.*

have been made elsewhere; for example, on the red-anchor *Leda* in the Schreiber Collection and on a gold-anchor vase (No. 485—1875) also at South Kensington. They occur constantly, however, not only on these early pieces in question but also on the later figures which bear the serial numbers of the Derby price-list and are therefore unquestionably of Derby manufacture. The "patches" clearly indicate a continuous factory practice, or perhaps even the custom of a single workman. A further proof of the origin of the class is furnished by the recurrence of the same models in later Derby. The *Falstaff* is one of these, and a remarkable confirmation of Mr. Rackham's conjecture was furnished by the occurrence of a mark on a figure of a *Bagpiper* of this class, in Mr. Wallace Elliot's collection.[1] This model is repeatedly found in all sorts of sizes and dates down to the closing of the factory,[2] and Mr. Elliot's specimen, which from its style seems to date from about 1760, bears the faintly incised mark *W D-Co*, reasonably regarded as an abbreviation of "William Duesbury and Company".

The figures belonging to this "patch family" form a coherent class with many other common characteristics. The colouring includes a very easily recognised turquoise-green with a tendency to become discoloured to a dirty brownish tone. Modelling of heads (and in particular noses) and the flesh-painting (with bright patches on the cheeks) are also distinctive; a "family likeness" is easily perceived. By style these figures seem to date from the period *c.* 1760–70, and confirmation of this is provided by a figure formerly in the Leverhulme Collection, marked *George Holmes did this figer 1765*.[3] Holmes was probably a "repairer" and

[1] Illustrated in *The Burlington Magazine*, *loc. cit.*

[2] There are two examples of different sizes in Mr. Herbert Allen's collection (Nos. 38 and 40), and two others, of nineteenth-century date, in the Museum collection at South Kensington.

[3] *Sale Catalogue*, Part 3 (New York, 1926), No. 112 (described as Chelsea); illustrated on p. 39.

A

B

C

About 1750–55.
(*Schreiber Collection.*)
See pp. 85 to 87.

A

B

C

About 1755–60. (*V. and A. Museum.*) See p. 91.

A

B

C

About 1760–65. (*Mr. Herbert Allen's Collection.*) See p. 91.

A

B

C

About 1760.
A and B are painted in colours, C in blue.
(*V. and A. Museum and Schreiber Collections.*)
See pp. 92 and 102.

perhaps the G. Holmes named in a list of hands working at the factory in 1787, quoted by Jewitt.[1] The class formed by far the greater part of the unmarked figures previously assigned to Chelsea, but it seems difficult now to understand how they could have ever been so confused. Not only do they differ in style, but their material is quite different. The soft greenish-toned glaze is absent; the paste has been proved non-phosphatic,[2] whilst Chelsea from 1758 contained bone-ash. But their owners hotly disputed (and perhaps still dispute) any other attribution than Chelsea![3]

If these lavishly gilded figures represent the Derby work imitating, and contemporary with, the later figures of Chelsea, what were the productions of the preceding years? The argument by a "throw-back" again helps. We find such a model as Kaendler's well-known *Lovers with a Clown*, familiar in the "patch" family,[4] occurring on a smaller scale and with different colouring in typical specimens of another class.[5] A smaller version of the model just mentioned is in the Schreiber Collection (No. 290). This earlier class of figures evidently aped the red-anchor Chelsea; their pale colouring,

[1] *Op. cit.*, vol. ii, p. 102.

[2] Analysis by Dr. Plenderleith of the *Man carrying a Keg* in the Victoria and Albert Museum (No. C 768—1917) shows no phosphoric acid. The full analysis is as follows:

Silica	68·5
Oxide of lead . . .	4·5
Alumina	5·5
Lime	17·6
Magnesia	2·5
	98·6

The magnesia may be due to soapstone, and if so this figure would be ascribed to a date after 1764. See p. 93 below, footnote.

[3] It is surprising that the partizans of particular factories should so constantly prefer quantity to quality. The average of excellence reached by the remaining authenticated Chelsea productions is raised by the withdrawal of those impostors "the patch-family"!

[4] An example from Mr. F. E. Sidney's collection is illustrated in W. King, *English Porcelain Figures*, Fig. 43.

[5] Most of them formerly ascribed to Bow, and, occasionally, to Longton Hall.

usually without gold, was the Derby version of the delicate tones of the London productions. A body of noticeably light weight and a strongly blued glaze are characteristic but not invariable features. Many of these figures were for long mistaken for Bow, but analysis again shows a non-phosphatic paste.[1] The same argument also helps to disprove the Derby origin claimed for the figure of a boy, marked with a cursive D, already mentioned under the heading of Bow.[2] Both in this and the subsequent period the applied flowers on the bases of the figures sometimes show centres in the form of a bun cut with a cross. This may be detected in the figures shown in Plate 36.[3]

It is by no means certain that figures of this "pale-coloured family" only began to be made in 1756 when Duesbury came to Derby[4] and the Nottingham Road factory was opened. Even after allowance has been made for the "lag" in the provincial imitation of a metropolitan fashion, the red-anchor style might well have been copied at the Cockpit Hill pottery for several years before this date. It is, I think, clear that such figures as those offered in the sale of 1756 could not have been the productions of a year-old factory: a tradition covering a longer period must be inferred.

Sufficient has been said to enable the collector to

[1] The analyses by Dr. Plenderleith of the *Diana* and the *Lady with a Lute* at South Kensington show:

Diana—		*Lady with a Lute*—	
Silica	74·1	Silica	70·4
Alumina	4·8	Oxide of lead	2·1
Lime	22·8	Alumina	5·4
		Lime	20·6
		Magnesia	1·3
	101·7		99·8

[2] See p. 68, and E. E. Hyam, *The Early Period of Derby Porcelain* (1926), p. 18, where this figure is claimed as Derby.

[3] This form of flower-centre does, of course, occur elsewhere, and is not by itself conclusive evidence. Staffordshire salt-glaze and Worcester porcelain figures show the same feature.

[4] We know that Duesbury was still "of Longton" in 1755.

identify the Derby figures of these two periods. As works of art their merit is decidedly a matter of opinion. Meissen models were copied no less constantly (as indeed the advertisements indicate) than at the other factories. The earlier "pale-coloured" family has occasionally the toy-like quality that helps to make a porcelain figure a delicious thing, but the chalky-looking paste and blued glaze are distinctly unpleasant. Delicacy of modelling is usually to seek. A pair of *Turkish Dancers* (Plate 36) and the *Musicians*—the *Lady playing a Lute* and a *Flute-player* (Plate 36 B), all at South Kensington (Nos. C 678 and 679—1925), are perhaps the best in the public collections. But in the later "patch" figures a stiff doll-like quality soon took possession, and the growing tendency to increase the scale of the models accentuates their clumsiness. The well-known group after Vanloo in the Schreiber Collection (No. 299) of a *Youth and a Girl with a Performing Dog* and the well-known *Minuet Dancers* (Schr. No. 297)[1] are characteristic and well-finished examples. Exact copies of Meissen models, such as the charming pair of a *Man carrying a Cock* and a *Woman carrying a Hen* at South Kensington (Nos. C 673 and 674—1925) and the *Mapsellers* and *Pedlars*, are among the best of the class. Pastoral figures with elaborate *bocages* were often fitted as candlesticks, and the applied flowers on these are sometimes very large and of a button-like form which occasionally helps to identify the rare pieces without other distinguishing marks. The three figures shown in Plate 37 (all from Mr. Herbert Allen's collection) are typical specimens of these Derby figures of the 1760's. The birds and animals cannot be compared for delicacy with those of Chelsea, and evidently soon became a "stock line" for the provincial market. Some of them, however, may date from the "Planché period": a group of two birds on a clumsy base in Mr. Herbert Allen's collection (No. 5) is an example, evi-

[1] Figured in many books on English porcelain as Chelsea.

dently early. *Miltons* and *Shakespeares* and *Britannias*, afterwards so popular, were already being made in this period.

THE USEFUL WARES AND DECORATIVE VASES OF THESE two periods show a link with the figures in the painting of flowers with stalks having a peculiar thread-like appearance (Plate 38 A): these are found quite early on the costumes of the figures, as on the pale-coloured *Diana* at South Kensington, already mentioned, and are very common later: Mr. Wallace Elliot's marked *Bagpiper* is painted with them. Another painter's hand is seen in the very large moths, beetles and other insects, copied of course from Meissen but treated in an individual and distinctive manner.[1] The "moth-painter's" hand is also seen in the sketchily drawn birds (Plate 38 B) and landscapes common on these pieces: there is a group of coffee-pots and jugs with this painting in the Schreiber Collection (Nos. 317 to 328, etc.). Characteristic miniature landscapes are seen on an inkstand at South Kensington (No. C 1148—1924). The moths, with the typical applied flowers and the "dirty turquoise" serve to identify as Derby the well-known pierced vases or perfume pots for long regarded as Chelsea, of which there are specimens at the British Museum No. II. 25), South Kensington (No. 2870—1901), and in Mr. Allen's collection (No. 45). A set of vases in the British Museum (Nos. IV. 1 and 2) with moths and birds by this painter and figure-subjects in Watteau style in panels reserved on a dark *gros bleu* ground has been usually regarded as Longton Hall on account of the tone of blue, but they are unquestionably of Derby origin, as the applied flowers and painting alone would

[1] Somewhat similar large moths are seen on Worcester porcelain of about 1765–70 (see Plate 64 B); a large red anchor occurs on some of these pieces, which probably date from the time of the Chelsea migration, and this is likely to cause confusion. A "frill vase", apparently of Worcester porcelain, painted with the Worcester large moths, with masks of the kind associated with "Tebo", was illustrated as Chelsea in *The Connoisseur*, vol. lxv (1923), p. 150.

show. Curiously enough the "patches" on the base of these vases were remarked upon by Nightingale, who did not, however, appreciate their significance. A plate in Mr. Allen's collection (No. 89), painted by the "moth-painter" and marked with a *red anchor*, should be mentioned here as an example seeming to support the former Chelsea attribution for this group. But the mark counts for little against the evidence of paste and glaze and painting, and it is probably a case of a pirated mark, as is another instance, the thoroughly Derbyish *Chatham* in the Schreiber Collection (No. 306), which has a gold anchor though it dates from about 1766.

It seems that Richard Holdship, who left Worcester in 1759, went to Derby and in 1764 offered Duesbury, among other things,[1] to teach printing in "Enamell and Blew"; but printing on existing examples of acknowledged Derby porcelain is exceedingly rare. Jewitt stated that he had in his possession letters from Holdship to his employer complaining that no work was given him for his presses, but showing an engagement that lasted at least until 1769. Jewitt further published an account for engraving plates for "small china" and other articles, done in 1771 by John Lodge for William Duesbury. It is evident, therefore, that some printed decoration was done on Derby china, though the glaze was probably too soft to be suitable for it. At present the chief examples described (there are none in the national collections) are a mug formerly in the Bemrose Collection, said to be printed in underglaze blue and marked under the handle with the word *Derby*, an anchor and a sun;[2] and a mug with a black print of George III. and Queen Charlotte, inscribed *Crowned March 1761* and marked with the anchor and *Derby*.[3]

[1] He was apparently interested in a soapstone mine and offered to the Derby proprietors the porcelain recipes including this ingredient. A small quantity of magnesia to be observed in the analysis of a Derby figure, given on p. 89, is perhaps to be accounted for by the use of soapstone at Holdship's instance, and if so the figure would be of a date subsequent to 1764.

[2] Bemrose, p. 140. [3] Binns (2nd edition), p. 69.

Jewitt declared[1] that this mark occurred on an engraved copper plate from Caughley, but it seems possible that both these pieces were printed by or for Holdship, if not at Derby, then at some other factory, for the purpose of providing specimens to be shown to the Derby proprietors.

THE FIGURES OF THE CHELSEA-DERBY PERIOD (1770–1784) represent a continuation of the earlier tradition of Derby rather than that of Chelsea. The use of the gold anchor on figures that are so unmistakably in the style of the former suggests that this mark cannot, as is often supposed, indicate the work done at Chelsea in the period. The Chelsea sales were, however, continued. The advertisement of a sale by Christie in 1772 was delightfully announced as "a Display of Elegance and Taste" that "reigns almost uninterrupted through the Articles that comprize this Sale. The Ornaments are a continued Variety of antique, select and peculiar Forms and Shapes, ætherial Colours and elaborate Decorations that alternately rise with increasing Beauty, and which distinguish Genius (British) not less conspicuous or meritorious than the Saxon or Gallic. Human Actions lively and naturally represented in many expressive and agreeable Characters; the Figures graceful, the Attitudes just, the Drapery loose and flowing, and finished with a nicety incredible; nor does the Table want its Requisites and Embellishments in all its various Occasions; the several Apparatus are contrived and adapted with much Skill, and painted and adorned with a luxuriant Fancy. Emulous to excell and happy to please, no Labour, no Expence have been spared; a chearful and vigorous Perseverance in the arduous Task, has, it is humbly presumed, brought this Porcelain to a Degree of Perfection that merits public Attention".[2]

[1] Vol. i, p. 273.

[2] Sale Catalogues of this and later dates (1773–85) are published in Jewitt, vol. i, pp. 75-83, and Nightingale, pp. 15-92.

The mark of a D intersected by an anchor, in gold, or more rarely in red,[1] belongs to this period, but was added as a rule only on table wares. Rare exceptions are the figure of *George III.* in the British Museum (No. II. 300) and the pair of figures of so-called *Vauxhall Singers* [2] of which Mr. A. H. S. Bunford has a marked specimen. An anchor and a D side by side is also known on a table service with hop-trellis pattern (Plate 41).[3] An anchor in red occurs on a dish at South Kensington (No. 2957—1901) in a Derby style too late to be ascribed to a date before 1770. The only mark usually found on the figures is a script *N* or *No* followed by a numeral referring to the Derby price-list, and occasionally a reference to the size (such as *small*). A useful extract from this list was published by Haslem.[4] The biscuit statuettes for which the factory was afterwards famous began to be made in this period,[5] and were similarly marked. Early specimens of these are in the Schreiber Collection (Nos. 422, 423 and 424), which is especially rich in Chelsea-Derby. In general, the figures of this time show rather insignificant modelling and an affected grace and sentiment in the fashion set by the Sèvres factory, but copied also by Meissen at this time. This style, with figures having abnormally large heads and studied attitudes, is often put down to Boucher, but it is questionable whether the Sèvres modeller Etienne-Maurice Falconet or the Meissen Michel-Victor Acier should be held responsible for its introduction. The *Boy and Girl dancing* (Schr. No. 348) are actually adapted from Sèvres models by Falconet, as are the two pastoral groups, the famous *Bergère des Alpes* and *L'Oracle* or *Le Nœud de*

[1] As on a basin at South Kensington (No. C 266—1922).
[2] An unmarked pair is in Mr. Herbert Allen's collection, No. 95.
[3] An example is in the V. and A. Museum (No. C 1272—1919).
[4] Pp. 170-181. Haslem included some notes and additions of his own, and the list must be used with caution. Another list is given in Bemrose, *Bow, Chelsea and Derby Porcelain*, p. 67: in this the numbering is different.
[5] At least as early as 1771: compare Nightingale, p. 19.

Cravate (Schr. No. 352) based on designs by François Boucher.[1] Another popular group (Schr. No. 355) is adapted from an engraving by Jacques Philippe Le Bas, after a painting by Boucher, entitled *Pensent-ils au Raisin*, now in the National Museum, Stockholm. The Schreiber Collection includes an impression of this print (No. 1820) as well as of that (dated 1772) of *Time clipping the Wings of Love* (Schr. Nos. 343 and 1819) engraved by Charles Phillips after Van Dyck. The Cupids and allegorical figures of the contemporary Louis Seize style were in fact much in evidence: *Cupid* as *Discretion* and as *Astronomy* (Schr. 344 and 345) and *Commerce* (Plate 39 A) are amusing instances. The *Boy with a Dog* and *Girl with a Cat* (Schr. No. 349) are similar to a pair described in the Sale Catalogue for March 29, 1773, as "Laughing figures enamell'd white and gold dressing a macarony dog and cat". Rare instances of the earlier Meissen-Chelsea style are the *Cupid in a Wig* (Schr. No. 358), and the *Bacchus* (Schr. No. 341), which is a rather weak and pallid version of a vigorous Meissen figure of about 1745. The group of a *Boy and Girl dancing*, in Mr. Allen's collection (No. 96), is a sentimentalised version of one by Kaendler. The exceedingly lively group figured in Plate 39 B is of rare quality in this period, and was doubtless inspired by the same modeller. The *Dwarfs*, of one of which there is a specimen in Mr. Broderip's gift at South Kensington (C 1132—1924), were from the same model as the "Callot figures" made at Chelsea, and appear in the price-list as a "pair grotesque punches". Many figures of popular personages were made in the style of contemporary monumental sculpture. The *George III.* in the British Museum, after Zoffany's picture now at Windsor Castle, painted in 1770 and engraved by Earlom in the same year, is to

[1] *Maquettes* of the original groups, known by the names given above, are preserved in the Musée Céramique, Sèvres. See Bourgeois and Le Chevallier-Chevignard: *Le Biscuit de Sèvres*, Plate 19, Nos. 110 and 481.

A

B

Chelsea-Derby figures. About 1770–80 (A is dated 1773).
(*Schreiber Collection and V. and A. Museum: Circulation Dept.*)
See p. 96.

A

B

C

About 1770–80.

B was perhaps made at Chelsea before 1770. A and B, *Mr. Herbert Allen's Collection*; C, *British Museum*.

See pp. 98, 99 and 101.

be dated between this and 1773 or 1774, by an entry in a catalogue of "Principal Additions" to the stock of the Bedford Street (London) warehouse of the factory: "Their present majesties the King and Queen, and royal family, in 3 grouped pieces in biscuit—the center piece represents the King in a Vandyck dress".[1] A complete set of these groups is in the collection of H.M. Queen Mary at Windsor Castle. The *John Wilkes* and *Marshal Conway* in the Schreiber Collection (No. 362), once called Chelsea, are late copies, of about 1775, of Derby figures made in the previous decade. The *Garrick as Richard III.* (Schr. No. 342) is a very feeble work, though attributed in the price-list to "Bacon", presumably John Bacon, R.A.,[2] who is known to have worked for Duesbury. The Chelsea-Derby figures are as a rule enamelled in insipid weak colours—amongst them unpleasant but distinctive pale "watery" greens and pinks are noticeable. The "dirty turquoise" of the earlier times gives place, however, to a much pleasanter clear colour inclining to blue (evidently from a Chelsea recipe), which provides a useful means of deciding the date of a piece when the model is common to both periods.

The formal flower-painting on the dresses of the Chelsea-Derby figures is often of the greatest delicacy and refinement, and the same quality marks the "useful wares" of this period, upon which rests the chief claim of Derby to an honourable place amongst the English china factories. These alone amongst the Derby productions carry on in any degree the fine Chelsea tradition. In fact a doubt as to their place of manufacture is even possible in the case of some earlier specimens, especially when these are marked with the anchor. That the gold anchor was used at Derby

[1] W. Bemrose, *Bow, Chelsea and Derby Porcelain*, p. 54.

[2] See also p. 56. Haslem (p. 43) quotes a letter from Mr. Henry Duesbury dated November 27, 1862, stating that a memorandum of his grandfather's shows a payment to Bacon in 1769 of £75 : 7 : 2 for models.

is proved by its occurrence on a piece marked also with the incised N.[1] In general, however, the Derby versions of Chelsea themes, like the designs newly created there, are less free in style and at times slightly mechanical in finish. The pseudo-classical style had scarcely appeared in England by 1770 and on this account the pieces with gilt-striped patterns [2] though sometimes marked with the gold anchor must be ascribed to the Chelsea-Derby period. From the weekly accounts of work done at Chelsea between 1771 and 1773, quoted by Jewitt, it would seem that toys were the principal articles made there after Sprimont's retirement. We read, for example, of "Cupid as a Bacchus", paid for by the three dozen at 3s. 6d.; the billing doves are "Double-doves" at 1s. A sad end for Sprimont's charming creations! Some workmen's names are given in the accounts, but they do not enable us to identify their work. The names of Barton, Boyer, Wollams (or Wolliams), Jenks (or Jinks) and Boarman (Boreman) are mentioned.[3] Claret and turquoise ground-colours on Derby pieces did not reach the level of quality obtained under the Chelsea management. We may conjecture that the Chelsea workman responsible for the claret-colour went to Worcester and not to Derby. On porcelain from the latter the colour always tends to a brownish tone. For this reason the classical Sèvres vases, of which one is figured in Plate 40 B, though rather late in style, are more likely to be Chelsea productions.[4] The dark mazarine-blue gave place to a large extent, towards the end of the Chelsea-Derby period, to an opaque enamel of a much brighter lapis-lazuli colour, imitated from the *bleu-de-roi* of Sèvres, but distinctive enough to be known as the

[1] A cup and saucer (Allen collection No. 67). Derby cannot, in fact, be distinguished from Chelsea in this period.

[2] First used on porcelain at Frankenthal. Derby copies of pieces in this style sometimes bear the Frankenthal mark.

[3] Jewitt, vol. i, pp. 179-186, and vol. ii, pp. 71 and 72.

[4] See p. 50.

"Derby blue". A border of this colour is seen on an important large bowl in the Schreiber Collection (No. 387) marked with a gold anchor and dated 1779, and painted with the arms of the Coopers' Company and with coopers at work. A bowl in similar style in Mr. R. W. M. Walker's Collection is painted with views of Chelsea and Battersea Churches before the rebuilding of the latter in 1776, and we may therefore with some probability regard these as belated Chelsea productions, made under Duesbury's management. The vase in the British Museum figured on Plate 40 C is a rare Derby production, its hybrid style combining the *rococo* with the classical.

Though the Sèvres influence is unmistakable and a thin-blooded elegance is the rule, the Derby table-ware of the Chelsea-Derby period (Plates 41 and 42), included some highly creditable work, employing a fine and practical material,[1] decorated in excellent if uninspired taste. The Derby patterns of this and the succeeding periods created a quite definite style which was not without influence on the other English factories. The swags and festoons, small detached sprigs of flowers, wavy lines and the often very charming monochrome painting of urns, vases and classical figures in grey or crimson monochrome are well represented at South Kensington in the Schreiber Collection, and more especially in the large collection bequeathed to the Museum by Mr. Sydney Erwood. Green monochrome painting of flowers was beautifully done; the work of a fruit and flower-painter of great ability is seen on a teapot (C 252—1922) and a sugar-basin (C 335—1922), as well as on the custard-cup figured in Plate 42 F (No. C 331—1922). The striped and wavy patterns resembling those of contemporary brocades are noteworthy. One of the most beautiful

[1] The soft and very pleasant glaze, however, was especially liable to craze. The paste from the time of the amalgamation with Chelsea contained bone-ash. An entry in the weekly accounts in Jewitt, already mentioned, refers to "bone-ashes to Derby £4 : 5 : 6".

of all the patterns is the simple black and grey husk (Plate 42 G). It should be mentioned here that some Worcester patterns were closely imitated at Derby and that these copies were not always marked. The well-known Worcester pattern with panels alternately containing pseudo-Japanese dragons and plants, and white rosettes reserved on a blue ground,[1] is sometimes found with the Chelsea-Derby mark. The other imitations are usually unmarked. The Derby "Queen Charlotte" or whorl pattern [2] has a dark mazarine-blue instead of the Worcester indigo, but in general these copies can only be distinguished by their glaze-quality and by the Derby gilding which seems to have been applied in a thicker condition, making fine brush-strokes difficult. It is very likely that Derby pieces of this kind are lurking in Worcester cabinets.

The earliest of the Derby painters whose names and work are known to us [3] is Edward Withers, and the painting on a dish and plate at South Kensington (Nos. 3047 and 3048—1901) is traditionally his. This so-called Withers style is marked by a still slightly conventionalised manner of outlining the petals of a flower. The little jug figured in Plate 42 is in this style. By the same hand are the flowers on a so-called Rodney jug (Schr. No. 408 and B.M. III. 18) made to commemorate that admiral's victory over the French under de Grasse in the West Indies on April 12, 1782.[4] This date is inscribed under thc spout, which is in the form of the head of Lord Rodney in a cocked hat.[5] A form of the familiar "Crown-Derby" mark, the crowned D, here in purple enamel, appears on this jug and seems

[1] Frank Lloyd No. 75, and Schreiber No. 575, are examples.

[2] See p. 167.

[3] See below, p. 108, for a discussion of the evidence for this and other attributions.

[4] A jug of this pattern, used by Derby workmen, is described by Haslem, p. 202.

[5] The type of spout, however, was evidently suggested by a Meissen coffee-pot. See *Festive Publication of the Meissen Factory* (Dresden, 1911), Fig. 97.

to have been used at times on Derby porcelain quite soon after the amalgamation. A set of urn-shaped vases and a ewer in the Allen Collection (Nos. 104 and 105: Plate 40 A) bear the same mark in gold: their classical forms indicate a date about 1775 and the painting on medallions reserved on a gilt-striped ground may well be the work of Zachariah Boreman (1738–1810), a landscape painter, and of Richard Askew, both of whom came to Derby from Chelsea.[1] The latter's earlier style is also seen in the figure subjects in Boucher's manner on a vase with a claret ground of poor quality, also in Mr. Allen's collection (No. 49). The charming grey and crimson *camaieu* painting of cupids (Plate 41 B),[2] already mentioned, is attributed to Askew by a tradition attached to a plate at South Kensington (formerly in the Jermyn Street Collection No. 3041—1901); this presumably represents Askew's second style.[3] A third manner is suggested by the traditional ascription of a plate at South Kensington (No. 3038—1901) with an elaborate painting of children and sheep sheltering under a tree (after an engraving published in 1790), but this is so different in handling that another artist seems perhaps more probable. Askew (Richard) had a son Robert, also a painter employed at Derby, and this work may be his. The fine covered cup in the British Museum (Plate 45 B) is in this style.

Blue-and-white porcelain such as was produced in quantity elsewhere seems to have been less favoured at Derby. Most of the little that is known seems to date from the Chelsea-Derby period; it is sometimes marked with the script N, but Mr. Hurlbutt has a piece

[1] See p. 49, for their work at Chelsea. Askew is recorded to have gone to Derby in 1772 (but may have returned to London), Boreman in 1783 (Jewitt, vol. ii, p. 98). For later work, see p. 112.

[2] As early as 1771 the sale catalogue of the joint factories included an item, "enamell'd in Cupids, after Busha".

[3] Jewitt, vol. ii, p. 99, gives a list of work done in Birmingham by Richard Askew in 1794 and 1795 for William Duesbury the second. The items were principally "coffee-cans" (cylindrical mugs) painted with "Cupeds" and classical subjects.

with a crowned D in blue, but a saucer in the V. & A. Museum (No. C 338—1922) is marked also with the crowned D in blue enamel. A strong violet-blue is characteristic. A few earlier pieces include some plates (Plate 38 c) decorated with applied rosettes in the style of the coloured wares of the 1760's: a dark inky blue is characteristic of these plates and dishes, which are often miscalled Chelsea. The "Derby Japan" patterns now made their first appearance and were as a rule in this period much more charming than the Japanese export porcelain, known as the "brocaded Imari", from which they were very freely adapted. I illustrate a specimen (Plate 42 I), of a pattern most frequently found, from the Erwood Bequest at South Kensington. This pattern was usually marked with an imitation Chinese seal-character, and was No. 3 in the Derby pattern-book to be mentioned presently.

William Duesbury died in 1786 and was succeeded by a son of the same name, who was manager until his death in 1796 or 1797, having in 1795 taken into partnership a miniature-painter named Michael Kean. The latter carried on the factory until 1811, when he sold it to Robert Bloor, previously clerk to the firm. In 1826 Bloor became insane and the factory was managed by James Thomason and Thomas Clarke in succession until its closing in 1848. The productions of these two periods, 1786 to 1811 and 1811 to 1848 respectively, are commonly known as "Crown-Derby" and "Bloor-Derby" china, from the marks in general use. The former, as we have seen, was introduced some years before the elder Duesbury's death; about 1782 it was modified by the addition of crossed batons and six dots. It was painted at first in blue, lilac or crimson-purple (puce); a similar mark was incised on biscuit figures, and the script N already mentioned continued in use until about 1800. The monogram DK, for Duesbury and Kean, is sometimes found, and porcelain so marked can be dated very precisely to the period of a few months between the date of Kean's admission to the partnership and that of the second Duesbury's death. In the "Bloor period" (from 1811) the Crown-Derby mark was painted in red, often very carelessly.[1] But after about 1820 various printed marks (such as BLOOR DERBY) were general,[2] and the crossed L's of Sèvres and the Meissen swords were not uncommonly imitated.

The soft biscuit-porcelain peculiar to the factory in the later Crown-Derby period was employed for a noteworthy series of groups and statuettes, generally in the classical taste. Of the Derby modellers it must be re-asserted that we know very little indeed. Many of their names and dates were discovered by the industry of Jewitt, but nothing of their work. The price-lists of models already mentioned give in only a few cases the names of modellers. John Haslem (nephew of James Thomason and a painter in the factory in its last period) recorded some traditions regarding their personal characters and their best-remembered works; but the attributions in more recent books on the subject are little more than guess-work based on these scanty and untrustworthy materials. Among the best of the modellers was evidently the temperamental John James Spangler or Spengler, a Swiss, son of Adam Spängler, director of the Zurich porcelain factory. Spangler worked intermittently at Derby in the last ten years or so of the eighteenth century and Jewitt[3] prints two agreements between him and Duesbury, dated 1790 and 1795. Bemrose's list, which dates from 1819, is supposed to cover the models in stock in 1795, and includes as Spangler's a

[1] It should be clearly understood that the red "Crown-Derby" mark belongs only to the Bloor period.

[2] See Appendix for particulars and dates of these. That printed marks were in use as early as 1818 or 1819 is proved by the Persian ambassador's service, of which a specimen in the British Museum bears the Mohammedan date corresponding to this year with the mark *Bloor Derby* in a ring surrounding a crown.

[3] Vol. ii, pp. 94-97.

group of *Belisarius and his Daughter* (No. 370), which Mr. Stuart G. Davis has shown to be copied from an original in *terre de Lorraine* modelled by Cyfflé.[1] The Zurich porcelain was made from *kaolin* from Lorraine, and this and other models perhaps came into Spangler's hands by the same channel. The same vigorous style is seen in the *Russian Shepherd* group (No. 387). Other models attributed to Spangler in Bemrose's list are No. 363, "Two pair female figures with dead bird", Nos. 11, 371, 373 and 381 (figures unnamed), and Nos. 123, 124 and 126 (vases). The *Diana* (No. 3012—1901, at South Kensington), after the *Diane Chasseresse* in the Louvre, and the set of three comprising *Bacchantes adorning Pan* (Herbert Allen, No. 114), the *Virgins distressing Cupid* (Plate 43), and the *Virgins awaking Cupid*[2] (Herbert Allen, No. 115) are delicately modelled pieces, declared by Haslem to be Spangler's work. The presence of groups with these or similar titles in sale catalogues for 1778 and 1782,[3] however, suggests that he may have been mistaken. It is significant that an illegitimate daughter of Spangler's was baptized at Zurich in 1783, and it is difficult to believe that he spent an interval there between periods of employment at Derby both before and after that date. The incident mentioned was apparently the occasion of his leaving Zurich: on the death of this daughter in 1801 Spangler was described in the register as a "vagabond" and his whereabouts were unknown. The set of three groups just mentioned was based on paintings by Angelica Kauffmann, the first two engraved by Bartolozzi, the other by W. Wynne Rylands in a print published in 1776, and the models may well have made their first appearance soon after this date. Others of the same series, enamelled in colours, are at South Kensington and at the British Museum.

[1] "Some English Pottery and Porcelain Figures connected with Alsace and Lorraine", in *The Burlington Magazine*, vol. li (Nov. 1927), p. 221.

[2] These are the titles in the price-list.

[3] Nightingale, pp. 52, 53 and 68.

A B C

D

Table-ware of the Chelsea-Derby period. About 1770–80.
(V. and A. Museum and Schreiber Collections.)
See pp. 99 to 101.

A B C

D E F

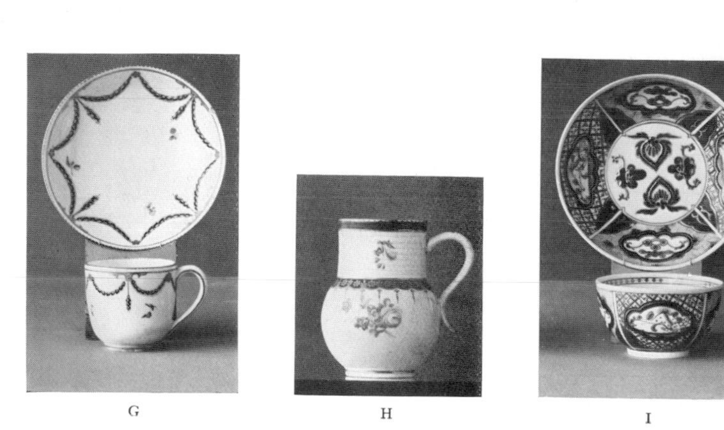

G H I

Table-ware of the Chelsea-Derby period. About 1770–80.
(*V. and A. Museum.*)
See pp. 99 to 101.

About 1780. Biscuit-porcelain group: VIRGINS DISTRESSING CUPID. (*V. and A. Museum.*) See p. 104.

A

B

C

About 1790–1800. Blue and puce marks.
A, probably painted by Banford; B, by Brewer; C, by Boreman.
(*V. and A. Museum, Mr. Herbert Allen's and Schreiber Collections.*)
See pp. 107 to 113.

Certain incised marks sometimes found on these figures were stated by Haslem[1] to be those of "repairers". Amongst these, Isaac Farnsworth is said to have used an incised star and Joseph Hill a triangle. Another modeller was Pierre Stephan, who came in 1770 and continued to work for the factory as late as 1795. He is said to have modelled a series of figures of English admirals and generals, and some of these are recorded to bear his name, incised on the base. One, said to represent General Drinkwater and formerly in the Waldo-Sibthorp Collection, is in biscuit; another in dark grey clay and apparently an original model, was formerly in the possession of Mr. J. B. Robinson of Derby, and later in the Alcock Collection. The *Lord Howe* is in the British Museum (III. 1).[2] A set of *Elements* is ascribed to him in the price-list. *Earth* and *Water*, in biscuit, are in the Allen Collection (No. 119), and *Fire*, enamelled in colours of the Chelsea-Derby period, is in the Museum collection at South Kensington (No. C 1289—1919). William Coffee had been a fireman at Coade's Artificial-stone Works at Lambeth, and after leaving the Derby factory manufactured porcelain on his own account for a short time, and later made terra-cottas and architectural pottery. The well-known *Shepherd*, of which there is an example in biscuit at South Kensington, is usually said to be his. It was adapted, by the addition of clothing, from an antique figure of Adonis in the collection of the painter Wright of Derby, sold after his death in 1797.[3] The companion *Shepherdess* is said to have been by Stephan, and the pair bore the number 396, not included in Haslem's list. Coffee's name is also attached in the price-list to several figures of animals and to a "Scotchman and his lass".

[1] *Op. cit.*, p. 150.

[2] Jewitt (vol. ii, p. 94), however, declares that the *Lord Howe* was modelled by Coffee, for whom see below.

[3] Haslem, p. 157. Wright is also said to have advised the factory on occasions in his lifetime. The clay-model for this *Shepherd* is in the Nottingham Castle Museum.

The finest kind of Derby biscuit was made towards the end of the century, especially during Kean's time. Haslem repeats a tradition that biscuit porcelain at Derby was actually Kean's invention, but unglazed porcelain was of course already being made in the Chelsea-Derby period. At its best, it was of ivory smoothness, with a slight film of glaze (technically, a "smear"), due to the intentional presence of volatile glaze-material in the kiln. The biscuit of the Bloor period was of inferior quality, tending to dryness. Associated with this, but not strictly Derby china, may be mentioned the porcelain made by George Cocker (*b.* 1794, *d.* 1868), a modeller who was trained at Derby but left about 1817, working for a time at Coalport and Worcester. He returned to the Derby factory for a short period,[1] and finally left to begin the making of china figures, animals, baskets of flowers, etc., on his own account, at first at Derby (between 1825 and 1840) and later in London. In 1853 he moved to Staffordshire and was for a time employed by Minton's. His biscuit has a dry and chalky surface, and is sometimes signed with his name, incised, but more commonly with a cross.[2]

THE GLAZED AND ENAMELLED FIGURES OF THE LAST fifty years of the factory were to a large extent repetitions of those of the previous periods, apparently supplying a large provincial market. Instances have already been given of figures repeated over as long a period as sixty years. The popular *Tailor on a Goat* and his companion (the "Welch Taylor and Family" of the price-list)[3] may be mentioned as examples of

[1] His work for Bloor includes a pair of kneeling figures, of which Haslem (*Catalogue of a Collection of China*, 1879, p. 29) cites the girl (with the title "Good-night, Mother") as one of the last figures issued at Derby. A pair of these figures is in the Herbert Allen Collection, No. 129. These execrable models were used again at Minton's.

[2] Similar biscuit figures were also made for a short time by one Robert Blore at Bridge Gate, Derby.

[3] Copied from Meissen models caricaturing the Saxon court tailor. See *Herbert Allen Catalogue*, No. 124.

models made in large quantities and several sizes. After the turn of the century, the modelling became more and more insignificant and the decoration tasteless and showy, with excessive use of hard, brassy gilding. The enamels of the later time often have a thick paint-like appearance probably due to a harder glaze. This unpleasantness of surface was further increased by the free use of such meretricious ornament as porcelain lace-work [1] of which there are examples at South Kensington and at the British Museum. In general, the later Derby figures are rarely worth the attention of collectors who are concerned with æsthetic qualities alone.

Edward and Samuel Keys (sons of the Samuel Keys who had been apprenticed in 1785) were the chief modellers whose work is known: some of their pieces are in the price-list given by Haslem ("Keys' Fancy Figures"). In particular, Edward Keys was responsible for the *Dr. Syntax* series, after Thomas Rowlandson's illustrations. There is a specimen at South Kensington (No. 385—1902). The forms of decorative vases shared the general bad taste. The elaborately modelled and applied flowers so popular at Coalport and elsewhere were also affected at Derby in the Bloor period. A "Peacock among Flowers" of this kind is named by Haslem as a work of John Whittaker, who was foreman modeller at the factory between 1830 and 1847. A specimen in Mr. Herbert Allen's collection (No. 130) is probably identical with this.

THE TABLE WARES OF THE CROWN-DERBY PERIOD maintained the fine tradition of their predecessors (Plates 44 and 45). The material remained of ex-

[1] Produced by dipping actual lace in a mixture of porcelain paste and water: the thread is burnt away in the kiln, and a model of the lace in porcelain is left. It was introduced at Meissen in 1763, and used at Derby, occasionally, as early as the Chelsea-Derby period: in the catalogue of the first sale (1771) a piece is described as "most curiously ornamented with lace". A pair of figures in the Allen Collection (No. 127) may be quoted as an example.

cellent quality but for the tendency to crazing. In addition to the sprays and garlands of the preceding period, sprig patterns (such as the familiar "cornflower" design of Paris porcelain) were especially popular (Plate 42 D).[1] This last was known as "No. 129",[2] from its number in the still-extant pattern-book: it was sometimes called the Angoulême sprig, since it is believed to have been first used at the Paris factory of the Duc d'Angoulême in the rue de Bondy. It was favoured also at Lowestoft, Pinxton and Worcester, in England. The gilt "sea-weed" and certain foliate and scrolled patterns only faintly recalling the classical style were characteristic Derby adaptations from Sèvres in the late eighteenth and early nineteenth centuries.[3] The fawn and pale red grounds were also of excellent quality and distinct from those of other factories if not actually earlier in date. Pale pink and yellow grounds of distinctive colour were also used. The wares were almost always marked, and there can seldom be any doubt about their attribution to Derby.

Much has been written about the styles of the Derby painters of this period. Their work, however, was very rarely signed, and our only real evidence is contained in two lists of patterns which have survived,[4] together with the ascriptions of certain pieces formerly in the collection at the Museum of Practical Geology in Jermyn Street and now at South Kensington. These in some instances embody traditions handed down by Haslem and other workmen in the factory. It should be remembered that in many cases Haslem had no personal knowledge of the workmen in question.

[1] A datable specimen, apparently rather late, is the jug in the Schreiber Collection (No. 418) with the initials of Daniel Parker Coke formed of these flowers, and apparently made to commemorate his re-election as member of Parliament for Derby in 1802.

[2] See Haslem, Plate 3 and p. 190.

[3] Samuel Keys the elder was an accomplished gilder, and one may conjecture that these patterns were his work.

[4] Published in part by Haslem, p. 185, and by W. Moore Binns, *The First Century of English Porcelain* (London, 1906), p. 138.

Jewitt gives a list of the names of the painters.[1] The rest is inference from very ill-established premises or else sheer conjecture.

The pattern-books are undated but apparently relate to a period towards the end of the eighteenth century. It should be borne in mind that even the names attached to certain patterns in them by no means prove that all pieces painted with those patterns were the work of the artists named. Pattern pieces by the latter may well have been kept at the works and copied by the others. And it is more than likely that the numbers have no reference at all to the subjects in the panels, but relate merely to the formal borders or diapering of the ground; the painting in the panels would be the work of any one of several hands. An undated document published by Jewitt[2] showed that at one time the Derby painters were instructed to add identification numbers to their work: this would scarcely have been needed had not several workmen painted the same pattern. Further, as the painters left their numbers would have been taken up by others, and without the date of the Jewitt instruction and the exact date of a piece it would be impossible to ascertain a painter's name from the number on it.

In spite of this uncertainty, the collector will find pleasure in classifying the interesting painting on the later Derby china, even if names cannot be attached to the several hands recognisable. Many pieces were evidently intended from the first to be "cabinet specimens"; the little cylindrical mugs known as "coffee cans" are often painted with miniature-like delicacy and care. Of the artists mentioned in the pattern-books Edward Withers belonged to an earlier tradition, and his style has been described on a previous page. Askew's work, too, is prominent on some of the most charming Chelsea-Derby porcelain and has already been discussed. The name of Billingsley (or

[1] Vol. ii, pp. 94-114. [2] Vol. ii, p. 103.

"Billensley") occurs several times in the pattern-book and his work is in fact of great importance. If not the creator of the naturalistic style of flower-painting, he was at least one of its first exponents. Instead of the simple direct brushwork of his predecessors he employed a style in which the lights were wiped out of washes of colour, and the whole treatment of shadows and details became softer and more "faithful to nature", though perhaps less appropriate as porcelain decoration. William Billingsley was born in 1758, apprenticed in 1775 and left the factory for Pinxton in 1796.[1] His work was evidently in favour with the firm's customers, since the London agent, Joseph Lygo, wrote at the time of his leaving that ". . . his going into another factory will put them into the way of doing flowers in the same way, which they are at present ignorant of". A dish from the Jermyn Street Collection, at South Kensington (No. 3045—1901), is an index of his style, which can be readily recognised if its peculiarities are once fully grasped. Another dish (No. 3046—1901) bears the pattern number 53, which is given in the pattern-book as by Billingsley. A plate (Plate 45 D) and a jug, also at South Kensington (Nos. C 175—1910 and 1—1873), and a ewer, a pair of vases and a flower-pot in Mr. Herbert Allen's collection (Nos. 166, 135 and 136) are further examples of his work. "The 'Prentice plate", painted by him and used by the younger painters as a copy, is in the Derby Museum, much worn. Billingsley's "number" was said to be 7, but pieces with this are variously painted and rarely in his style. The number does, however, occur on a ewer and basin in Mr. Frank Hurlbutt's collection,[2] which may reasonably be attributed to him. The painting on a dish in the Derby Museum,[3] declared by Haslem

[1] His later work is described under that heading and that of Nantgarw on pp. 198, 200, and 205, 213.

[2] Illustrated by a water-colour drawing in F. Hurlbutt, *Old Derby Porcelain* (1925), Frontispiece.

[3] F. Hurlbutt, *Old Derby Porcelain*, Plate 54.

to be Billingsley's, corresponds with a sketch also believed to be his, published by Bemrose.[1] A successor of Billingsley's, William Pegg "the Quaker", was famed for an even closer fidelity to Nature, and a large tureen at South Kensington (No. 3068—1901), with the Jermyn Street ascription to him,[2] is painted in the now familiar "botanical" style. He sometimes adopted the practice of adding on the reverse of the piece the name of the flower depicted. A plaque signed by Pegg is illustrated in *The Connoisseur*, vol. x (1904), p. 190.[3]

Figure-painting was done by several hands. Askew has already been mentioned. James Banford's name also appears several times in the pattern-lists, and a cup and saucer from Jermyn Street (No. 3000—1901: Plate 44 A) with the figure of a girl, are ascribed to him. The number on this cup (239) is in the pattern-books as "Hope by Banford", and though the subject on the cup is different, it is customary to regard painting in this style as his. In a letter, however, he spoke of his work in "any line of painting", and he was evidently more than the figure-painter he is generally represented to have been. The pattern-books describe classical, allegorical and landscape subjects as by him. His wife Bernice seems also to have painted porcelain. The Brewers, John and Robert, were artists of some repute, apart from their painting on porcelain. John Brewer began to work for Duesbury in 1782, but only in 1795 removed to Derby. The accomplished paintings of shipping seen on some of the best Derby china are believed to be his: their style is that of a watercolourist, and a list of his work given by Jewitt includes several items of shipping, but many other subjects

[1] *Bow, Chelsea and Derby Porcelain*, Plate XVI.

[2] There was another, later, William Pegg, who also worked at Nantgarw and subsequently designed for calico prints. But this ascription cannot possibly refer to him, as the tureen has the *blue* mark.

[3] Pegg worked at Derby for two short periods only, from 1796 to 1801 and from 1813 to 1820, twice abandoning china-painting on the ground of conscientious scruples regarding the "making of a likeness of anything". His actual work is consequently somewhat rare.

also! The customary attribution of a single class of decoration to each well-known painter is evidently a false one. A fine seascape probably by John Brewer is painted on a cup and saucer in the Allen Collection (No. 162: Plate 44 B); in the same series is a pair of vases (No. 136) with camp scenes presumably of the kind attributed to "Brewer" in the pattern-books, and perhaps by John or Robert. Many delicate miniature landscapes on cylindrical coffee cups are also probably by Brewer.

Most of the painters seem to have painted birds, and there is no evidence by which to identify Complin's (which figure largely in the pattern-book) or Dodson's, which were rather later and stated by Haslem to be "somewhat heavy in colour"; Cuthbert Lawton has repeatedly been said (following a note of Jewitt's) to have painted the hunting subjects; but these were also painted by others, and in the pattern-books "a bird on a tree" is alone put down to him.

Zachariah Boreman, first of the landscape painters, came from Chelsea[1] in 1783 and continued to work at Derby until 1794. The striped vase figured in Plate 40 C shows his earliest ("Chelsea") style. In his better-known manner (developed only at Derby) details were drawn in monochrome and coloured with low-toned washes, as in the work of Paul Sandby and the early water-colourists. Several pieces in the National collections are plausibly attributed to him. Two plates in the Schreiber Collection (No. 413: Plate 44 C) are very charming examples; and a fine cabaret with pink ground in the Herbert Allen Collection (No. 161) is painted with a series of typical Derbyshire landscapes by him. No. 178 in the pattern-book is described in "Near Crich by Boreman", but a cup at South Kensington (No. 3026—1901) is also inscribed "Near Critch"

[1] See pp. 49, 101, and 98, footnote. A signed plaque of uncertain origin, dated 1797, painted by Boreman after leaving Derby, is in the V. and A. Museum. His name is erroneously given by Marryat as Beaumont.

A B C

D

About 1790–1800. Lilac and crimson marks.
A, B (perhaps painted by Askew) and C are in the *British Museum*; D (probably painted by Billingsley) is in the *Victoria and Albert Museum*.
See pp. 101, 107 to 109.

A

B

C

Later Derby porcelain. Red marks.
A. About 1810. B. About 1820. C, painted by Thomas Steele. About 1830.
(*Mr. Herbert Allen's Collection.*) See pp. 114, 115.

though it has the number 230—yet another indication of the need for caution in the use of the pattern-books for purposes of identification. Boreman is also said to have painted birds, which would show the same quiet tones as his landscapes. Haslem states that the landscape-painting of "Jockey" Hill, a contemporary, whose name like Boreman's appears several times in the pattern-books, differed from the latter's only in the use of stronger local colour, "with greens and yellows rather prominent", and it is probable that their work is often confused. A painter named William Longdon is said to have used the number "8", and a landscape on a cup and saucer in the British Museum (III. 23) is so marked, but according to Haslem (p. 230), William Longdon was chiefly employed in painting the "Chantilly sprig" pattern. There were, however, two William Longdons, father and son, the latter apprenticed in 1790.

The bloor period was marked by artistic decline in all respects. Financial difficulties led to the sale of a large accumulation of imperfect pieces (known in the trade as "seconds"). Latterly, too, the glaze was harder, the body approximating to the normal Staffordshire type. The factory had lost the pre-eminence it may justly be claimed to have held during the last two decades of the eighteenth century. We find Bloor in 1817 advertising in Staffordshire for painters of those "Japan patterns" which include some of the worst of his productions, at once crowded, showy and tasteless. The flower-painters [1] largely deserted naturalism for a mannered style, adopted also at times at Coalport and Rockingham and in Staffordshire, particularly at Spode's. This was perhaps the invention of the younger Steeles of Derby, and is at all events conveniently associated with them. Thomas Steele (*d.* 1850, aged 79), their father, painted highly coloured fruit with care and

[1] Haslem (pp. 34-36) gives a list of the hands working at Derby in 1832.

skill,[1] and his flowers were still in the Billingsley tradition; but his sons Edwin and Horatio developed a style with hard, facile drawing, associated with a conventional colouring in which a sharp pink, a foxy red and a deep orange are conspicuous. Their work is often minutely finished, but the naturalism of the earlier work has frozen into mannerism. At South Kensington there are well-authenticated examples of Thomas Steele's fruit-painting (a plate numbered 3036—1901), and a vase in Mr. Allen's collection (No. 152, Plate 46), and a vase decorated with flowers by Horatio Steele (No. 3008—1901), as well as a number of other examples in his style. A dessert-service made for Queen Victoria is said to have been painted by Horatio Steele: a specimen from this at South Kensington (No. 3040—1901) has panels painted with birds, reserved on a chrome-green ground. Both Edwin Steele and his father worked for a time at the Rockingham factory, and Horatio went to Staffordshire. Leonard Lead (*b.* 1787, *d.* 1869) worked in the same style: two plates in Mr. Allen's collection (Nos. 179 and 194: Plate 46 B) show his manner, which is marked by smooth-curved flower-stems. Moses Webster (1792–1870) was a flower-painter with an individual style inclining to the older naturalism. Apprenticed at Derby, he worked for a time for the London enamellers Robins and Randall, decorating much Nantgarw porcelain for them,[2] and returning to Derby about 1820. "Crushed hat-roses" (a phrase of Mr. Rackham's) well indicates a quality of his painting, which is, however, free in style and shows a sensitive touch. A bold example on Derby china at South Kensington (a plate numbered 346—1854) is in an unusual purple monochrome. The arabesques of the cups and saucers figured in

[1] A famous dessert-service made for the Earl of Shrewsbury was painted with fruit by him. He subsequently went to Davenport's at Longport. His method obviously depended on the use of the finger in smoothing away brush marks.

[2] See p. 209.

Plate 46 maintain the excellent tradition of the earlier period.

Of the later landscape-painters George Robertson (*fl.* 1800–20) was probably the painter of a set of vases at South Kensington (Nos. 888 to 890—1905) and a cup and saucer and a dish in Mr. Herbert Allen's collection (Nos. 169 and 185): his style shows a monotonous, coarse stippling and thick colour. Jesse Mountford, who left Derby for Longport in 1821, was perhaps the painter of a set of three vases in the Allen Collection (No. 143: Plate 46), with minute stippling and a certain cleanness of style in rendering rocks and buildings. Daniel Lucas, who came from Longport, was the chief landscape-painter in the later years of the factory, and is represented at South Kensington by a set of vases formerly in the Joicey Collection (Nos. C 1280 to 1284—1919): his rendering of foliage with small hard touches and his shaky tree-stems help to distinguish his work, which is very common. But there is little real individuality in this later landscape-painting: the now stronger colours have the thick, paint-like quality already remarked upon.

William Corden (1797–1868) was among the first of the painters to employ porcelain for decoration in the manner of contemporary oil-paintings. He left the Derby factory about 1820 and began business as a painter of miniature portraits on china, and a little later he was engaged at the Rockingham factory to decorate a service ordered by William IV. A painting of his of *The Death of Cleopatra* is on a plate at South Kensington (No. 335—1902). The logical medium for this branch of art was found in the china plaques used by John Haslem during the last years of the factory: there are two of his works at the Victoria and Albert Museum.

On the closing of the old Derby works in 1848 a few of the hands started a small china-factory in King Street, Derby, under the management of Bloor's clerk, William Locker. Locker was succeeded by Stevenson,

Sharp & Co., Stevenson & Hancock, and by Sampson Hancock alone. In 1876 another, entirely new, company opened a factory in the Osmaston Road with the style of the "Royal Crown Derby Porcelain Company". Both establishments still exist, and their marks are given in the Appendix.

CHAPTER V

LONGTON HALL

A PORCELAIN FACTORY WAS CONDUCTED FOR A SHORT period in the middle of the eighteenth century at Longton Hall, near Stoke-on-Trent, Staffordshire, by William Littler, who had previously been successful in the manufacture of salt-glazed stoneware. The little direct information we have concerning this factory is contained in brief accounts in Simeon Shaw's *History of the Staffordshire Potteries* (1829) and Ward's *History of Stoke-on-Trent* (1843). The first of these is an untrustworthy authority, and the date (1765) given for Littler's first attempts towards the manufacture of porcelain is obviously an error, as will be seen from the advertisements I shall shortly quote. Ward [1] only mentions that Littler succeeded in making china of good quality, but at great financial loss.[2]

The existence of the factory was rediscovered, after having been forgotten for many years, by J. E. Nightingale,[3] who found advertisements of its productions in contemporary newspapers of dates between 1752 and 1758. The earliest of these, which first appeared in

[1] P. 50.

[2] It is also possible that the Longton factory was referred to in a passage in the Letters of Dr. Pococke (published by the Camden Society in 1888 under the title *Travels through England of Dr. Richard Pococke*), describing a visit in 1750 to Newcastle-under-Lyme, a town not far from Longton. Dr. Pococke spoke of a potter "from Limehouse" who was making much porcelain at the time of his visit. See an article by Mrs. E. MacAlister in *Apollo*, January 1927.

[3] *Contributions*, pp. li-lxvi.

Aris's *Birmingham Gazette* of July 27, 1752 (and was repeated later), does not specify the nature of the "Porcelain or China Ware" made and offered for sale by "William Littler and Co. at Longton Hall near Newcastle". A dealer's advertisement in the *Manchester Mercury* of December 10-17, 1754, announces "the first produce of the Factory at Longton near Newcastle in Staffordshire of useful Porcelain or China Ware".[1] As far as is known, no further advertisement appeared before April 1757, when "new and curious Porcelain or China . . . of the LONGTON HALL MANUFACTORY" was announced in the London *Public Advertiser*, "consisting of Tureens, Covers and Dishes, large Cups and Covers, Jars and Beakers, with beautiful Sprigs of Flowers, open-work'd Fruit Baskets and Plates, Variety of Services for Deserts, Tea and Coffee Equipages, Sauce Boats, leaf Basons and Plates, Melons, Colliflowers, elegant Epargnes, and other ornamental and useful Porcelain, both white and enamell'd". An advertisement in Aris's *Birmingham Gazette* two months later speaks also of "Variety of Services for Deserts with Figures and Flowers of all Sorts, made exactly to Nature". The latest-known advertisement appeared in the same newspaper in the following year and specifies "Services of Dishes and Plates, Tea and Coffee Equipages, and great Variety of Services for Deserts, Beautiful Essence Pots, Images, Flowers, Vases, etc. with fine Blue and White Ribb'd, Fluted and Octagonal Chocolate Cups and Saucers, Tea Sets etc." offered for sale by "William Littler and Co.".

It has been suggested[2] that William Duesbury, who was described in the unsigned and presumably Derby agreement of 1756[3] as "of Longton", was in some way connected with the Longton Hall factory; and a descendant of his, writing in 1865,[4] asserted that Dues-

[1] Thanks are due to Mr. Francis Buckley for the discovery of this advertisement.

[2] Nightingale, p. lvi.

[3] P. 82.

[4] *Derby Chronicle*, quoted in Nightingale, p. lv.

bury was proprietor of "china works at Chelsea, Bow, Longton and Derby". The late date at which this statement was made would discount its value, but it has been said[1] that the writer was a member of the firm of solicitors who had acted for Duesbury's family for several generations, and a certain amount of weight must therefore be allowed to the assertion. Nevertheless it is unlikely that Duesbury was proprietor of the Staffordshire factory, at all events in 1757, as both Derby and Longton Hall held public sales concurrently in the spring of that year. It is significant that in 1758, the last year in which the Longton Hall advertisement appeared, the Derby proprietors doubled the number of hands employed,[2] and this gives colour to the suggestion that the former establishment was then purchased by Duesbury and some of the material transferred. It was stated, however, in an advertisement of a sale[3] of the Longton Hall stock at Salisbury in *The Salisbury Journal* of September 8, 1760, that "the partnership is dissolved", and this may perhaps indicate that the manufacture had continued until shortly before that date.

An earlier connection between Duesbury and the Staffordshire factory is established by his work-books,[4] in which entries for dates between 1751 and 1753 show him to have enamelled "Staffordshire figars" and other objects, presumably of pottery or porcelain. The name of "Littler and Co." appears in an account book of his for 1751,[5] and the articles in question may have been of salt-glazed stoneware, such as we know Littler to have made, though their appearance in lists containing Chelsea and Bow specimens seems to show that they were of porcelain.

[1] Bemrose, *Longton Hall Porcelain* (1906), p. 7.
[2] P. 84.
[3] See a letter from Norah Richardson in *The Connoisseur*, vol. xxxiv (Dec. 1912), and an article by Mrs. E. MacAlister in *Apollo*, Jan. 1927.
[4] Bemrose, *Bow, Chelsea and Derby Porcelain* (1898), pp. 7-17.
[5] Bemrose, *Longton Hall Porcelain* (1906), p. 7.

No recognised mark is positively known to have been used at Longton Hall, and the identification of the porcelain produced there depends principally upon the occasional similarity which may be presumed to exist between it and Littler's productions in salt-glazed stoneware. No other porcelain is known to have been made in Staffordshire at the time, and any distinct and coherent body of pieces apparently dating from the 1750's and showing an indisputable connection with the Staffordshire wares of the time may be assigned to Littler with fair probability. The identification of the Longton Hall porcelain is in fact one of the most fascinating exercises in argument by resemblances.[1]

It was stated by Shaw [2] that Littler had discovered a method of dipping pieces of stoneware in a glaze of special composition producing a blue colour of exceptional richness and brilliancy, and a very important covered dish and a pair of plates of porcelain in the British Museum are decorated with a colour apparently of the kind described by Shaw; they are, moreover, further painted over the blue in opaque white enamel in a manner never seen on porcelain known to have been made elsewhere. This white enamel on blue is in fact not uncommon on Staffordshire salt-glazed wares of this time. These pieces also bear a mark resembling crossed L's, one of them reversed, in combination with three dots. The mark is not unlike and may be a copy of that of Vincennes and Sèvres, but may equally well have represented the initials of "Littler, Longton".[3] Two sauce-boats in the Herbert Allen Collection at South Kensington (No. 499) were made in a mould

[1] Longton Hall porcelain is perhaps the most difficult of all to identify correctly, and specimens are often found mistakenly classified as Bow or Liverpool or even Chelsea, whilst early Derby pieces are commonly regarded as Longton Hall.

[2] *Op. cit.*, pp. 168 and 169.

[3] A somewhat similar "mark" in the field of blue-painted designs is of fairly frequent occurrence. See Plate 47 and Appendix, p. 263. It is difficult to explain; both forms can scarcely represent crossed L's, since they sometimes occur on the same piece.

A

B

C

D

Blue-painted ware. About 1752.

(*V. and A. Museum.*)

See pp. 121, 122.

C

B

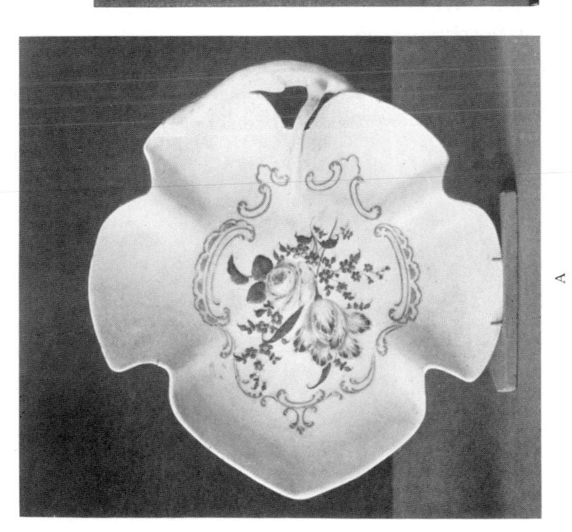

A

Painted in colours. About 1755. (*V. and A. Museum.*) See pp. 122 to 125.

A

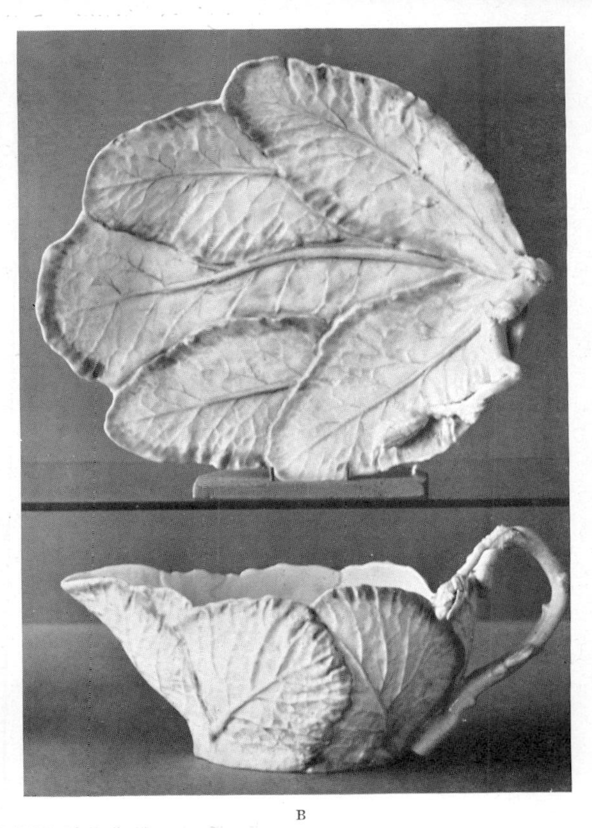

B

Painted in colours. About 1755. (*V. and A. Museum.*) See pp. 121, 123.

A

B

C

About 1755. (*V. and A. Museum and Schreiber Collections.*) See p. 128.

used also for salt-glazed ware,[1] and may on that account be presumed to be of Littler's manufacture. The painting in purple on these is unusual in colour, but by the same hand as a number of pieces to be ascribed to the factory on other grounds, as will be mentioned later; a bunch of broad strap-leaves, some of them turned over at the top, was a favourite motive of this painter; the peculiar crude landscape with building on one of these sauce-boats is also repeated on other Longton specimens. And their paste and glaze are also important as evidence regarding the porcelain produced at the factory. Certain other pieces of not dissimilar paste and glaze, such as the teapots (Schr. No. 443 and C 267—1918), a sauce-boat (C 1242—1924: Plate 49), and a butterboat (No. C 561—1924: Plate 47 B), all in the form of folded leaves, resemble in style much earthenware made in Staffordshire in this period. The handle of the Schreiber teapot is in fact of a form quite peculiar to Staffordshire. The sugar-bowls in the form of melons (Schr. No. 444) are further instances, and it is to be noted that "leaf basons" and "melons" were in fact mentioned in the Longton advertisements. Such articles were of course made at most European china-factories, but these specimens show a distinctive Staffordshire character, and may reasonably be regarded as of Longton Hall manufacture.

In addition to the important pieces at the British Museum already mentioned, there are in the collections at South Kensington several pieces bearing the crossed L's believed to be Littler's mark. In the Schreiber Collection are two plates, moulded in relief with overlapping leaves, the rims painted with a brilliant uneven blue. Similar plates and dishes are in the adjacent room, numbered C 683, 684—1924 (Plate 47 D). The crossed L's in two cases appear on the face of the dishes in the field of the design, as well

[1] Both a mould or "block" (No. 2165—1901) and a salt-glazed sauce-boat (No. 3047—1852) are in the Museum collection at South Kensington.

as on the back. The small tureen figured in Plate 47 A shows well the manner of applying this "Longton blue".

A mug of Staffordshire shape (C 1245—1924) with indefinite moulding and a bright blue border resembling that on the double-L-marked dish in the British Museum is, like it, painted with bouquets and sprigs of flowers, in which pink roses are prominent, the petals clearly but tremulously outlined in a distinctive manner.[1] Painting by the same hand assists in the identification of many specimens of the manufacture, including at South Kensington a mug (C 947—1924: Plate 48 B) and a characteristic basin in the outline of a fig leaf (C 787—1917). The painting on a pair of vases of fantastic form, with handles in the shape of monsters (C 1336, 1337 — 1924), and two small *rococo* vases (C 1144, 1145 — 1924) is earlier in style than that on the others, but perhaps by the same hand. They are likely to be the "essence pots" of the advertisement. A *rococo* specimen painted in blue only and figured in Bemrose[2] is said to be marked with the double L's. The form is repeated in an amusing large and very prickly vase in the Schreiber Collection (No. 445), decorated with applied flowers and, on the cover, a small figure, which provide links with other specimens and more particularly with the figures of the same origin. This vase is also painted with a bird in a landscape by the same hand as similar compositions which appear on a not uncommon class of plates and dishes. Amongst these, in the collection at South Kensington, are several plates moulded in relief with strawberries and leaves

[1] Mr. O. Glendenning has pointed out to me that the two mugs with this painting in the Edinburgh Museum, inscribed *Over Hailes*, and for long attributed on the ground of a tradition to a Scottish manufacture at Musselburgh, are actually of Longton Hall porcelain (compare Hobson, *Catalogue*, p. xviii, and Mrs. Willoughby Hodgson, *How to identify Old China*, Plate 24 and p. 95).

[2] *Longton Hall Porcelain*, Plate XLVI, No. 4 (formerly in the Merton Thoms Collection). It should be noted that many of the pieces illustrated in Bemrose's book are wrongly ascribed to Longton Hall.

(Plate 48 c); others of the same pattern are painted with the peculiar roses just described, and this serves to confirm the attribution of the whole of this group of pieces to a single factory.[1]

A further chain of argument may be put together from pieces at South Kensington. The style of landscape-painting seen on the leaf teapot in the Schreiber Collection already mentioned appears again on a plate (C 710—1925: Plate 49) the rim of which is moulded in the form of leaves and painted with a peculiar yellowish-green enamel often seen on pieces attributable to Longton. A pair of plates from the same mould in the Allen Collection (No. 500) show primitive flower-painting, probably by the same hand as the specimens with roses described above. The melon-tureens (Schr. No. 444) and the "Staffordshire" leaf-sauce-boats (C 1242—1924: Plate 49) provide further instances of this yellowish-green colour.

The blue-painted porcelain, apart from the marked pieces and those exactly resembling them (such as a covered sugar-bowl at South Kensington numbered C 726—1924[2]), may also be identified with the aid of the coloured flower-painting already described. The unusual handle of a mug with this decoration (C 947—1924: Plate 48) is repeated on another,

[1] This bird- and flower-painting should be carefully distinguished from the somewhat similar work, perhaps from the same pattern-books, appearing on Worcester and Liverpool porcelain. See pp. 172 and 195.

[2] Analysed by Dr. H. J. Plenderleith with the following result:

Silica	65·1
Oxide of lead	trace
Alumina	10·7
Lime	19·3
Phosphorus pentoxide	2·2
Magnesia	trace
Sodium and potash	not estimated
	97·3

The small quantity of phosphoric acid shown in this analysis may have been accidentally introduced with the alkali or some other ingredient, and does not prove the regular use of bone-ash as at Bow and elsewhere.

rather crudely painted with a Chinese landscape in blue (C 808—1924); and blue-painting, perhaps by the same hand, is seen on a sauce-boat moulded in relief in imitation of basketwork (C 460—1924), a form of decoration found also on a cup painted with the presumed Longton Hall birds (C 534—1919). The butterboat in the form of folded leaves (C 561—1924: Plate 47 B) is of a type peculiar to Staffordshire, as is the plain white teapot (C 267—1918) in the same case. Another type of leaf-sauce-boat (C 452—1924: Plate 47 C), of a shape which originated at Meissen,[1] is distinguished in the Longton versions by a transverse ribbing of the handle and by the pendent fruit attached to it.

The distinctive handle just mentioned is found also on another mug, in Mr. Wallace Elliot's collection,[2] painted with flowers in *famille rose* style; a teapot at South Kensington (C 688—1920), of salt-glaze shape with crabstock handle, was painted by the same hand. A dish (C 233—1915: Plate 48 A) of characteristic Longton paste and shape is decorated with flowers within a border of *rococo* scroll-work in enamel once white, but now discoloured to a dull brown. A border in white enamel on blue, composed of the same elements, is also known.[3] The shape of this dish is similar to that of many other Longton specimens. A dish in Mr. and Mrs. Donald MacAlister's collection [4] is a kindred fig-leaf shape and has a green twig handle of a kind much favoured at Longton; it is painted by the hand mentioned above with birds and plants, among which appears the bunch of strap-like leaves already referred to as occurring on Mr. Allen's sauce-boats painted in purple. The strawberry-and-leaf moulding was an especial favourite at Longton,

[1] Compare Adolf Brüning, *Porzellan*, Berlin, 1907, abb. 47.
[2] See *The Connoisseur*, vol. lxxix (Sept. 1927), p. 15.
[3] Bemrose, *Longton Hall Porcelain*, Plate 6.
[4] Figured in *Apollo*, Jan. 1927, Fig. V.

and was even applied to jugs, as in a charming specimen in the London Museum.[1]

The peculiar handle already pointed out (Plate 48 B) again helps in the identification as Longton Hall of a class of mugs for long regarded as Liverpool on account of the printed decoration they bear, which is sometimes signed by Sadler of that place.[2] Such a specimen at South Kensington (No. 3612—1901) has a handle almost identical with that illustrated here; and another very similar mug (No. C 8—1920) has been analysed [3] and proved to contain a high proportion of lead such as is also present in some figures attributable to Longton, to be mentioned presently. The very small quantity of phosphoric acid present also in other presumed Longton specimens is again found in this analysis in exactly the same quantity. Paste and glaze also agree in appearance (including the "scum line")[4] with other Longton pieces. This analysed mug is of a shape with grooved foot for long held to be typically Liverpool, and a similar shape certainly does occur in porcelain from that city. But a mug of this very form at South Kensington (No. C 991—1924) is painted with birds by the same hand as those on the piece figured in Plate 48, and the curious bunch of leaves again appears.[5] But though the material of the mugs seems proved as of Longton origin, it may seem difficult to account for the presence of Liverpool prints upon them. We know, however, that Wedgwood, at least as early as 1764, sent wares by road to Liverpool to receive printed decoration, and some Staffordshire salt-glazed plates printed with fable-subjects in brick-red may well belong to the later

[1] Figured in *Apollo*, Jan. 1927, Fig. VIII. A deep bowl of fig-leaf outline decorated with the same moulding was sold as Bow at New York in January 1927 (Tom Cannon Collection, No. 89).

[2] See p. 192.

[3] *Analysed Specimens*, No. 9.

[4] See below.

[5] Another mug of the same form at South Kensington (No. C 183—1916) has the Longton *famille rose* flowers mentioned above.

1750's. That porcelain made in Staffordshire may also have been sent in the same way is thus by no means impossible, and the links with Longton Hall here detailed make it impossible to resist the conclusion that this was done.[1]

The body of porcelain thus assembled on grounds of style is in general characterised by a hard-looking and heavy but glassy paste, with pale-greenish translucency, generally not free from imperfections, and a glaze usually of cold tone and often with a surface quality not unlike that of paraffin-wax or candle-grease. Flat bases are common, and the paste has sometimes been manipulated in a way suggesting the consistency of dough. Long spur marks are commonly but not invariably present, and where glaze meets body at the foot there is often a dark line like that left by dirty scum on water. The rich streaky blue and yellowish green may almost be regarded as peculiar to the factory, though not by themselves conclusive evidence of origin. Dull size-gilding of poor quality was sparingly used. These indications, with the moulded leaves and peculiarities of form, the white enamel and the characteristic flower-painting, should enable the collector to recognise members of the Longton Hall family.

Figures are known from the advertisements to have been made by Littler, but with the exception of two small models of pug-dogs, painted in underglaze manganese-purple, now in the Hanley Museum and illustrated in Bemrose [2] (similar but unmarked pieces are at South Kensington, Nos. C 24 and 660—1925), no figure bearing the presumed Longton Hall mark is known to exist at the present time. A specimen so marked (and a very important one if the mark should prove genuine) was, however, sold at Christie's (Merton Thoms Collection) in February 1910, de-

[1] Dr. Sadler may have bought undecorated Longton stock on the closing of the factory.

[2] Bemrose, *Longton Hall Porcelain*, Plate 15.

scribed as a "Figure of a Sportsman with Gun, Dog and Dead Bird, 6¾ in. high".[1] Apart from the evidence of the so-called Longton blue and green, the attribution of a certain coherent class of figures to this factory rests upon the evidence (for what it is worth) of the applied flowers and the rather crudely modelled figure with star-diapered skirt, on the large "prickly" vase already mentioned. These flowers, like those often found on the bases of the figures in question, are of a form quite peculiar in English porcelain, and markedly double, unlike the large flat flowers of early Derby porcelain, or the smaller ones of the Chelsea bases, which often have the centres painted with rings of dots. Bow flowers are of more various forms, but are, as a rule, quite different from these, which are of very constant occurrence on this class of figures. That the modelling of these applied flowers was left to the individual fancy of the repairer is shown by the occurrence of quite different forms on the Plymouth and presumed Longton versions of the same models.[2] It is noteworthy that the Longton flowers are very exact copies of those favoured at Meissen. It must be admitted that the flowers on the bases of the figures are never precisely similar to those on the vase, though sufficiently close to suggest they are the work of the same hand, perhaps at a rather later date.

The group of *Boys feeding a Goat* (C 709—1925 and B.M. IV. 7) is decorated with patches of dark blue not unlike that on the marked dishes. A coloured version of the same model in the Schreiber Collection (No. 435) shows flesh-painting of peculiar quality, seen also on a pair of figures of a *Girl with a Basket* (C 674—1920) and a *Boy with Flowers* (Schr. No. 439).[3]

[1] See *The Connoisseur*, vol. xl (March 1910): Auction Sale Prices.

[2] See p. 228.

[3] From Meissen originals. See Album of the Royal Saxon Porcelain Manufactory, Plate 3, No. 15.

The former has been analysed [1] and shows a composition markedly different from that of the sugar-bowl mentioned above. It seems likely, however, that most of the figures of the class here ascribed to Longton Hall represent the later work of the factory for which the earliest receipt may have been considerably modified.[2] The presence of lead, due perhaps to the use of flint-glass cullet in the frit, makes them heavy in the hand, a feature which helps to distinguish them from the contemporary and not altogether dissimilar Derby figures. The chemical composition of a group of *Samson and the Lion* (No. C 1335—1924 and B.M. No. IV. 6) is very close to that of the other analysed figures; and a differently coloured specimen of the same model in Mr. Broderip's gift at South Kensington (C 1334—1924: Plate 50 B) shows also patches of the dark streaky "Longton blue". The excellent modelling of these figures, which rank amongst the best made in England, is particularly evident in the skilfully rendered heads, of a type quite different from those on any specimens known to have been made elsewhere. These distinctive features are seen again in a large figure of *Britannia* (Schr. No. 436 and B.M. I. 18) for long ascribed to Bow,[3] with a base picked out in dry crimson and decorated with crude transfer-prints roughly coloured. Others of this class in the Schreiber Collection are a *Market Woman selling Butter* (No. 432: Plate 50 C), a *Seated Musician* (No. 430: Plate 50 A) and a *Boy holding Grapes* (No. 434), all apparently original compositions with a decidedly Staffordshire flavour. Their modeller, who showed a strong preference for seated figures half turned to right or left, was perhaps the "Dr. Mills, a tolerable modeller" of

[1] *Analysed Specimens*, No. 8.

[2] It is possible, too, that a differently composed body would be used for figures to secure plasticity and stability in the kiln.

[3] So ascribed in Mr. Hobson's *Catalogue* of 1905. It should be noted that a large proportion of the pieces ascribed to Longton in the British Museum Catalogue would now be called Derby.

Shaw's account.[1] Fairly close copies of Meissen models include a *Turk* (Schr. No. 438) [2] and the *Negro and Turk leading Horses* (Schr. No. 441).[3] The modelling of the animals may be compared with that of a group of a *Boy on a Galloping Horse* (Schr. No. 440). The distinctive looped flower-stalks (like the applied flowers, exactly copying the Meissen) on the base of the last recur on a plain white figure of a *Turkish Lady* (C 559—1922),[4] companion to the *Turk* mentioned above, and this pair of figures is known in Staffordshire salt-glazed stoneware.[5] A figure of *Winter* (Schr. No. 437) similarly occurs in both materials.[6] The whole family of figures thus holds together in a remarkable way.

In their painting, most of the figures show a distinctive manner of outlining the eyelashes, generally in red, and costumes are commonly not flowered as in the productions of other factories, but decorated with star- or formal diaper-patterns, like the costume of the important little figure on the large prickly vase previously mentioned (Schr. No. 445). A harsh, thick, paint-like red frequently appears, as well as a strong dry crimson much used to outline the scroll-work of the often rather clumsy bases.

It is noteworthy that the models of the *Boys with a Goat* and of a *Seated Man and Woman* in the Museum collection at South Kensington (Nos. C 707, 708—1925), which show the patches of peculiar dark blue and the characteristic posture, appear also in Plymouth porcelain.[7] It has been suggested [8] that the sale at Salisbury mentioned above may well have come to the

[1] Simeon Shaw, *op. cit.*, p. 198.
[2] Compare Berling, *Meissner Porzellan*, Fig. 82.
[3] Compare Berling, *op. cit.*, Fig. 97.
[4] Formerly ascribed to Bow, but tested and found non-phosphatic.
[5] Both are represented in the Schreiber Collection, No. 858.
[6] A specimen is in the British Museum. See R. L. Hobson in *The Burlington Magazine*, vol. xxxvii (Aug. 1920), Plate facing p. 84.
[7] See p. 228.
[8] By Mrs. E. MacAlister, I think.

notice of William Cookworthy in the course of a journey from Plymouth to London, when he would have passed through Salisbury, and that the use of the same models for both Longton Hall and Plymouth figures would be explained by his purchase of a part of the Longton stock.[1]

A CLASS OF LATER PIECES TO BE ASSOCIATED WITH Littler includes the cups and saucers (such as C 1092—1924 at South Kensington), and other pieces, painted with Chinese figure-subjects in which a strong pink colour is prominent. This decoration is identical with that on a well-known tea-poy in the Hanley Museum to which is attached a memorandum [2] stating that it was presented to the Museum by Enoch Wood, to whom it was given in 1809 by William Fletcher, who remembered it being "made by Mr. William Littler at Longton near Stoke, about fifty-five years ago, say in 1754". This harder porcelain is very different in material and painting from that of the classes here ascribed to Longton Hall. It is possible that the Hanley tea-poy is a specimen of the porcelain made by Littler as manager of the factory of John and Ralph Baddeley and Thomas Fletcher at Shelton,[3] and this view is perhaps confirmed by the name of the person by whom it was given to Enoch Wood.

[1] Mr. Wallace Elliot has a blue-bordered plate of the familiar L-marked type (illustrated in Hobson, *Worcester Porcelain*, Plate 87), painted in the middle with "dishevelled birds" by the same hand as certain Bow, Plymouth and (more commonly) Worcester pieces. If this is the hand of a wandering painter, it is perhaps possible that he conveyed the moulds from Longton to Plymouth? Against this is the fact that while the Longton plate itself dates from the early 'fifties, its decoration must be nearly twenty years later, and I have on another page given the evidence for the view that this painter did not travel at all, but worked in a London enameller's shop, probably Giles's.

[2] Quoted in full in Bemrose, *Longton Hall Porcelain*, p. 68.

[3] See Simeon Shaw, *op. cit.*, pp. 199 and 204, where, after a description of Littler's venture at Longton Hall, he states that "Mr. Littler at a subsequent period was manager of a porcelain manufactury at Shelton for Messrs. Baddeley & Fletcher until its early discontinuance".

CHAPTER VI

LOWESTOFT

THE FAME ENJOYED BY THE MODEST CHINA-WORKS AT Lowestoft, in Suffolk, is scarcely due to the intrinsic merit of its actual productions. By a notorious mistake the early editions of Chaffers ascribed to the factory a great deal of hard-paste that could only have been made in China. The name "Lowestoft", however, still clings to the class of Chinese porcelain painted with bouquets of pink roses in a style, it is true, not unlike that of the Suffolk factory. And it is a curious fact that some at least of this "Chinese Lowestoft" was actually copied at Canton from specimens of Lowestoft china. The so-called Redgrave pattern of peonies and rocks, and the familiar "Chinese" figures in red, pink and green, as well as the shaded pink roses, are not at all uncommon in collections of Chinese porcelain; there are specimens in both the national museums in London. So popular has the type painted with roses become that it has been faked in Paris in quite recent times, a remarkable instance of the copying of copies, three times removed from the original.[1]

It is perhaps superfluous to state at the present day that not only was no hard-paste ever made at Lowestoft, but Chinese porcelain was not even decorated there to

[1] These fakes (which are hard-paste) are excellent imitations: they often bear, however, a red mark perhaps intended for a seal character, but showing a quite un-Chinese cursive twist.

any considerable extent: the Chinese tea-pot in the Schreiber Collection (No. 819), marked *Allen Lowestoft* and painted with the Crucifixion is not an instance to the contrary, since this subject is by a Chinese hand, copied from a European print in the same manner as the rest of the so-called Jesuit china. The mark itself (with perhaps the flowers on the lid) was added by Robert Allen (*b.* 1744, *d.* 1835), a painter in the Lowestoft factory in 1757, its manager in 1780, and after its closing proprietor of a small enamelling establishment in the town.

The Lowestoft factory was in Bell Lane (now Crown Street) and was founded in 1757 after an unsuccessful attempt at china-making in the previous year. The first partners were Messrs. Walker, Browne, Aldred and Richman.[1] Robert Browne evidently took a leading part in the manufacture, and according to tradition he is said to have learned the secret of the Bow porcelain by taking employment there as a workman. The fact that the Lowestoft body contains bone-ash and is chemically the same as that of Bow lends colour to this story. By 1770 the firm was Robert Browne and Company, and had a warehouse in Queen Street, Cheapside, London. The factory was closed about 1802. The manufacture was always a comparatively small one, and never employed more than seventy hands at most. Its comparatively long life accounts for the abundance of the surviving specimens.

Much lowestoft china is readily recognised, but its kinship with Bow sometimes leaves room for doubt, particularly in the case of the blue-and-white. The documentary pieces, however, are numerous and serve to establish a few fairly well-marked types. It was the obliging practice of the factory to mark certain pieces—tea-poys, inkstands and the like, doubtless made for visitors to the town—with the words "A

[1] Gillingham, *An Historical Account of the Ancient Town of Lowestoft* (1790), p. 112.

Trifle from Lowestoft".[1] A dish with powdered blue ground in the British Museum (No. XI. 1) is painted with a view of Lowestoft Church. Dated and inscribed pieces, evidently made to order, are not uncommon, and enable us to fix the sequence of the Lowestoft types. A list of dated pieces is given by Church,[2] and there are several in the British Museum, with dates ranging from 1765 to 1795. Moulds and wasters were found on the factory site in 1902, and impressions from some of these are also in the British Museum (Nos. XI. 22 to 51).

No recognised mark was used, but those of other factories were imitated as freely as their designs were copied. The Worcester crescent[3] and the Meissen crossed-swords are not only found on pieces attributable by style to Lowestoft, but they were found also on fragments discovered by Mr. Spelman on the factory site. More significant than any other marks are the numerals and letters written in blue on the inner side of the foot-ring. The placing of these workmen's marks is almost peculiar to Lowestoft, and pieces so marked were again found on the site.[4] The foot-ring itself is also very characteristic, an inverted broad-based triangle, not at all undercut, well seen in Plate 54.

The paste is naturally very like that of Bow, but the glaze is generally thinner and not so liable to the iridescence and slight discoloration at the foot which marks the Bow porcelain, though this is sometimes present. On the other hand, the glaze seems to have been especially absorbent; discoloration in patches to a pale brown is frequently seen in the tea-cups. A certain peculiar soft thinness and lightness is noticeable in many Lowestoft bowls and cups. This quality is quite distinct

[1] Compare, for instance, British Museum, XI. 6 and 17, and Schreiber Collection, No. 455. "A Trifle from Yarmouth" is also found.

[2] *Op. cit.*, p. 87.

[3] The crescent in the sky in some Lowestoft designs is of course not a mark, but copied from a Chinese design.

[4] The mark of a cross scratched in the paste should be mentioned as having been found on a waster from the site (see Spelman, *Lowestoft China*, Plate 58, Fig. 1); but see p. 147.

from the hard crisp thinness of early Worcester, and may be described as a toy-like quality, not altogether unexpected in a factory so much concerned with "Trifles" and mementoes. Toy tea-services do in fact figure in the Lowestoft productions.

The abundant blue-and-white is generally of mediocre quality; an even-toned rather dark blue, never very strong and sometimes quite grey, is characteristic. On the best pieces (such as the wonderful bowl figured in Plate 52) the blue is remarkably pure and luminous. As far as we know, printing in blue was never practised at Bow, and all pieces of the Bow and Lowestoft paste so decorated must be ascribed to the latter factory.[1] The numerous moulds found on the site confirm the attribution of many pieces decorated in relief. A typical pattern shows slight painted decoration in blue in panels reserved on a moulded surface (Plate 51 E). A coarse wicker-pattern was much used, and baskets of open-work with rosettes at the intersections were copied from Derby, whilst the well-known large "cabbage-leaf" jugs of Worcester are often found copied in Lowestoft china. That figured in Plate 52 is of a typical Lowestoft form, differing from the Worcester, and was doubtless made for the landlord of a Stag Inn or White Hart. The familiar flower-bud knob on tea-pot lids is at Lowestoft usually closed, but at Worcester half-open, though this rule is of course not infallible. That a powdered blue ground was made at Lowestoft is proved by the dish in the British Museum, painted with Lowestoft Church, noteworthy for an uneven and indefinite outlining of the panels. A similar saucer-dish at South Kensington (No. C 797—1917) has a trace of a numeral within the foot-ring. Shape, character of glaze and stronger tone of blue all point to a Bow origin for the well-known powdered-blue plates and dishes marked with four or six imitation Chinese characters.[2] In

[1] This is confirmed by numerals within the foot-ring, which occur on printed pieces.
[2] Often claimed for Lowestoft. See p. 76.

general, the Lowestoft decoration is more meagre and less fantastic than the Bow, though not without a touch of imagination in the variations played upon the borrowed themes. For the rest the blue-and-white designs (Plate 51) are of great variety, inspired by all sorts of sources: Chinese scenes, *chinoiseries* in the French manner, copies of the "pine-cone" pattern and other Worcester transfers, as well as much unpretentious slight flower-painting and feathery scrolls. On occasions—as on the pieces made for weddings and presentations and the like—the painting could be of a quality far in advance of that on the usual run of the factory's productions. Mr. Wallace Elliot's beautiful bowl (Plate 52), evidently made for presentation to a ship's captain, is a case in point.[1] The blue-and-white dish (No. C 403—1924, at South Kensington) figured in Plate 51 shows what is probably a Chinese lake-scene adapted to resemble an English harbour: the queer clouds are a fanciful touch, taken over from the Chinese and altered in the best Lowestoft manner.

The coloured wares of the first twenty years of the factory belong to only a few types, most of them very easily recognised. Chinese subjects are the most common. The well-known pattern of conventional rocks and flowering peonies, in red and blue,[2] adapted from a Chinese original, is, for some reason never recorded, attributed to one Redgrave, a painter at the factory in its earlier period. Mr. Spelman gives a list of the painters, but apart from Redgrave's none of their work

[1] It is inscribed "Success to the Frances" and "Captain Osborn from Colchester". Painting in blue by the same hand appears inside a wedding-bowl figured by Spelman (Plate 90), made for "Mr. and Mrs. Dance"; this is painted on the outside in colours, an unusual feature. Mr. Herbert Read has suggested to me that this style, with figures and sometimes ships, with rich scroll-work borders, was probably copied from Bristol delft, in which such designs are not uncommon. The fact that both Bristol and Lowestoft are seaports makes this not unlikely: some specimens would be brought by seamen.

[2] No. C 662—1917 at South Kensington is an example in green, red and blue. Two cups and saucers in blue alone figured in Plate 51 are of course versions of the same theme.

has ever been identified. And there appear to have been three Redgraves! Other Chinese red-and-blue designs (which include also the Worcester "whorl pattern"[1]) can only be distinguished from Bow by the general characteristics I have described. Quite characteristic of Lowestoft are some designs of Chinese figures (Plate 54 E). The light red in these tends to a brown and is neighboured by a rather strong pink and a bright turquoise blue and green, giving a delicious discord. The collector will quickly learn to recognise this colouring, as well as the red-brown horizontal dashes on which the sketchily-drawn Chinese ladies and children stand. Like the rather similar subjects used at Worcester, these were freely copied from examples of the so-called Mandarin porcelain so largely exported from China in the second half of the eighteenth century, and these same Lowestoft designs were themselves copied in China, as I have said. The favourite globular shape of the Lowestoft teapot (Plates 52 to 54) was also a close copy of Chinese "export porcelain" and this may perhaps help to account for the error of "Chinese Lowestoft". This Lowestoft teapot was more nearly spherical as a rule, and had a higher foot than the similar copies made at Worcester and Bristol. The Lowestoft jugs and coffee-pots are usually of an easily recognisable form, with a handle that returns outwards with a "kick" at its lower end, and is usually provided with a knob or thumb-rest above.

The bouquets of pink roses and other flowers by one prolific hand are marked by a stiff shading of the petals sometimes in nearly parallel lines (Plates 53 and 54). A similar manner is seen in some Salopian decoration, but with a harder, more precise, quality. The two may be compared at the Victoria and Albert Museum, which is by Mr. Broderip's gift very rich in Lowestoft of all kinds. The mug and small vase in Plate 53 show some

[1] Sometimes known as "Queen Charlotte's pattern": copied also at Derby. See pp. 100 and 167.

A B C D E F

Pieces painted in blue; F is painted also in red. About 1760–70.
(*V. and A. Museum.*) See pp. 134, 135.

A

B

C

Painted in blue. About 1760–70. (*Mr. Wallace Elliot's and the Schreiber Collections.*) See pp. 134 to 137.

A

B

C

D

Painted in colours. About 1760–70.
(*V. and A. Museum.*)
See p. 136.

A B

C D E

Painted in colours. About 1760–1800.

(V. and A. Museum.)

See pp. 136, 137.

rarer Lowestoft painting with a more sensitive touch than is usual. Certain diapers, mainly a sort of trellis-pattern in red or pink regularly dappled with darker spots, also help to identify the Lowestoft types. Hexagonal cell-diaper, sometimes in blue alone but occasionally in red and blue, was a favourite Lowestoft border. All these diapers were of course copied from Chinese porcelain. On the more ambitious pieces, the spaces between the panels are filled with close gilt scroll-work in another Chinese style, also adopted at Worcester.

Among the most charming of all Lowestoft porcelain are the bowls, represented here by the fine blue-and-white specimen from Mr. Wallace Elliot's collection already mentioned (Plate 52), made to order for farmers' celebrations, elections, weddings and the like. They are sometimes painted in blue inside and in colours without,[1] and bear such inscriptions as "John and Eliza Remnant"; "Success to the Jolly Farmer 1774". Commemorative pieces, in fact, formed an important part of the Lowestoft china. "Birthday plaques" (small china discs with a name and date) and inscribed mugs are not uncommon. Some of the owners have been identified amongst residents in Lowestoft and relatives of the proprietors,[2] but it is probable that many pieces were painted to the order of visitors to the town.

The *rococo* and Chinese styles persisted at Lowestoft long after they had given place to pseudo-classicism elsewhere. During the last ten or fifteen years of the factory, the "Angoulême"[3] and other "sprig" patterns such as were fashionable on Paris porcelain began to be used; a piece dated 1795 in the British Museum is typical. Some slight designs in black and gold (Plate 54 B) are not without charm, but in general this later

[1] A punch-bowl so decorated is illustrated in Spelman, *Lowestoft China*, Plate 89.

[2] See F. A. Crisp, *Catalogue of a Collection of Lowestoft China*, London (privately printed), 1907.

[3] See p. 108.

porcelain is undistinguished and of little interest to the collector.

A class of figures has sometimes been ascribed to Lowestoft on the evidence of fragmentary moulds found on the factory site.[1] The type, however, is on the one hand totally unlike the normal Lowestoft porcelain, and on the other quite indistinguishable from that made in Staffordshire.[2] The modelling, which closely resembles that of the well-known earthenware figures made by the Wood family, and the strong colouring, which includes distinctive browns and yellowish greens, all point to a Staffordshire origin for these.

[1] Spelman, *op. cit.*, p. 61.
[2] See p. 239.

CHAPTER VII

LOWDIN'S BRISTOL FACTORY

BRISTOL is a town with an honourable place in the history of English pottery and glass, and both manufactures are likely to have led to experiments in porcelain-making. Porcelain of some kind was evidently made there as early as 1750, when Dr. Pococke in a record of his travels[1] mentioned a manufacture "lately established" at "Lowris China House by one of the principal (*sic*) of the manufacture at Limehouse which failed." Dr. Pococke had previously seen at the Lizard a vein of soapstone which he had described as an ingredient of the porcelain made at this Bristol factory. The "principal" of "manufacture at Limehouse" may perhaps have been associated with the Bow factory,[2] where an attempt had been made in 1744 to use under patent a china-clay imported from America, doubtless the same material as that mentioned in a letter from William Cookworthy in 1745.[3] Cookworthy was a Quaker apothecary with near relatives at

[1] Letters, published by the Camden Society in 1888 under the title of *Travels through England of Dr. Richard Pococke,* Oct. 1750: "We went nine miles to the south near as far as Lizard Point to see the soapy rock which is a little opening in the cliff, where a rivulet runs over a vein of soapy rock into the sea, the lode or vein running along the bottom of the valley . . . there are white patches in it, which is mostly valued for making porcelane, . . . and they get five pounds a ton for the manufacture of porcelane now carrying on at Bristol . . . ."

[2] Both Bow and Limehouse are in the east of London, not far distant from each other. See pp. 54 and 117. Limehouse porcelain (if it ever existed) has not been identified.

[3] See p. 54.

Bristol,[1] and Edward Heylyn, who had been named in the Bow patent, was a copper merchant of Bristol and London, and quite likely to have been the "principal" mentioned by Dr. Pococke. An advertisement of the Bristol china in 1750[2] mentions a Mr. Lund, evidently an agent for the factory. This was probably Benjamin Lund, a brass-founder and subsequently the patentee of a process of copper manufacture. Lund was a Quaker whose wedding was witnessed by Champions of the generation before that of Richard, Cookworthy's successor in the hard-paste manufacture eventually established at Bristol. A connection may thus be reasonably conjectured between Cookworthy, Heylyn and Lund. As early as 1764, Sarah Champion[3] referred to Cookworthy as "the first inventor of the *Bristol* china works", and Cookworthy may well have been the leading spirit of the earlier as of the later factory at Bristol.

The factory referred to by Pococke was presumably that conducted at a glass-house formerly owned by William Lowdin[4] and situated at Redcliffe Backs, Bristol. An advertisement of 1752[5] announced that the Bristol china manufactory was then to be "united with the Worcester Porcelain Company". As late as 1755, however, some of the productions remained unsold at the firm's warehouse in Castle Green, which also continued in use until 1757 as an agency for Worcester porcelain.

A FACTORY IN WHICH MATERIALS OBTAINED FROM Cornwall were said to be used is mentioned in a letter

[1] See p. 220.

[2] Pountney, pp. 192 and 193. The advertisement announced the extension of the works and offered to engage apprentices "of either sex . . . to be learned to draw and paint . . . the said Ware, either in the *India* or *Roman* taste, whereby they may acquire a genteel subsistence".

[3] Owen, p. 15.

[4] "Lowris" in the published letters of Dr. Pococke is a copyist's error for "Lowdin's". An advertisement in a newspaper of 1745 (Pountney, p. 187) mentioned "the glass house, consisting of several tenements lately in possession of William Lowdin".

[5] *Bristol Intelligencer*, July 24, 1752.

from Richard Champion dated from Bristol in February 1766 [1] as "set up here some time ago". Whether this factory was a continuation of Lowdin's or a separate undertaking is uncertain.[2] A plate dated 1753 with initials said to be those of John Brittan, afterwards foreman at Champion's Bristol factory, was described by Nightingale,[3] and a bowl traditionally believed to have been made by Brittan for a relative and dated 1762[4] was destroyed in the fire at the British Section of the Brussels Exhibition of 1910. Brittan had been apprenticed to Cantle the Bristol potter in 1749, and in his evidence before the Committee of the House of Commons in 1775 [5] claimed to have had "great Experience of several China Manufactures"; his work at Lowdin's and its conjectured successor may perhaps have been meant.

WE ARE FORTUNATELY ON FIRM GROUND IN identifying some of the earliest of the Lowdin's china. There exist a number of copies of a figure of a *Chinaman*, apparently cast from a Chinese specimen, stamped on the back near the base with the word *Bristoll* in raised letters and the date *1750*. One of these is in the Victoria and Albert Museum.[6] It was evidently no accident that Dr. Pococke selected for remark the "beautiful white sauceboats adorned with reliefs of festoons which sell for sixteen shillings a pair"; these form the greater part of the Lowdin porcelain which has survived, and several are known bearing the same mark as the *Chinaman*. Three of these marked sauce-boats are in the Victoria and Albert Museum (Nos. 3151—1901: Plate 55 B, C 472—1924, C 1297 — 1924), and two are in the British Museum

[1] Owen, p. 11. See also p. 222 below.
[2] See also p. 147.
[3] Pp. lxxiv and lxxxv.
[4] The inscription F.B. (for Francis Brittan) and date are figured in Owen, p. 14.
[5] In support of Champion's patent. See p. 222.
[6] No. C 1300—1924. Another is in the British Museum.

(Nos. VIII. 1 and 52).[1] They are moulded in relief from a silver model, as are two others with the same mark—butter-boats rather than sauce-boats—in Mr. C. H. B. Caldwell's collection.[2] Though all these are obviously earlier in date than many other moulded sauce-boats, the latter are no less certainly attributable to Lowdin's factory or its continuation at Worcester.

All these specimens show a decidedly hard-looking paste, and some of them have indeed been erroneously described as hard-paste porcelain. They are, however, essentially soft-paste, and are actually no harder than the normal Worcester porcelain of the next thirty or forty years, of which they were in fact the forerunners. The minutely pitted and in the earlier specimens very bubbly glaze shows in the marked pieces a strong tinge of blue or a greyish tone. This is due either to a deliberate bluing of the glaze with cobalt or to the conditions of firing by which the blue used for the underglaze painting has "flown" in the kiln. The enamel-painted specimens show on the contrary that warm ivory tone in the glaze (probably due to the lead in it) which is so pleasant to modern eyes but which seems to have been regarded as a shortcoming in the eighteenth century.[3] The ideal of the English potter was evidently Chinese "export porcelain", which constantly shows a tendency to a cold greenish or bluish tone, especially in the blue-and-white.

The forms were to a remarkable extent moulded from silver.[4] The wavy rim of a sauce-boat (Plates 55 and 56), two peculiar handles—one angular (Plate 58), the other with a rosette at the junction with the body—and moulding with foliate scrolls in relief leaving

[1] An analysed specimen shows 13 per cent. of magnesia, equal to 40 per cent. of soapstone. See *Analysed Specimens*, No. 24.

[2] Illustrated in Pountney, Plate 48.

[3] Dr. Pococke described the porcelain as having a "yellow cast, both in the ware and the glazing".

[4] To a much greater extent than at the Bow factory, to which many of the pieces here ascribed to Bristol were ascribed.

panels reserved for painting are very distinctive features commonly found. Pickle-trays in the form of scallop-shells were also made in quantity. A specimen of this shape in the Victoria and Albert Museum (No. C 962—1924) is painted in underglaze manganese-brown, a rare colour found also on a marked specimen of the *Chinaman* in Mr. Caldwell's collection;[1] this is a further proof of the origin of the class.

The painting in underglaze blue (Plate 55) is commonly blurred and sometimes almost indecipherable. An artless version of the Chinese landscape, with palm-like plants and horizontally shaded water, is constantly seen; a structure resembling a mast with yards is also characteristic. Another favourite design includes ruins or a classical pyramid (Plate 55 A). A feature distinguishing Lowdin's china from all others is the manner of painting the inside of the rim of the sauce-boats with festoons of flowers or Chinese "emblems", with a shell commonly painted inside the lip. This feature is found on both blue-and-white and coloured porcelain from Lowdin's factory and seldom found elsewhere.[2]

If the decoration in blue is sometimes without much merit, the painting in colours is often of the greatest charm (Plate 56). One painter in particular used a very thin brush with remarkable skill, and his Chinese figures amid furniture and trellises, and very distinctive birds and flowers include some of the most graceful brushwork seen on English porcelain. There is a good group of these pieces in Mr. Broderip's gift in the Victoria and Albert Museum, from which the specimens figured on Plate 56 are drawn. The blue painting on the *Bristoll*-marked sauce-boat figured in Plate 55 B may perhaps be recognised as the work of this artist; if it is, we have a further proof of the

[1] Pountney, Plate 46.

[2] In Bow examples (such as that in Plate 31) the effect is quite different, and the favourite Lowdin's shell is absent.

origin of the whole class with fine-brush painting. Sauce-boat-forms similar to but not absolutely identical with the marked specimens are of course very common (compare Plate 55 B and 56 D). Another painter's hand is seen in some charming flower-painting on a *Bristoll*-marked sauce-boat in Mr. Wallace Elliot's collection.[1] Two other sauce-boats decorated with festoons in relief from the same mould as this, at South Kensington (No. C 1297—1924) and at the British Museum (Nos. VIII. 1 and 52),[2] have the *Bristoll* mark painted over with a green leaf, perhaps, as Mr. Elliot suggests, because they were not made there, but at Worcester, though the mould automatically reproduced the mark. A little bulbous-shaped hexagonal bottle in the Schreiber Collection (Plate 57) is painted in colours with a subject of acrobats and tumblers to be seen also on Bristol opaque white glass, and is evidently by the same hand—a confirmation (if one were needed) of the Bristol origin of the group. The birds by the same hand on the mug in Plate 57 are also a common decoration on Bristol white glass.[3] This hand is often claimed to be that of Michael Edkins, but this is open to question. The only documents, if such they can be called, for Edkins' work are a delft plate with the initials MBE[4] (said to be those of Michael Edkins and Betty, his wife) and a white glass tea-canister figured in woodcut in Owen (p. 379), "authenticated" by William Edkins, his grandson.[5] I do not think these pieces are painted by the same hand as the porcelain figured in Plate 57, but the differences of material make the comparison inconclusive. But though the hand is

[1] Illustrated in colours in *The Connoisseur*, vol. lxxix (October 1927).

[2] Described as hard-paste in the *Catalogue*.

[3] Compare a vase (No. C 670—1921) in the Victoria and Albert Museum.

[4] In the V. & A. Museum, No. 3125—1901. Figured in an article by Brig.-Genl. Sir Gilbert Mellor in *The Connoisseur*, vol. lxx (1924), p. 76.

[5] A similar glass canister is in the Schreiber Collection, No. 423 (vol. iii, Plate 47).

A

B

C

D

E F G

Wares painted in blue. About 1750–55.
B is marked Bristoll in relief.
(*V. and A. Museum.*)
See pp. 141 to 144, 253.

Wares painted in colours. About 1750–55. (*V. and A. Museum.*) See pp. 143, 144.

A

B

C

Pieces with painting similar to that on Bristol white glass. About 1750–55.

A is in *Mr. Wallace Elliot's Collection*, B in the *Schreiber Collection*, D in the *V. and A. Museum*.

See p. 144.

A B C

Transfer-printed wares. About 1750–55. (*V. and A. Museum and Schreiber Collections.*) See pp. 145, 146.

not proved to be that of Edkins, it is commonly recognisable on porcelain of Lowdin's type.

Transfer-printing in black is seen on sauce-boats of forms obviously akin to those of the Lowdin specimens. At their best, the impressions are clean and of warm satisfying colour, though the enamel tends to rest on the surface with a very slightly sticky appearance, unlike the impressions on Worcester china of rather later date, where the colour is perfectly incorporated with the glaze. The engraving itself has a certain "primitive" charm which I find more attractive than much of the technically perfect Worcester printing. The dish, butter-boat, and little pickle-tray in the Victoria and Albert Museum, figured in Plate 58, may be considered typical.[1] If we were to accept the view that Lowdin's factory came to an end in 1752, as the advertisement quoted above would seem to show, this transfer-printing would be among the earliest of all. But it is of course quite possible that many of these printed pieces were made at Worcester shortly after the removal. Whether any of the engraving is the work of Robert Hancock is decidedly open to question. While in general effect it is very different from his signed work on Worcester porcelain, in line and handling it is sometimes not unlike it. The accidents of firing the prints in this early period make it difficult to recognise an engraver's hand with any certainty. We may conjecture that the earliest prints are the rather sooty and over-inked little landscapes, squirrels and shields, of which there are several examples in Mr. Broderip's gift at South Kensington. The charming little print (Plate 58 c) of a boy teaching a girl to play the flute (which we find also on later quite certain

[1] A mysterious signature, "*Rhodes pinxit*", *painted* on the print on a dish (No. 466) in the Schreiber Collection, should be mentioned here. In addition to the printed decoration the dish has a painted green edge, and the name is presumably that of the workman who added this. In any case it cannot be connected (as was formerly believed) with David Rhodes, the enameller of Leeds and London.

Worcester pieces) is of a very different character. Its sensitive line long ago recalled to the writer of the Jermyn Street Museum Catalogue those etchings actually cut with a diamond on porcelain, and coloured black, by Canon Busch of Hildesheim, which are among the most charming examples of the German "outside decoration" of the eighteenth century, or *Hausmalerei*, as it is usually called. Neither of these styles bears much resemblance to Hancock's signed work, but the beautiful little landscape shown in Plate 58 B is, I think, quite definitely in his style. In technique, however, it is not so assured as his Worcester work, and we must assume that prints of this type were done in the period of a few years before 1757, perhaps even before 1752. The print on the butter-boat shown in Plate 58 A is also of this earlier style. But whether printed pieces of this class, or indeed any of the others discussed in this chapter, should be called Lowdin's or Worcester it is of course impossible to say.

It is unlikely that a small factory could have produced in the space of little more than two years[1] so large a quantity of porcelain as the number of these printed and other pieces implies. And it is important to remember that the continuity between Lowdin's and Worcester would in any case make a sharp division impossible. Many specimens, plainly either of Lowdin's or of Worcester china, must necessarily remain as of uncertain origin, not to be definitely attributed to either factory. The moulds of the presumed Lowdin's pieces (such as the butterboat moulded with landscapes in Plate 55 C) evidently continued in use at Worcester for a long time, whilst the Lowdin's blue very closely resembles the distinctive Worcester colour to be described in the next chapter. The workmen's marks found on Lowdin's pieces further include several (such as the arrow with a ring on the shaft on the coffee-

[1] As stated above, the factory was said by Dr. Pococke in 1750 to have been "lately established".

cup figured in Plate 56 A) which are common on undisputed Worcester specimens of rather later date.

ANOTHER CLASS OF PIECES OF LONG-DISPUTED ORIGIN is also by body and glaze quite obviously related to both Lowdin's and Worcester. These specimens usually bear certain incised marks—a cross[1] or one or two short strokes, or a short cut made with a sharp blade on the inner side of the foot-ring. In addition, a number of marks of uncertain significance were painted in blue or colours. A few forms were constantly repeated: a nearly cylindrical mug with spreading base (Plate 55 E and G), the handle of which often shows signs of parting from the body, leaving incipient fissures within; another mug, of the form shown in Plate 55 F; a pear-shaped jug with lip and scroll handle; and a sauce-boat in the form of folded leaves, copied from Meissen.[2] The painting is often decidedly amateurish, with "fine-brush" work which is distinct from that seen on Lowdin's china. An analysed specimen shows 10 per cent of magnesia, equal to 30 per cent of soapstone.[3] It has been conjectured by Mr. Bernard Rackham[4] that these pieces were perhaps made at Worcester after the transfer of Lowdin's works, from a special composition indicated by the incised marks.

Several other links with Worcester are noteworthy. A mark resembling a trident-head in blue, sometimes found on the "scratched cross" pieces, also occurs on a cup almost certainly made at Worcester.[5] Other marks (such as an arrow with a ring on the shaft) are

[1] An incised cross is of course a natural and common mark on porcelain of all kinds and not by itself evidence of origin. A waster with this mark was found at Lowestoft (see p. 133). A red-painted cross occurs also on a mug in the Schreiber Collection of the class here discussed, and will perhaps suggest the hand of Champion, who used a similar mark later.

[2] These sauce-boats are fairly common: there are three pairs in Mr. Herbert Allen's collection, Nos. 30, 31 and 32.

[3] Normal Worcester porcelain shows 11 to 13 per cent of magnesia; a *Bristoll*-marked sauce-boat, 13 per cent. See *Analysed Specimens*, Nos. 24-36.

[4] *Herbert Allen Catalogue*, p. 55.

[5] See *Analysed Specimens*, No. 26

common on this class and on Worcester and Lowdin's. A pear-shaped jug in the Schreiber Collection (No. 461), in addition to the usual incised marks, has also a script capital *L* (or a small *h*)[1] incised under the base, and is painted with figures and flowers which seem to be by the same hand as the early Worcester jug in the Schreiber Collection (No. 490), here illustrated in Plate 59. A jug in the Frank Lloyd Collection (No. 386), quite certainly Worcester, with the arms of Chalmers and the date 1759, is of the typical "scratched cross" pear-shape. The Worcester design, afterwards known as the "Reynolds" pattern,[2] also appears on mugs of this class (such as Schr. No. 460).

Links with Bristol, on the other hand, are not lacking: a *Bristoll*-marked sauce-boat at South Kensington (No. C 1297—1924) has the additional mark of an incised stroke. A peculiar blue-painted scroll on the handles of jugs is to be found on fairly certain Lowdin's pieces as well as on the "scratched cross" family. Painting in blue is in general similar. Marks under the handles[3] are a singular feature of both.

A cup in the possession of Mr. W. W. Winkworth, dated 1753, with initials perhaps intended for *J. B.* (John Brittan?) but equally to be read as *T. B.*, shows the usual Lowdin characteristics, and the painting in blue includes the mast-like tree to which I have referred. To judge by Nightingale's description, his dated "John Brittan" plate may have been very similar to this piece. One of a pair of plates in the Schreiber Collection (No. 469), with early-looking transfer-prints coloured over, has the incised stroke: exactly similar prints appear on a little hexagonal bottle of the same shape as that painted with acrobats by a Bristol hand mentioned above.

The peculiar marks so common in this class resemble

[1] The *L* could possibly stand for Lowdin's, though this is unlikely. The piece was ascribed by Lady Charlotte Schreiber to Liverpool, and by M. L. Solon to Longton Hall.

[2] See p. 167.

[3] See Appendix, p. 264.

alchemists' signs and may perhaps suggest the invention of Cookworthy, whose leaning in the same direction is shown by the mark unquestionably used at Plymouth on his hard-paste china. It is, I think, highly probable that the use of Cornish soapstone in English porcelain was due to Cookworthy's researches and inquiries. He was thoroughly familiar with the *Letters édifiantes et curieuses* written by the Jesuit missionary Père d'Entrecolles from the Chinese porcelain town of Ching-tê Chên, where soapstone (*hua shih*, slippery stone) is described as an ingredient sometimes substituted for *kaolin* in the Chinese manufacture. The incised marks on this "scratched cross" family may well have indicated special bodies made at Bristol after 1752, or perhaps "tried out" at Worcester from soapstone obtained from fresh localities in the course of experiments towards a true hard porcelain. Alternatively, Richard Champion (who was, as we know, interested in china manufacture at least as early as 1765[1]) may have been concerned in the making of some of these experimental pieces. The links with Worcester would be naturally explained by the migration of hands from an experimental Bristol factory to the established Worcester works. In any case, a West of England origin seems proved for all these pieces.

[1] See p. 222.

CHAPTER VIII

WORCESTER

THE WORCESTER CHINA MANUFACTURE stands apart in several respects from the other English ventures of the eighteenth century. Alone of all these it has survived with a record of continuous activity down to the present day. It largely created its own fashions, and the usual criteria for dating do not apply to its earlier work as surely as elsewhere. Its *rococo* was never as wild or its somewhat belated neo-classical as severe and precise as at other factories.

The origins of Worcester china have been mentioned in the previous chapter, dealing with Lowdin's factory. It seems highly probable that the use of soapstone was learnt from the Bristol inventor, Cookworthy or another, though the transfer to Worcester was not advertised until 1752. The "Worcester Tonquin Manufacture", as it styled itself, was established at Warmstry House [1] in 1751. In June of that year articles were signed by fifteen gentlemen "to discover for the benefit of themselves and the other subscribers the real true and full art mistery and secret [of porcelain making] by them hitherto invented and found out". One of these subscribers, Dr. John Wall (*b*. 1708, *d*. 1776), has generally been given the credit of the initiative, and his name has become attached to the first and by far the

[1] A view of Warmstry House and a description of the works appear in *The Gentleman's Magazine* for August 1752. The factory was again described by Valentine Green in his *Survey of the City of Worcester* (1764).

A

B

Painted in colours. About 1755.
(*Schreiber Collection.*) See p. 155.

A B C

D

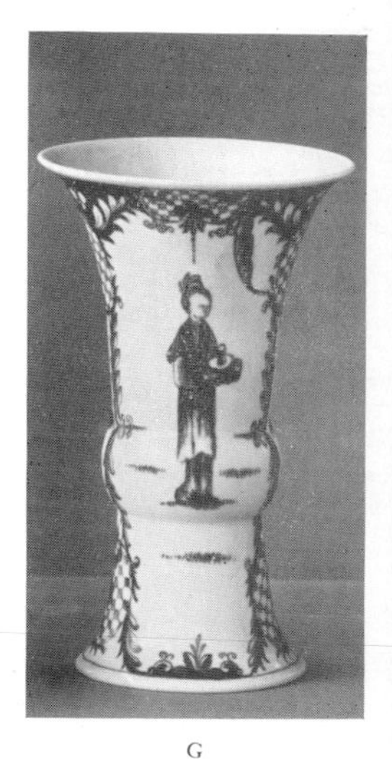

E F G

Blue-and-white wares. About 1755–70.
(*V. and A. Museum and Schreiber Collections.*)
See pp. 155, 157.

most important period of the factory. But it is more probable that the leading part was played by William Davis, "apothecary", the first manager and a large subscriber, and it is perhaps no coincidence that a James Davis should have been a tenant of Lowdin's Bristol glass-works from 1745.[1] It may be conjectured that Davis was the chief "arcanist", whilst Robert Podmore and John Lyes also shared the secret, and special payments were to be made to them.[2] In the list of subscribers should be remarked the name of Edward Cave, founder of *The Gentleman's Magazine*. Several laudatory references to the Worcester china are to be found in the magazine, and though London advertisements were rare in the earlier period it is unlikely that any opportunities for publicity were lost. An article on the porcelain in *The Annual Register* for 1763, quoted by Mr. Hobson,[3] has all the air of an inspired puff, with its concluding remark commending the factory to the attention of the "Society for Encouraging Arts and Manufactures".

Its history has been comparatively uneventful.[4] The original company was reconstituted in 1772; shares were held in the new concern by Robert Hancock the engraver,[5] but he was bought out two years later. Dr. Wall died in 1776, though by a convenient fiction the "Wall period" is extended to 1783, when on the death of William Davis the concern was bought by Thomas Flight, the firm's London agent, for his sons Joseph and John, and at the same time Robert Chamberlain seceded and founded a rival factory in Worcester.

[1] Pountney, p. 203.

[2] " . . . the better to engage their fidelity to keep such part of the secret as may be entrusted to them."

[3] *Worcester Porcelain*, p. 26.

[4] Binns, with Victorian optimism and complacency, was gratified "to find the finest productions and the most prosperous results in perfect accord".

[5] Other shareholders were John Wall senr., Rev. T. Vernon, W. Davis senr., W. Davis jnr., and Richard Cook, chinaman, of Fleet Street, London.

John Flight died in 1791, and in the next year Martin Barr was taken into partnership. *Flight and Barr* became *Barr Flight and Barr* (1807) and *Flight Barr and Barr* (1813) on the admission of younger members of the Barr family. In 1840 Chamberlain's factory, which had at first only decorated [1] but afterwards actually made porcelain, was amalgamated with the older company. In 1847 the original premises at Warmstry House were abandoned in favour of Chamberlain's works. Walter Chamberlain and John Lilly were the proprietors in 1848, and in 1850 W. H. Kerr joined the firm, which became *Kerr and Binns* in 1852, and the still-existing Royal Worcester Porcelain Company in 1862.

The factory for a long time adopted no regular mark, though a script *W* was occasionally used. A crescent, stated by Binns to have been taken from the Warmstry arms, is common enough on Worcester china to be regarded as a factory mark, but it has been so often imitated elsewhere [2] that it is of little use by itself as proof of origin. The "fretted square", an invention in the manner of a Chinese seal character somewhat resembling the Union Jack, is not uncommon and is fairly trustworthy.[3] These marks were as a rule painted in blue under the glaze: the crescent, however, was sometimes printed in blue on printed wares, when it was commonly shaded, and occasionally towards the end of the Wall period and in the subsequent Flight period it was painted in enamels or gold. As at other English factories, the Meissen and Sèvres marks as well as Chinese characters were commonly imitated. Forgeries of the Chelsea mark are not unknown.[4]

But early Worcester china itself is perhaps the most

[1] Usually Caughley (Salopian), but sometimes also New Hall porcelain.

[2] Particularly at Caughley, Bow and Lowestoft.

[3] It is copied, though rarely, in blue enamel on Salopian imitations of Worcester types: compare a cup and saucer at South Kensington, No. C 1051—1924, and also on Bow copies of scale-blue (see p. 79).

[4] These and other imitations are reproduced in the Appendix.

distinctive of all eighteenth-century porcelains. With the exception of Lowdin's, and to a slight extent Chaffers' Liverpool porcelain, which was virtually an offshoot of Worcester, it is unlike any other. It is hard-looking, though actually melting at a fairly low temperature; the lead glaze is invariably even and smooth ("close-fitting" is Mr. Rackham's happy word) and inclined to be thin, never collecting in pools or masses at the foot. Some collectors are in the habit of regarding as an infallible sign of Worcester origin the dryness of the edges and the thinness of the obviously brushed-on glaze on the base of a piece; but these are characteristics sometimes found elsewhere, and are occasionally absent in genuine Worcester. It may however be asserted that the Worcester body and glaze were so well suited that the latter never "crazed".[1] The glaze often has a decidedly greyish or bluish tone, due to a minute quantity of cobalt used to counteract the yellow tinge given by the lead. The greenish hue by transmitted light of early Worcester china is due rather to this "blueing" of the paste and glaze than by the soapstone used in the body.[2] Iron present as an impurity in one of the materials would also produce a greenish tone.[3] Salopian porcelain also contained soapstone, but commonly gives a warm yellowish tone to transmitted light. Kiln losses were evidently less than in most soft-paste manufactures, and the proprietors constantly laid stress on the cheapness of their wares. It is rare to find a Worcester piece that has needed to be ground level at the foot, as was so often the case at Chelsea and Derby. The material was indeed very practical, withstanding hot water much

[1] "Crazing" and "crackle" are the names respectively used for the accidental and intentional production of a network of lines due to a splitting-up of the glaze. The effect is due to a difference in the amount of contraction of body and glaze on cooling.

[2] A typical Worcester analysis shows about 13 per cent of magnesia due to soapstone. See *Analysed Specimens*, Nos. 26-36.

[3] See Donald A. MacAlister, *loc. cit.*

better than most other artificial porcelains.[1] And this practical quality was characteristic of the ware in other ways. The amusing extravagances of Chelsea and Bow were for the greater part carefully avoided, and neatness and "English good sense" prevailed in the shapes of the useful wares to which the factory largely confined its attention for the first fifteen or twenty years. The characteristically well-proportioned forms and careful finish are quickly recognised by the collector. "Not good enough for Worcester" is often the deciding comment on a doubtful piece. The decoration commonly strikes the same note, but a certain *naïveté* in the rendering and combination of Meissen, Chinese and Japanese motives gives the ware a very distinct charm, particularly in the earliest period, before the advent of painters from Chelsea brought a more pretentious style.

The firm usually disposed of its wares to retailers, and until 1769 held no public auction-sales with catalogues such as assist us in identifying the productions of other factories. The first exhibition of the china was announced for September 20, 1752, "with a great variety of ware, and at a reasonable price". London advertisements of 1756 [2] merely make known to us the existence of the firm's warehouse in Aldersgate Street in the City of London. A sufficient number of dated pieces have survived, however, to enable the sequence of styles to be inferred.

The earliest style is naturally a continuation of that of Lowdin's factory, with a considerable Meissen influence. The moulded early Bristol sauce-boats have their counterpart in such silver forms as that of a charming jug in the Schreiber Collection (No. 490: Plate

[1] In the *Handmaid to the Arts* (1758) it was stated that "a manufactory at Worcester has lately produced, even at very cheap prices, pieces that not only work very light, but which have great tenacity, and bear hot water without more hazard than the true China ware".

[2] *The Public Advertiser*, March 20, 1756; also Aris's *Birmingham Gazette*, February 27, 1758.

Painted in underglaze blue; *TF* mark. Height: $15\frac{1}{2}$ in.
About 1775. (*Schreiber Collection.*) See p. 156.

A B C

Painted in colours. About 1760. (*V. and A. Museum and Schreiber Collections.*)

See p. 158.

59 A). This is also painted with rather artless landscapes in colours (faintly recalling those of Meissen) which may well be by the same hand as those on the L-marked jug described in the last chapter.[1] A more definitely German style of painting is seen on some of the elaborately moulded pieces that date from this early period. A plate in the Schreiber Collection (No. 491: Plate 59 B) has a little group of figures and sprays of flowers in colours evidently copied from a Meissen model. But the well-known figure-subject depicting sportsmen with queer-looking dogs [2] is quite likely to have been copied through the medium of a Chinese version of a Meissen design. Such Chinese copies are not uncommon [3] and show precisely the same shading and dotting.

The Lowdin's tradition of forms moulded from silver was perhaps continued through the influence of Samuel Bradley, a silversmith, who was one of the original subscribers. An important document for the earliest styles is provided by a white tureen formerly in the possession of Mrs. George Barr,[4] dated 1751 in blue. This is moulded in relief (there are similar but not identical moulds in the Worcester Works Museum), and another in Mr. Dyson Perrins' collection [5] exactly corresponds with it but is painted in blue and has proved on analysis to contain soapstone. Many early specimens are in the public collections (Plate 60)—some moulded with *rococo* scrolls, others with ribbed patterns interrupted by flowers. Little cups were formed of overlapping leaves, again in silver style. These and the horn-shaped flower-holders and sauce-boats moulded with landscapes, the large dishes with shells and scrolls

[1] P. 148.
[2] Frank Lloyd, No. 133, a sugar-bowl and a tray (Schr. No. 495) are examples.
[3] There is a specimen at South Kensington (No. C 1062—1924), in Room 143.
[4] Illustrated by Binns, p. 43.
[5] Hobson, *Worcester Porcelain*, Plate 16.

on the rims, and many others, all speak of silver originals.[1]

The analysed tureen in Mr. Dyson Perrins' collection is additionally important since it proves the Worcester origin of much blue-and-white formerly ascribed to Bow. The painting on this tureen is unmistakably like that on many pieces bearing a mark resembling the letters T and F conjoined which was at one time believed to be the monogram of Thomas Frye of Bow. The mark is probably no more than a copy of a Chinese character, "a maimed version", as Mr. Hobson says, of that for *yü* (jade), a very common mark on Chinese porcelain. The Worcester underglaze blue even at this time already shows its characteristic tendency towards a dark indigo tone, a feature constantly noticeable in the abundant blue-and-white of the next twenty years. Valentine Green, writing in 1795, declared that the early Worcester was chiefly blue-and-white; and it was certainly much made, probably supplying a large provincial market. There is usually little difficulty in distinguishing it. The hexagonal vase in the Schreiber Collection (Plate 61) is typical of the better kind of Worcester blue-and-white and is finely painted: it bears the TF mark, and it seems astonishing now that the distinctive paste and glaze and tone of blue of these pieces should not have prevented their ascription to Bow. On the other hand, much of the abundant Bow blue-and-white ware with powdered-blue ground was (and still is, I am afraid) wrongly ascribed to Worcester. Powdered blue certainly was made at Worcester, but the soft glaze and rich blue, the shapes, and the characteristic imitation Chinese characters of the marks on the Bow pieces [2] clearly distinguish them from the Worcester, which have the usual qualities I have already described. A

[1] Compare also dish and pierced basket in the Schreiber Collection (Nos. 633 and 480).

[2] See p. 76 and Appendix, p. 260. Lowestoft, of course, comes into question as well, see p. 134.

cup and saucer at South Kensington (No. 3271—1901: Plate 60) is a typical piece of Worcester with powdered-blue ground, marked with both crescent and fretted square. The powdered blue made at Caughley is naturally harder to distinguish, but the ground is inclined to be paler and, as Mr. Rackham has pointed out, the form of foot-ring is different.[1]

THE DECADE BEGINNING ABOUT 1755 SHOWS A FULLY-developed Worcester style in being. Documentary pieces for this period are fairly numerous. Two large jugs dated 1757 are in the Corporation Museum at Worcester.[2] They are moulded in relief with overlapping "cabbage" leaves in a style afterwards very familiar in Caughley and Lowestoft as well as in Worcester china. It should be noted that the mask-lip-spout, which is a common feature of the later jugs in this form, is here absent. The painting includes the arms of the city of Worcester, with figures emblematical of Commerce and Justice, and borders of feathery crimson scroll-work probably suggested by Meissen but very characteristic also of Worcester and helping us to identify and date many pieces belonging to this period.

The date 1759 is inscribed on an important mug in the British Museum (Frank Lloyd Collection), which bears also the name of Lord Sandys, Dr. Wall's guardian. This mug is of a characteristic Worcester shape, somewhat resembling a bell, and is painted by one of the most accomplished of the artists whose work gives such distinction to this period of Worcester. The rare figure-subjects (as on this piece) with the landscapes, birds and flowers also by his hand are the Worcester counterparts of the Chelsea fable-painter's work. One of this artist's favourite subjects shows an owl on a branch mobbed by other birds, with a characteristic distant landscape in which three or four Lombardy poplar trees

[1] See p. 187.
[2] Hobson, *Worcester Porcelain*, Plate C.

are a common feature. His work may be well studied in the Schreiber Collection at South Kensington, as on the typical oviform Worcester vases (such as No. 496: Plate 62 A) with domed lids having the half-open flower-bud knob which is characteristic of early Worcester.[1] The hand of this "painter of the Lord Sandys mug" is sometimes recognisable in the shields of arms surrounded by the deliciously treated *rococo* scroll-work which is one of the most attractive features of this early Worcester porcelain (Plate 63). A beautiful mug of this kind in the Schreiber Collection (No. 500: Plate 63 C) is painted with a crest and flowers in lilac, grey and crimson monochromes. A jug in the Frank Lloyd Collection (No. 386), with the arms of Chalmers, has a beautiful little landscape in lilac and the date 1759. Scroll-work even more beautiful is seen on the little cups and saucer painted with no less charming flowers (V. & A.M. No. 3210—1901: Plate 64 A). Worcester flowers in this period are obviously inspired by Meissen, but quite fresh and individual in treatment. Two other styles of flower-painting are shown in Plate 62: that on the vase seems to be by the hand of the "painter of the Lord Sandys mug". These flowers are sometimes seen rather arbitrarily painted over the vine- and lettuce-leaf dishes and the plates moulded in relief with rose-leaves and flower-buds, all of them adaptations of Meissen forms. The last-named relief pattern is commonly associated with the "blind Earl" of Coventry, who, however, did not lose his sight until 1780, long after the earliest date of this pattern. Plate 64 B shows a specimen of about 1765–70, painted in colours.[2] This relief pattern certainly remained in use over a long period, and it seems to have been the Worcester practice to name designs, years after their introduction,

[1] Other distinctive Worcester forms of this period are a globular teapot usually not so high in the foot as at Lowestoft, and a pear-shaped coffee-pot.

[2] The large moths on this and other Worcester pieces of this time should be carefully distinguished from the somewhat similar insects which mark a class of early Derby porcelain. See p. 92.

after distinguished patrons who happened to favour them.[1]

The work of another talented painter may best be studied in the charming "Chinese" landscapes in crimson monochrome, naïvely set in a yellow ground with borders and scattered flowers in the Kakiemon style (Plate 65 A). A date for a yellow ground of this type is provided by a mug in Mr. Wallace Elliot's collection with a silhouette portrait of Dr. Wall inscribed *J. W. 1761*.[2] The hand of this "painter of the Chinese landscapes" may often be recognised in the blue-and-white.

THE PRACTICAL AND AT TIMES DISTINCTLY COMMERCIAL bent of the Worcester proprietors is made plain by their quick adoption on a large scale of transfer-printing. We have no record of the date at which the process was first introduced at Worcester, and portraits of Frederick the Great dated 1757 are the earliest unquestionably Worcester prints. These are the work of Robert Hancock (*b.* 1730, *d.* 1817),[3] round whose name controversy has for long raged, the difficult question of whose early work I have discussed on previous pages.[4] We know, however, for certain that he was at Worcester or working for the factory at the latest by the date of these portraits.

Most of Hancock's prints for porcelain were not even newly adapted from designs in other media, but were merely versions of work by other engravers. Many of the prints used by him in this way cannot now be found, but one may conjecture that a collection of work by F. Vivares furnished him with much material.

[1] A list of named patterns of this kind is given in Hobson, *Worcester Porcelain*, p. 129. The name was occasionally much too *early* for the porcelain, as in the case of the service in the style of the 1770's named after Lady Mary Wortley Montagu, who died in 1762.

[2] Illustrated in colours in *The Connoisseur*, vol. lxxix (October 1927).

[3] Biographical details and a catalogue of his work as a mezzotint engraver and painter are given in A. Randal Ballantyne, *Robert Hancock and his Works* (London, 1885).

[4] See pp. 73 and 145.

No original engraving of the famous *Tea-Party* has ever been found, but the design has a decidedly French air and the comparable *L'Amour* is known to be after a French print.[1] Many engravings signed by Hancock were included in the popular collections published by Robert Sayer in the 1760's and 1770's under such titles as *The Ladies' Amusement* and *The Artist's Vade-Mecum*, though it by no means follows (as is often supposed) that their dates of publication in this form give the earliest dates for the porcelain on which they appear. The prints may well have been in use for porcelain decoration for many years previously. Indeed, Binns long ago suggested that their appearance in Sayer's publications was due to their sale to him by Hancock, who evidently owned some of the plates, since he took them with him to Caughley and Staffordshire; and a curious Staffordshire enamel (Schr. Collection No. 406) bears an engraving signed *R H Worcester*, though the signature is concealed by herbage painted over it in dark brown.[2]

Some of the prints, in addition to the signatures *R. Hancock fecit*, *R. H. fecit* and *Hancock fecit*, bear a monogram of R and H with an anchor. The last is by general consent the rebus device of one or other of the brothers Holdship, who were apparently in charge of the printing department of the factory: a printed basket at South Kensington (No. 3222—1901) bears a device of two crossed anchors, possibly with reference to the two brothers. Richard Holdship, a glover, was a large subscriber to the original company, and his brother Josiah also held shares. The former left Worcester in 1759, and in 1764 offered his "process of Printing enamell and Blew" to the Derby proprietors.[3] The significance

[1] See Ballantyne, *op. cit.*, p. 5.

[2] An enlarged photograph of this concealed signature is reproduced in Mr. Bernard Rackham's article on Hancock in *The Burlington Magazine*, vol. xxvi (1915), p. 155.

[3] See p. 93 and Jewitt, vol. i, p. 233, and vol. ii, p. 89. Holdship is also said to have offered the Worcester recipes for porcelain, indicating the use of

A

B

C

About 1760. (*Frank Lloyd and Schreiber Collections.*)

See p. 158.

A

B

A, marked with the crossed swords. About 1760. (*V. and A. Museum.*) See p. 158.
B, "Blind Earl's" pattern. About 1765–70. (*Frank Lloyd Collection.*)
See pp. 92 and 158.

of the monogram has been the subject of much discussion. For long believed to be Holdship's mark, it was declared by Mr. Hobson [1] (who had at one time held the other view) to be no more than another form of Hancock's signature. But its presence on a piece signed by Hancock in full, as for example on the well-known dated mugs with portraits of Frederick the Great,[2] is strong evidence in favour of the older view. There is little likelihood that a print would bear two signatures of one engraver, though it has been suggested that the full signature was added by Hancock when he found that his initials were being mistaken for those of Richard Holdship.

Some verses which appeared in *The Gentleman's Magazine* of December 20, 1757, "Inscribed to Mr. Josiah Holdship" and referring to the portrait of Frederick the Great, included the lines:

> What praise is thine, ingenious Holdship, who
> On the fair porcelain the Portrait drew.

This couplet was reprinted in the *Worcester Journal* in January 1758 with this addition:

> Hancock, my friend, don't grieve tho' Holdship has the praise,
> 'Tis yours to execute, 'tis his to wear the bays.

Such a commentary could have had little point had not the manager of the printing-shop taken advantage of his position to add his mark to that of the engraver; but there seems to have been some confusion between Josiah and Richard. The interpretation of the monogram as Holdship's involves the corollary that plates which bear it cannot have been engraved after

---

frit and glass and two sorts of "soapy rock" ("the process of making porcelain ware delivered by Richard Holdship to John Heath and William Duesbury, Dec. 31st 1764"). According to Holdship, tin-ashes were used in the Worcester glaze. The Derby proprietors do not seem to have used the recipes to any considerable extent; but see p. 89.

[1] *Worcester Porcelain*, p. 74.

[2] Such as Schr. No. 622.

1759, when Holdship left Worcester, though they may perhaps have remained in use for some years longer, if we may assume that he did not take them all away with him.

I have chosen to illustrate the best qualities of "Worcester transfer" typical versions of *L'Amour* and of "the two milkmaids", with a charming specimen of a less familiar subject (Plate 66 B). The touches of brushwork in delicate scrolls of black or crimson, which often frame the subjects, occur only on the earlier prints of the Hancock period, which ended with his departure in 1774. On the whole, early Worcester printed china is the best of its class ever made in England. Technical excellence is allied to fine taste in the placing of the transfers, and the modest wares deserve a place beside the best achievements in domestic pottery of Josiah Wedgwood, of which they are in a sense the counterpart. They are evidence, it may be, of a commercialising tendency, but in themselves by no means negligible or without charm.[1]

The prints were executed in lilac and (more rarely) in red, as well as in the usual brown or black. The last were referred to in the catalogues of 1769 as "jet-enamelled". In an important section of the printed class the prints are further decorated by washes of colour, not always with pleasing effect, and such pieces are often marked with crossed swords in overglaze blue. It is highly probable that this style was the work of the "outside enameller" J. Giles, whose name appears as

[1] An artistically unimportant small class of Worcester porcelain, which may be mentioned here, takes the form of tokens printed in black with a "promise to pay bearer" one or two shillings, signed by W. Davis; on the reverse are the initials W.P.C. (for Worcester Porcelain Company). They were evidently made on account of the prevalent baseness of the currency at the time. As pointed out by Mr. Hobson (*Worcester Porcelain*, p. 126), Binns was in error in supposing that these porcelain discs all date from 1763. They may have been made at any time after the introduction of printing until the death of Davis in 1783. There are specimens in the British Museum (Nos. V. 87 and 87 A), and an illustration is in Hobson, *loc. cit.* Similar tokens were made at Pinxton.

the purchaser at the Worcester sale of 1769 of several services of "jet-enamelled" porcelain.[1] Giles had in the previous year advertised as "China and Enamel Painter" and "Proprietor of the Worcester Porcelaine Warehouse" that he had a "great Variety of white Goods by him", and that customers could have pieces "painted to any pattern they shall chuse". The Worcester factory proprietors responded to this advertisement a little later, describing their own goods and referring to "some of their Ware . . . advertised at another Room, painted in London". Giles's advertisement was then repeated, but with the omission of the words "Proprietor of the Worcester Porcelain Warehouse". To judge by the wording of his advertisements it seems probable enough that Giles decorated Worcester china in other ways besides colouring transfer-prints, but this work has never been certainly identified. Mr. Hobson mentions[2] vases with blue ground and blank panels, which he thinks may be unfinished pieces from Giles's workshop, and I shall have occasion to revert to this question when discussing the Worcester painters of a later period.

A small class, usually ascribed to Worcester, that may be associated with the transfers has Chinese figures printed in brown outline filled in with washes of colour. These pieces generally have borders of cresting or *lambrequins* in underglaze blue, in a style much favoured at Liverpool and used also at Caughley, and some pieces of this unattractive class may well have been made there. A sauce-boat with this decoration at South Kensington[3] is marked with an incised cross, but differs in other respects from the "scratched cross group" of the last chapter.

When Hancock left Worcester in 1774 he took some at least of his plates with him; in that year the Caughley factory announced that they had secured his

[1] Nightingale, p. 95. [2] *Worcester Porcelain*, p. 20.
[3] No. C 1199—1924.

services.[1] The Worcester printing then declined in importance, though Hancock's pupil [2] James Ross produced some good plates. A feature of the printed wares of this later period is the gold line encircling the edges, never seen on pieces of Hancock's time. Towards the close of the eighteenth century prints after Angelica Kauffmann and Bartolozzi were made by the newly introduced process of glue-bat printing.[3] These were usually in the fashionable stipple, but line-engravings continued to be used occasionally as late as 1809, the probable date of a flower-pot in the Schreiber Collection (No. 678). Groups of shells and bunches of flowers were virtually novelties in this later printing.

It was at one time believed that printing in underglaze blue was not in use at Worcester until 1770, when a strike of blue-painters is alleged to have taken place,[4] and printing in blue that can be ascribed to an earlier date is certainly rare; but the process was presumably known at Worcester in 1759, when Holdship left, since he was able to offer it to the Derby people, though this was not till five years later. Worcester blue-printing has all the neatness characteristic of the other wares, but is otherwise undistinguished. Designs persisted over a long period. One pattern in particular — a group of conventionalised fruit,[5] including an object resembling a pine-cone but perhaps meant for a strawberry—enjoyed the distinction of being copied, not only in printing on Caughley [6] and Lowestoft

[1] Jewitt (vol. i, Plate 3) illustrates some of Hancock's engravings, printed from Caughley plates which have on them the C and S marks of that factory.

[2] An earlier assistant, who left when Ross came in 1765, was Valentine Green, mezzotinter and historian of Worcester. His work on porcelain was never signed.

[3] See p. 7.

[4] Binns (1st edition), p. 87. The statement was, however, omitted without explanation from the second edition.

[5] Schr. Nos. 487 and 488.

[6] The suggestion that Worcester china was printed in blue at Caughley is discussed on p. 189.

china, but in laborious brushwork on Chinese porcelain.[1] Dates are rarely found on this class, and a mug at South Kensington (Schr. No. 489), printed with flowers and a butterfly, is incised *July 31, 1773*, and is therefore important as a document. The yellow ground on an often-mentioned blue-printed dish at South Kensington (No. 3230—1901) is most probably a later addition.

AMONG THE MOST CHARACTERISTIC OF ALL WORCESTER inventions were the so-called Japan patterns, which continued to be made from the earliest days until well into the nineteenth century. The favourite Kakiemon "partridge" and other designs, also found on Bow and Chelsea, were perhaps taken at second-hand from Meissen versions, but are fairly close copies as a rule. They long remained in use. Most of the versions of Oriental designs, however, deserve to rank as creations of the English painters. It is unnecessary to enumerate here the very many designs freely adapted from both Chinese and Japanese sources: they are particularly well represented in the Frank Lloyd Collection. Three typical designs in use at an early period may be selected for mention. A figure-subject evidently adapted from the so-called "Mandarin porcelain" shows ladies at a table or otherwise employed, in panels set in a ground often diapered in red or gold.[2] A rich clear turquoise adds greatly to the charm of these pieces. Plate 67 shows two of these subjects. A pattern adapted from the *famille verte*, with a kylin in the middle, and border panels containing rocks, flowering plants and mythical animals,[3] is often known as the "Bishop Sumner pattern", but the only bishops of that name living in the second half of the eighteenth century were born as late as 1780 and 1790. This and kindred designs con-

[1] A specimen of this kind (No. C 594—1924) may be seen at South Kensington with the other Chinese porcelain copied from European models.

[2] Nos. 24 to 26 in the Lloyd Collection, or No. C 1076—1924 at South Kensington.

[3] No. 2 in the Lloyd Collection.

tinued to be made until the end of the century[1] and even later, in coarsened quality with rougher drawing. A simpler and very charming type, only faintly recalling the Chinese style and virtually a Worcester invention, is marked by panels of springing foliage stylised with much grace and vivacity. A tea-service in the Lloyd Collection (No. 11: Plate 67 D) is of this kind, and the same qualities are seen in many red-and-green Japan patterns, such as that on a cup and saucer with powdered-blue ground in the Schreiber Collection (No. 518). We may ascribe these pieces chiefly to the second decade of the factory: the simple decoration on a coffee-cup in the Frank Lloyd Collection (No. 73), which is related to these, includes the inscription *Nancy Squier 1764*. The cup and saucer figured in Plate 67 A, with a Chinese lady surrounded by feathery scrolls, was perhaps copied from a Chinese version of a Meissen decoration, and is typical in its naïve combination of Eastern and Western motives.

Of Chinese derivation again is a singular type found only at Worcester amongst the English factories, with Chinese and other subjects "pencilled" in black or lilac. These pieces were doubtless inspired by the Chinese porcelain "painted in ink", as a Chinese list describes it,[2] often with copies of European prints. A whole series of Chinese pieces painted in this way with the goddess Juno is in the Victoria and Albert Museum. The familiar subject of a Chinaman riding on an ox is often copied on Worcester (Schr. No. 511); and a tray in the Museum collection at South Kensington shows a European floral design rendered at second-hand through the medium of a Chinese imitation. Mr. Hobson has pointed out a saucer in the Worcester Factory Museum, with a gentleman and a lady fishing, which was certainly copied in this way from a Chinese

[1] A dish, No. C 1017—1924, at South Kensington, is a late example.

[2] Compare the *List of Decorations used on Imperial porcelain in the reign of Yung Chêng*, No. 40.

version of a European print. A saucer at South Kensington (No. 3991—1901: Plate 65 B) is pencilled in lilac with Chinese figures in a very soft and pleasant style. A beautiful Meissen-Chelsea landscape style, akin to this and adopted at Worcester, employed a similar pencilling in black coloured over with a wash of green: examples are in both the national collections.

A design in Oriental style long popular at Worcester and found also on Lowestoft and Derby consists of vertical or spirally curved panels alternately red on white and white on blue, with gilding (Plate 68 A). This is stated by Mr. Hobson to be derived from a Chinese design, but the only Chinese examples I have met appear to be themselves copies of this pattern. It was variously known as the "whorl", "spiral", "catherine-wheel" and "Queen's pattern".[1] The so-called "Sir Joshua Reynolds' pattern"[2] with a pheasant on a turquoise-blue rock is another free adaptation of a Japanese design.

MANY OF THESE INVENTIONS, HOWEVER, DID NOT reach their fullest splendour until the next period, which may be said to begin with the arrival of hands from Chelsea about 1768. It is likely enough that workmen may have migrated during one of the earlier periods of inactivity at Chelsea, and the "painter of the Lord Sandys mug" has even been claimed as a Chelsea man on account of the similarity between his flowers and those on some "raised-anchor" dishes. This resemblance seems rather to be due to their common Meissen model. As evidence of the later migration, however, we have not only Worcester tradition (Binns

[1] It is so named in the Sale Catalogue of 1769. This "Queen's Pattern" should be clearly distinguished from the "Queen Charlotte's Pattern" or "Royal Lily", chosen in 1788 at a visit to the factory by George III. and his Queen. This later pattern, also of Chinese derivation, is in blue with gilding, with radial panels of conventional floral designs in outline. Herbert Allen No. 323 is an example. It was also used at Caughley and I believe is still made at Worcester.

[2] No. 96 in the Frank Lloyd Collection; No. 537 in the Schreiber Collection is an especially charming plate.

mentions the names of Willmann, Dontil,[1] Duvivier, Mills and Dyer [2]), but the style of at least one Chelsea painter can be recognised on the actual porcelain. Moreover, the advertisement of 1768, already mentioned in connection with Giles, stated that the proprietors had "engaged the best painters from Chelsea, etc.", adding that "any orders will be executed in the highest taste and much cheaper than can be afforded by any painters in London".

Two public auction sales were held in 1769, following the Chelsea fashion. Of the first, held by Burnsall, no catalogue has survived, but the announcement in *The Public Advertiser* [3] makes clear the ambitious nature of the china offered: "Table and Desert Services, Leaves, Compotiers, Tea and Coffee Equipages, Baskets, Vases, Perfume Pots, Jars, Beakers, Cisterns, Tureens, Porringers, Bowls, &c., in the beautiful Colours of Mazarine Blue and Gold, Sky-blue, Pea-green, French-green, Sea-green, Purple, Scarlet and other Variety of Colours, richly decorated with chased and burnished Gold; and many other Articles both useful and ornamental. The whole enamelled in the highest Taste, and curiously painted in Figures, Birds, Landscapes, Flowers, Fruits, &c." Seven months later another sale, apparently of less pretentious wares, was held by Christie; extracts from the Catalogue of this with prices and purchasers were published by Nightingale.[4] Many items may be recognised amongst the porcelain surviving.

The coloured grounds perfected at Worcester at this time rank among the best ever made.[5] The Chelsea

[1] The suggestion recently put forward that this painter gave his name to the "dontil" or scalloped gilt border on porcelain can scarcely be accepted. The French *dentelle* is more probably the source of the word.

[2] Compare p. 56.

[3] May 5, 1769. Nightingale, p. lxxviii.

[4] P. 94.

[5] It should be remembered that at Meissen every ground colour subsequently used in the course of the century was employed, at least tentatively, before 1750. Even the pink of the *famille rose* was used by Böttger *before* it appeared on Chinese porcelain. But soft-paste was capable of giving greater depth and richness to the colours.

A

B C

A. Mug, painted in crimson, yellow ground.
B. Saucer, painted in lilac.
C. Teapot, painted in black.
About 1760.
(*V. and A. Museum and Schreiber Collections.*)
See pp. 159 and 166.

A B C

Transfer-printed wares. About 1755–65.
(Schreiber and V. and A. Museum Collections.)

A

B

C

D

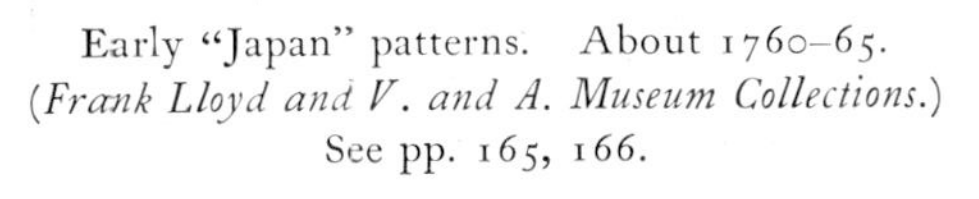

Early "Japan" patterns. About 1760–65.
(*Frank Lloyd and V. and A. Museum Collections.*)
See pp. 165, 166.

A

B

C

About 1765–75. Later "Japan" patterns.
A is marked with the fretted square, B and C with four imitation Chinese characters.
(*Frank Lloyd and Schreiber Collections.*) See pp. 167, 174.

About 1770.
(*Frank Lloyd Collection.*) See p. 174.

A

B

About 1770–75. Pink-scale and dark scale-blue border and ground.
B is marked with the fretted square.
(*Frank Lloyd and Schreiber Collections.*) See p. 170.

A

B

C

About 1770–75. A has a pea-green ground; B a pink-scale border.
(*Frank Lloyd and Schreiber Collections.*)
See pp. 170, 172, 176.

A

B

About 1770–75. The ground-colour in A is dark blue.
(*Frank Lloyd and Schreiber Collections.*) See pp. 172, 173.

dark blue was never equalled, it is true, and the evenness and richness of the Sèvres grounds were in most cases beyond the reach of the English factory. The Chelsea claret-colour was sometimes obtained successfully, and I have already mentioned, in my account of Derby, the probability that the workman responsible for this colour at Chelsea migrated to Worcester and not to Derby on the closing of Sprimont's factory. It was not very much used, however, and was probably uncertain and costly. But the Worcester turquoise and lavender and above all the pea-green were thoroughly mastered and of very fine quality. Moreover, the Worcester method of breaking up the ground-colour by reticulation, fish-scale pattern and diapers, such as the tiny circles resembling shagreen and called by the Chinese "fish-roe", may almost be regarded as an invention, though the device had been used on Turkish pottery of the sixteenth century and to some extent on Chinese porcelain. That pink-scale was used as early as 1761 is shown by a dated specimen in the Dyson Perrins Collection,[1] and it is stated on the authority of a family tradition that a tea-poy [2] with scale-blue is as old as 1763. The earlier specimens of this last and most famous ground show a bold pattern, outlined with a brush on the powdered (underglaze) colour, which was of the usual dark indigo tone. Later a smaller, less definite and obtrusive scale was produced by wiping away the lights. Yellow- [3] and brick-red-scale [4] were used in the same way. Worcester gilding admirably continued the Chelsea tradition, and has never been surpassed. The slightly dull gold was applied with the greatest delicacy in scrolls, foliage and lace-work in *rococo* style, whilst bolder masses were chased with a metal point in the Sèvres and Chelsea manner. Plates 70, 75 and 76 show some excellent specimens.

[1] Hobson *Worcester Porcelain,* Plate 59, Fig. 2.
[2] Hobson, *op. cit.,* p. 114.
[3] Frank Lloyd No. 148, and V. & A.M. C 1268—1919.
[4] Frank Lloyd No. 29.

The most famous and costly of all Worcester china is that painted in panels set in the coloured grounds with the so-called exotic birds, fantastically coloured, and originally an invention of the Meissen factory. The classification of the several painters' work in this style is one of the most interesting studies open to the lover of Worcester china. At the head of these unnamed artists may be placed, appropriately enough, a Chelsea man with a decided style of bold, fluent brush-strokes, who also painted fruit and flowers (Plates 70 and 71). His work on Chelsea, Worcester and imported Chinese porcelain may be well studied in adjacent cases in the Schreiber Collection at South Kensington. His birds are always drawn with a peculiar freedom and verve. The heart-shaped dishes, No. 183 (Chelsea) and No. 540 (Worcester), are comparable pieces, though the former is more carefully finished.[1] The differences in colouring are of course accounted for by the differences of glaze and the local sources of the enamel colours. The cut fruits and fig with calyx in this painter's work have been noted by Mr. Hobson, but as these were doubtless copied from a pattern-piece (probably of Meissen china) they would not be his special property.[2] On the two heart-shaped dishes (Schr. No. 540) they are combined with birds, and again on No. 543 and other plates in the Schreiber Collection they are seen in company with his characteristic flowers. It was evidently his practice to draw with a full brush, and a peculiar "wetness" is always noticeable in his work. His flowers are seen especially often on services of the *feuille de choux* and "hop-trellis" patterns copied from Sèvres.[3] A plate and cups and saucers with *bleu de roi* panels in the

[1] Some Chelsea dishes with mazarine ground in the Emily Thomson Bequest show birds which come near to his Worcester work. For his Chelsea work, see p. 47.

[2] Mr. Hobson accepts, I think wrongly, the late Robert Drane's identification of this painter with a Meissen artist.

[3] Frank Lloyd No. 183 (a deep plate) and Schreiber No. 544 (a plate) are examples.

Schreiber Collection (Nos. 602 and 603), which may well be as late as 1780, show his later style, now grown rather weak and insignificant.

One of the most distinctive of these styles of bird-painting is that of an artist who came from Plymouth and Bristol, the "Mons. Soqui" of Cookworthy's biographer Harrison, described by Prideaux as an "excellent painter and enameller . . . from Sèvres".[1] His manner is in some respects an imitation of that of the Sèvres bird-painter Evans, and is usually marked by rather strong colour in thickly stippled brushwork, and by the introduction of a faintly coloured distant landscape with shadowy trees. Many Worcester pieces by him are in the British Museum and at South Kensington,[2] though the Schreiber Collection includes none. The plate from Mr. Allen's collection (Plate 73 A) is a typical example.

I have already mentioned the "painter of the dishevelled birds" in connection with Bow and Longton Hall porcelain.[3] The fact that his work is found also on Plymouth and Worcester china as well has suggested that he may never have travelled at all, but worked at Giles's shop in London decorating porcelain of different makes bought in the white.[4] Against this view is the unlikelihood of white Plymouth porcelain being available in this way, to any extent, though white Plymouth shell-salts, such as are also found decorated by him, have survived (see Plate 87). It is noteworthy that the gilding on some pieces with his painting (such as the teapot figured in Plate 73 B) is rather crude, and the finish of some of them (such as a basket-work dish,

[1] The name is also given as Saqui and Lequoi. His style was first identified by Mr. Bernard Rackham. See *The Burlington Magazine*, vol. xxv (1914), p. 104. For his work at Plymouth and Bristol, see p. 231 below.

[2] Such as No. C 173—1910 (a plate) at South Kensington and No. 233 (a vase) in the Frank Lloyd Collection.

[3] Pages 79 and 130.

[4] I made this suggestion myself in an article in *The Morning Post* some two years ago, and I find that Mr. Wallace Elliot had independently come to the same conclusion.

Schr. No. 546) often markedly inferior to the usual Worcester work in the period. A plate by him in the Herbert Allen Collection (No. 262) is on the other hand beautifully finished. Good gilding in the Worcester factory style is also seen on some pieces painted by him marked with the gold anchor and usually regarded as Chelsea. There is a cup and saucer of this kind in the British Museum (others are in the London Museum) with a pale pinkish "claret" ground of very poor quality: it is of unmistakable Worcester paste. A pair of crocus pots (Frank Lloyd No. 250) painted by him has a very rough scale-blue ground. On the whole, therefore, the evidence seems to point to the "painter of the dishevelled birds" as a Giles's man. In 1770 Giles advertised "Mazarine and Sky Blue and Gold curiously enamelled in Figures, Birds, Flowers, etc." The painting just described may be part of this, but we may wonder what were the other wares offered. It is of course possible that Giles sold Worcester-decorated pieces as well as those done to order by his own painters.

Another prolific painter (Plate 71 A)[1] had a special fondness for rendering the plumage of his birds by dots, and their eyes by well-defined circles (several others, however, tended to do this, but not in so marked a degree). His style suggests facility, and is not free from hardness. The stiff S-shaped curves of the outlines of his birds and a frequent use of *red* foliage make his style easy to recognise. Quite distinct again are the birds (Plate 72 A) painted by an artist using a smudgy brush-stroke, largely avoiding the dots of most of the painters. His foliage usually has a blunt spikiness, easily recognised.[2] Still another hand was responsible for the slender-legged, plump birds often confused with those of the supposed Soqui, but depicted in landscapes

[1] See also Schr. Nos. 552 and 554, and Frank Lloyd No. 252. This painter's style was closely copied at Liverpool (see p. 195), and the birds on Longton Hall porcelain (Plate 48) were perhaps painted at an earlier date from the same engraved copies.

[2] See also Schr. No. 550 and Frank Lloyd No. 265.

more clearly indicated, with trees like billowy clouds (Plate 72 B). The differences between their styles will be made clear by a comparison of the two specimens illustrated here in Plates 72 B and 73 A, both probably painted from the same copy. The practice by which several painters freely copied the same subject seriously complicates the problem of identification. The collector will doubtless recognise other hands besides those indicated here.

The hand of a Bow (and perhaps also Chelsea) painter is suggested by some Worcester versions of the Kakiemon "partridge pattern". Several specimens with this design brought together by the late Robert Drane[1] included an oviform Worcester vase and an octagonal plate described as Chelsea, on both of which a partridge is rendered with a peculiar humped back, probably indicating the same hand. But the possibility of a common Meissen example should be borne in mind. The same feature is seen on Bow versions in Mr. Broderip's gift at South Kensington. Amongst the painters of the beautiful and unmistakable[2] "Worcester Japan" patterns of this period should be noted the master of the fretful-looking birds who appear in the midst of tufty red and green willows and scattered strange rocks and "jewels". These patterns — the "wheat-sheaf", "crab", "pheasant" and the rest, painted chiefly in red, green and gold, and full of the most fanciful detail—are actually far removed in both spirit and design from their Japanese examples. The "old mosaick Japan" and "fine old Japan fan pattern" (all these names are from the Sale Catalogue of 1769) are, on the contrary, fairly exact renderings of the "brocaded Imari". The "Japan star-pattern" is more likely to be the chrysanthemum design (such as Frank

[1] Hobson, *Worcester Porcelain*, Plate 30 and p. 60, where the Worcester specimen is erroneously described as Bow.

[2] But exact copies of some were made at Derby, though rarely. See p. 100. The soft glaze of the copies and the thicker, rather clumsy, gilding reveal their Derby origin to a critical eye.

Lloyd No. 60 or Plate 68 B) than that with slight conventional stars, much less Japanese, to which the name is attached by Mr. Hobson. The "fan pattern" was probably that with radiating panels (Plate 68 C). Of the more elaborate of these inventions I illustrate (Plate 69) a superb hexagonal vase from the Frank Lloyd Collection (No. 76), with an S-shaped object suspended from a showering, scintillating tree, which may be presumed to be the "fine old rich dragon pattern" of a specimen in the Catalogue, where it is described as having a "bleu Celeste" border, doubtless the clear turquoise often found with these designs. These hexagonal vases are among the most highly prized specimens dating from this period. They seem to have given trouble in the making and it is not unusual to find them collapsed at the shoulder or otherwise misshapen.[1] It has often been remarked that some lack of plastic quality in the Worcester paste forbade the more elaborately modelled pieces, figures and the like, such as were made elsewhere, though the practical bent of the Worcester management alone would perhaps account for the abstention. The mishaps of the hexagonal vases, however, suggest that the view approaches the truth. The wandering repairer "Tebo" [2] was at Worcester at some time in the 1770's, and the *rococo* "frill vases" which are the most fancifully modelled of any Worcester things were apparently made on his initiative; there are specimens with his mark in the Schreiber (No. 571: Plate 74 B) and Frank Lloyd Collections (No. 125). They are very similar to those in Bristol china, presumably also by "Mr. Tebo". One may guess, too, that the sweetmeat stands in the form of shells and rocks [3] were also his work, and perhaps also the basket-work dishes with vine-leaves in relief,[4] again identical with Bristol

[1] An example of the kind, printed and coloured over, is in the Schreiber Collection (No. 668).

[2] See pp. 66 and 227 for a discussion of his identity and of his work at Bow, Plymouth and Bristol.

[3] No. C 632—1925 (V. & A.M.).

[4] Frank Lloyd No. 137 and Schr. No. 570.

specimens. More classical in feeling and perhaps rather later in date are the baluster- and urn-shaped vases with festoons of applied white flowers, such as Frank Lloyd No. 126 and A; they were perhaps copies of Meissen pieces. Those just cited are painted with flowers *en camaieu* in the "dry" blue quite peculiar to Worcester, a very brilliant colour with a curiously matt surface.

In spite of the presumed technical difficulties a few figures were undoubtedly made at Worcester, and their identity was finally established after much conjecture by an analysis by Mr. Herbert Eccles, which proved the presence of magnesia from soapstone.[1] It had long been known from an advertisement of 1769[2] and from the diary for 1779 of Mrs. Philip Lybbe Powys that figures were actually made at Worcester, and the crescent-marked figures, of which a large number exist, were held to be Worcester productions in spite of their obvious resemblance to late Bow specimens.[3] Analysis has only given the last item of evidence to a case which might well be considered proved on style alone: the characteristic Worcester dry blue, the "close-fitting" glaze and the unmistakable gilding are all present on the identified specimens. But up to the present the only Worcester figures which have been recognised are a *Gardener* (Plate 74 C) and his companion and two *Turks* (Plate 74 A).[4] Figures were presumably made during the whole period of ten years between the two dates I have quoted, so that others must surely remain unidentified in English cabinets. Mrs. Powys also left us a description of the modelling of the "little roses, handles, twists and flowers" which were used on the

[1] See an article by Mr. William King in *The Connoisseur*, June 1923.

[2] In *The Public Advertiser*, December 1769, "Jars, and Beakers, Figures . . . Bowls, Basin and other articles".

[3] Analysis had proved them phosphatic.

[4] The others are reproduced in W. King, *English Porcelain Figures*, Figs. 61 and 62. There are *Gardeners* at S. Kensington and at Bloomsbury. Trapnell Collection No. 459, which I have not examined, is perhaps another Worcester figure.

china baskets she saw made at Worcester. "Pierced baskets with green handles" are also mentioned in the Catalogue of 1769: a specimen in the Schreiber Collection (No. 545) is painted inside with fruit by the "Chelsea painter". Three different types of these baskets are in the Frank Lloyd Collection (Nos. 122 to 124): all have applied flowers of precisely the same character as those on the figures—a final proof of the origin of the latter, if one were needed.

Another Chelsea style of painting adopted at Worcester in this period is seen in the "Watteau" figure-subjects. Several hands are recognisable in these. One style is seen on a curious pattern-plate in the Frank Lloyd Collection (No. 340), painted with specimens of three designs. Five other figure-pieces in the Lloyd Collection (Nos. 341 to 345) are by the same hand as the pattern-plate and show the same free and attractive style. One of these, a mug (No. 341: Plate 71 B), is also an example of "peacock-scale" in pink. One of the other patterns on the specimen plate is a gadroon- or petal-design in plain gold lines which is virtually a Worcester invention, though perhaps ultimately of Japanese derivation, as has been asserted. Another figure-painter is represented in the Lloyd Collection by a coffee-pot (No. 354) with a Pillement Chinaman amid *rococo* scrolls, and a cup and saucer (No. 355), the former with a bold scale-blue ground of the early type. Another cup and saucer is in the Schreiber Collection (No. 538: Plate 75 A). It is tempting to see in this work the hand of the Chelsea painter who decorated the Emily Thomson tea-service at South Kensington, though slight differences make the identification not quite certain. As I have said in my chapter on Chelsea, this painting has been wrongly ascribed to John Donaldson, whose rather dull style on Worcester china is known from signed pieces.[1] Red-

[1] Signed specimens in Sir Samuel Scott's collection are illustrated in Hobson, *Worcester Porcelain*, Plate 80.

A

B

About 1770–75.
The grounds are dark blue. A is marked with a crescent.
(*Mr. Herbert Allen's and the Schreiber Collections.*) See p. 171.

A

B

C

About 1770–75.

The figures are in *Mr. Dyson Perrins' Collection*, the vase in the *Schreiber Collection*.

grave [1] stated that he "painted some vases sent to him in London from the Worcester china-works", and the more elaborate figure-pieces, such as that on a large hexagonal vase in the Lloyd Collection (No. 353), are possibly his. Mr. Hobson has pointed out a similarity in the features to those on an engraving by J. Finlayson entitled "The Newsmongers after Donaldson"; the fact that the birds and flowers on this vase are not by the same hand as the figures, also points to this attribution, since vases with blank panels are known,[2] and we may conjecture that these were sent from the factory to London for the addition of figure-painting that was never done. The work of another miniature-painter, Jeffrey Hamet O'Neale, whose address in an exhibition catalogue of 1765 was "at the China shop, in Oxford Road", is unmistakably in the style of that fascinating *Hausmalerei* (as distinct from factory painting) which is so much more common in Germany than in England. Crude, O'Neale's work may be in an academic sense, but its *naïveté* and sincerity give it a certain charm. Signed pieces are not uncommon. The Frank Lloyd Collection includes a set of three vases (Nos. 347 and 348) as well as an important unsigned vase (No. 349). O'Neale's favourite subjects were hunting scenes in the style of Wouwermans (with delightful impossible horses), unconsciously humorous classical scenes, and landscapes, marked by a curious red-brown rock first pointed out by Mr. Hobson.

THOUGH WORCESTER WAS TO SOME EXTENT INDEPENDENT of the changes in metropolitan fashions, the Meissen and Chinese styles of its first twenty-five years gradually gave place to the pseudo-classical and a modified and much anglicised Louis Seize. Towards 1780 we find the Sèvres green-and-gold "mignonette" (Plate 76 A), hop-standard and trellis styles becoming popular, and shapes began to tend towards fluting

[1] *Dictionary of Artists of the English School.*
[2] See R. L. Hobson, *Worcester Porcelain*, p. 20.

and severity. The fluted egg-shaped vase with small stopper is a characteristic Worcester shape exemplifying the change of taste. The gold-striped ground in Chelsea-Derby style was another rather belated manifestation. A rather dry manner of flower-painting, imitated from Sèvres, with festoons and clusters commonly without the usual bunch of stems of the older style, now began to be preferred. The hand responsible for some of the best "French flowers" (Plate 75 B and C) was also the painter of the monochrome sprays in "dry blue", as on an unusual teapot in the Schreiber Collection (No. 606). A brilliant *bleu de roi* enamel, rather similar to the contemporary "Derby blue", appeared at this time. It is perhaps best displayed in those pieces, such as the teapot in the Schreiber Collection figured in Plate 76 B, decorated chiefly with the still-incomparable Worcester gilding. Pieces decorated in gilding alone are not uncommon (Plate 76 C). The familiar turquoise husk-pattern is distinctly of this later style, though we find it on pieces with blue grounds and painting of birds suggesting a continuance of the earlier manner.

To this last phase of the Wall period belong the numerous patterns with urns in monochrome, groups of fruit, and landscapes with hard bright clouds.[1] The fruits and landscapes are very distinctive, but so common that it is scarcely possible that they are the work of a single hand, though the style and certain patterns are alike in all. The often-remarked spotting on the fruits is a feature, but two varieties may be distinguished: the pale summarily rendered specimens, as on a teapot in the Schreiber Collection (No. 590), and the rather unpleasant objects in over-strong colouring on a moulded jug in the same collection (No. 598). The commoner landscapes with their emphatic colours are often very charming, but not to be compared with the earlier Worcester work in the same field. But the

[1] The Lord Henry Thynne Service (Frank Lloyd No. 203) and the tea-service in the Allen Collection (No. 218) are typical.

hand of a painter gifted above the others may be detected in a mug (Plate 77) in the Schreiber Collection (No. 592), at a glance seeming like many others, but with a decidedly more sensitive touch. Mr. Alfred Hutton has a set of rare and charming plates, apparently by the same hand (Plate 77 c), which are unusual at this date in the scale of the landscapes. The mug with a delicately painted figure-subject, also shown in Plate 77, is of about the same date as these. A strange-looking pattern apparently of this period is a naturalistic representation of festooned blue drapery with a gilt fringe. A sugar-basin in Mr. Allen's collection (No. 222) has this decoration. Two reeded teacups in the Schreiber Collection (No. 486), with dark-blue and gilt decoration and the year 1782 inscribed in gold, should be mentioned as documents for date in this period.

After the change of management on the death of William Davis in 1783,[1] the good taste which had governed the work began to give place to pretentiousness and an elaborate pomposity. It may fairly be said that for the next quarter of a century Worcester fell definitely behind the Derby factory, which was then creating a distinctive style in the decoration of table-wares. Doubtless the stock patterns were repeated so long as the older painters continued at work and the demand lasted,[2] but by the end of the century dull classical forms were the rule and naturalistic flower-painting followed the fashion set by the Derby factory. Pearled and beaded borders, gadrooned edges and massive gilding were characteristic of the dress services ordered by distinguished patrons in the early-nineteenth century and detailed with such pride by Binns. A

[1] The marks of the Flight and later periods are given on p. 266.

[2] The lowest stage of the Kakiemon partridge pattern is seen in certain specimens marked with the incised B of Barr. In these roughly painted pieces the gilding is replaced by a greenish-brown enamel. An example at South Kensington is numbered C 1082—1924. A somewhat similar colour was, however, occasionally used in the same way in the earlier period.

Derby influence may also be detected in the gilt palmette and formal patterns which at the beginning of the nineteenth century were fashionable borders for the minutely rendered landscapes and figure-pieces.

James Pennington was a figure-painter who worked at Worcester for a long period at the end of the eighteenth and beginning of the nineteenth centuries. A beaker painted with a boy holding a mug of beer, in Mr. Herbert Allen's collection (No. 317), has been attributed to Pennington, but the figure of Hope on the service made for the Duke of Clarence in 1792 is better authenticated: specimens are at South Kensington (No. C 990—1922) and in the British Museum (No. V. 84). The portraits of George III. and Queen Charlotte on a service in the Worcester Corporation Museum are also said to be his work.[1] The most celebrated of these later figure-painters was Thomas Baxter (*b.* 1782, *d.* 1821), the son of a china-decorator who had a workshop at No. 1 Goldsmith Street, Gough Square, Fleet Street.[2] Baxter is known to have worked for Flight and Barr between 1814 and 1816; he then moved to Swansea,[3] returning to Worcester in 1819, and working for both factories until his death in 1821. Baxter was very versatile, and his work may be admired for its skilful technique. Three very important signed works by him[4] at South Kensington are dated 1802, 1808 and 1809. None of these is marked, but all seem to be of Chamberlain's porcelain, and were perhaps decorated in London. The earliest, a vase and cover (No. C 257—1919), is painted in brownish monochrome with a scene from *Hamlet*, and

[1] Hobson, *Worcester Porcelain*, Plate 103.

[2] A water-colour of his father's china-decorating studio, painted by Baxter in 1810, is in the Victoria and Albert Museum (Room 140); it is reproduced in Dillon, *Porcelain*, Plate 47.

[3] See p. 207 for his work at Swansea.

[4] These are part of an important gift by Mr. Herbert Eccles, which includes a number of very good Baxters, "authenticated" by a nephew of Humphrey Chamberlain. Some work of his pupils also included is interesting for comparison.

provides a document for the identification of many pieces of his earlier figure work. The other dated specimens are plates (Nos. C 258 and 259—1919) painted with apple-blossom and with shells. His work is always distinctly stippled or in short curved brush-strokes; the earlier specimens are more strongly coloured than the elegant later pieces, generally of figures, which are in fact sometimes in grey monochrome, like the beaker illustrated in Plate 78 B. Baxter's stippled background seems to distinguish his shell-pieces from those usually attributed to John Barker. The evidence for this artist is of the slightest (amounting to a few words of Binns'),[1] and we do not know whether he worked for Flight and Barr or for Chamberlain's, or for both. The better work in this style is on Chamberlain's porcelain, and shows feathers and shells painted with minute fidelity to nature upon a white ground. A set of vases in Mr. Herbert Allen's collection (No. 349) and a plate in the Museum collection (No. C 1505—1924) show this style at its best. This we may presume to be Barker's as the better and therefore more likely to be famous. Inferior painting, marked by feeble streamers of seaweed and a background stippled rather in Baxter's manner but distinct from his, appears on Flight and Barr porcelain of rather earlier date. It is perhaps earlier work of Barker's. A pair of plates in Mr. Allen's collection (No. 335) and some little vases (Nos. 301 and 302) are examples. Birds were sometimes copied from text-books of natural history, but about 1800 one Davis imitated the earlier style of the supposed "Soqui", and exotic birds continued to be painted occasionally for a long time.[2]

[1] It has even been suggested that his existence is a myth, springing from a misspelling for Baxter.

[2] A plate (Herbert Allen, No. 326) is probably by Davis. These "exotic bird" pieces are not likely to be mistaken for the earlier work. Imitations (virtually forgeries) of this class of Worcester were made at Tournay and in Paris in the nineteenth century. The copies made by Booth of Tunstall and still sold by them of course are earthenware; the scale-blue grounds are transfer-printed.

The painting of porcelain to imitate marble was in keeping with the classical tendencies of the period. Gilt "seaweed" patterns distinct from those of Derby and of an all-over character, and grounds striped or vermiculated in gold (Plate 78 C), were favourites at Worcester; but by about 1790 the fine dull gold of the earlier time had given place to the hard and brassy mercury-gilding. Black stipple-prints associated with gilt vermiculation were a characteristic decoration of about 1810. The short period of employment of Billingsley and Walker between 1808 and 1811 had no influence on the Flight and Barr style. The first reverberating kiln used at Worcester was, however, installed by Walker during their stay.

The taste in decoration shown at CHAMBERLAIN'S was on the whole worse than at Flight and Barr's. The earliest work of the factory is probably often mistaken for Salopian china:[1] a marked plate at South Kensington (No. C 416—1920) is a rare example of Chamberlain's porcelain of a date apparently before the end of the eighteenth century. Baxter's and Barker's styles I have spoken of; those of Humphrey Chamberlain, junior, and his brother Walter[2] are perhaps worth mention. A laborious minuteness was the most famous quality of Humphrey's work: it was proudly said that the brush-strokes could not be discerned, even with a glass. His sporting subjects were probably his best. In the Allen and Schreiber Collections (Nos. 372: Plate 78 A, and 612) are a jug and a plate with copies by Humphrey Chamberlain of engravings by J. Scott after W. B. Daniell in *Rural Sports*, published in 1801–2. A plate in the British

[1] It will be remembered that at first Chamberlain only decorated white porcelain from other places, including Caughley and New Hall. A marked specimen, with decoration in the Chinese *famille verte* style of the "Bishop Sumner" service of Dr. Wall's time, has proved on analysis to be true hard-paste, obtained most probably from the New Hall factory.

[2] A panel painted with flowers in the Allen Collection (No. 358) is reputed to be his work.

Museum (No. V. 88) is inscribed on the back *Beating for a hare*. Perhaps the worst of all Messrs. Chamberlain's productions were the gaudy "Japan" vases of about 1810–20, though passable versions of the old "Worcester Japans"[1] had been made at a rather earlier date. Brilliant gilding was applied in profusion, and a salmon-coloured ground was particularly favoured.

The identification of FLIGHT and BARR and CHAMBERLAIN's Worcester china is generally made easy by the marks, but in their absence the hard-looking and slightly grey paste and glaze are sufficiently distinctive to be recognised. Notes upon its dating will be found in the Appendix dealing with the marks. The incised B is said to indicate a paste improved by Martin Barr, doubtless by the addition of bone-ash, and though by the early-nineteenth century both factories had adopted a porcelain formula approximating to that of the modern Staffordshire body, analysis of a dated piece[2] has proved that soapstone continued to be used at least occasionally as late as 1823.

The later productions of the combined factories are beyond the scope of this book. A full and nearly contemporary account of their work and that of the later Royal Worcester Porcelain Company will be found in Binns and in Jewitt,[3] as well as in Mr. R. L. Hobson's monumental *Worcester Porcelain* (1910), where all the later work of the factories is fully described.

A third Worcester factory of no great importance was founded in 1800 by Thomas GRAINGER, a nephew of Humphrey Chamberlain, with whom he had served an apprenticeship as a painter. He did not make porcelain at first, but decorated wares brought from elsewhere, usually from Caughley. About 1812 he took his brother-in-law into partnership, and their produc-

[1] Compare Allen Nos. 367 and 378.

[2] *Analysed Specimens*, pp. 17 and 38.

[3] Vol. i, pp. 240-254, where their "wondrous state of perfection" is fully described. "Neither in ancient nor in modern specimens", writes Jewitt, "have such exquisitely beautiful works been produced."

tions, marked *Grainger Lee and Co.*, resemble those of Chamberlain's factory. This and other marks of the firm are given in the Appendix. Two mugs of Grainger's porcelain at South Kensington (Nos. 3301—1901 and C 20—1915) are datable by the painting of the Worcester Regatta of 1846 upon one of them.

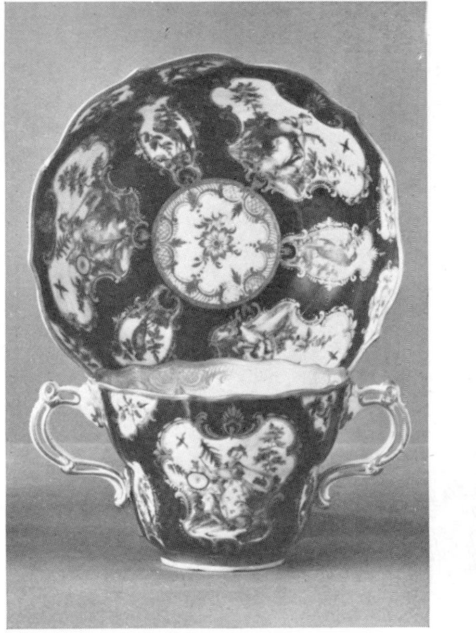

A

B

C

About 1775.

A has a scale-blue ground and a fretted-square mark; B, a dark blue ground and a W mark; C, a yellow ground.

(*Schreiber Collection.*) See p. 178.

A

B

C

About 1775–80.

B has the fretted-square mark; C, the crossed swords.

(*Schreiber and V. and A. Museum Collections.*)

See pp. 177, 178.

A

B

C

About 1775–80.

A. *Schreiber Collection.* B. *Mr. Herbert Allen's Collection.*
C. *Mr. Alfred E. Hutton's Collection.*

See p. 179.

A

B

C

CHAMBERLAIN'S PORCELAIN.

A, painted by Humphrey Chamberlain. About 1810. B, painted by Thomas Baxter. About 1820. C. Jug. About 1810.

(Mr. Herbert Allen's Collection.)

See pp. 181, 182.

CHAPTER IX

CAUGHLEY

A pottery was in existence at Caughley, near Broseley, on the Shropshire bank of the Severn, soon after 1750. In 1754 the works were leased to a Mr. Gallimore, whose daughter married Thomas Turner (*b.* 1749, *d.* 1809), who had been in the service of the Worcester china factory.[1] Turner became proprietor of the Caughley works in 1772, when new premises are said to have been built,[2] and porcelain began to be made there from this date.[3] A "Salopian china warehouse" was opened in Portugal Street, Lincoln's Inn Fields, London, about 1783 or a little earlier.[4] In 1799 the works were purchased by John Rose, a former apprentice of Turner's and proprietor of the successfully competing factory at Coalport on the opposite bank of the Severn. The Caughley factory, much diminished, continued to be used for making biscuit porcelain, which was glazed and decorated at Coalport, whence materials and plant were finally transferred in 1814. Doubtless much of the china necessarily classified as Salopian was decorated at Coalport in this final period.

The chief marks used at Caughley were the initials C and S, printed or painted in underglaze blue. The

[1] Jewitt, vol. i, p. 264. [2] Chaffers, *op. cit.*, 3rd edition, p. 559.

[3] Jewitt, vol. i, p. 267, quotes an advertisement of 1775, stating that "the porcelain manufactory erected near Bridgnorth . . . is now quite completed".

[4] Hobson, *Catalogue*, p. 103.

former sometimes resembles the crescent of Worcester (which was also freely copied in its various forms): the latter stands for "Salopian", the name by which the porcelain was generally known. The word "Salopian" was itself sometimes used impressed in full, in capitals or small letters. Imitation Chinese characters and disguised numerals somewhat resembling them are also found. An impressed star is proved as a Caughley mark by its occurrence with the blue C. The unusual mark of a lion rampant is similarly proved by its association with one or other of the recognised marks. An impressed circle centrally placed, though scarcely to be regarded as a mark and found also on other wares, is of very common occurrence on Salopian porcelain.

Salopian china is exhaustively represented at the Victoria and Albert Museum, particularly in Mr. Alfred Darby's large gift of upwards of a hundred and fifty pieces.

The earliest porcelain made at Caughley naturally resembled that of Worcester, from which it is sometimes not easily distinguished. A typical piece marked with a disguised numeral showed on analysis [1] the presence of soapstone, but in smaller quantity than in Worcester china. Salopian porcelain, particularly that painted in colours, often (but not invariably) shows a yellowish or brownish tone by transmitted light, in contrast to the greenish tone of much Worcester. This is evidently due to the absence of the "blueing" used at Worcester, and from the same cause Salopian china is usually whiter, or of creamy colour in contrast to the greyish hue of the other. Turner is said to have been an engraver under Hancock at Worcester, as well as a pottery chemist, and much of the earlier ware is printed in blue, often of a violet tone of peculiar brilliancy. A paler and quite distinctive misty tone is also noticeable in many pieces. Amongst the printed designs were the so-called "willow-pattern"

[1] *Analysed Specimens*, No. 39.

and the "Broseley Dragon", both supposed to have been invented and engraved by Thomas Minton.[1] Printing over the glaze is not so much in evidence, though it was advertised in 1775[2] that Robert Hancock was then associated with the factory, apparently as a partner or agent, as well as engraver. Jewitt published[3] impressions of some Caughley engraved plates, one of them bearing both a C and an S, and unmistakably in Hancock's style. A blue-printed jug in Mr. Darby's gift at South Kensington (No. C 78—1921) is dated 1776.

A documentary piece for the earlier painting in underglaze blue is a jug at South Kensington (No. 3147—1852), painted with a bouquet of flowers and inscribed *James Kennedy 1778*. Powdered-blue grounds with painting in blue in reserved panels was done at Caughley, as at Bow and Worcester. An unquestionable Salopian specimen (C 1301—1924) at South Kensington has the impressed mark and three simulated Chinese characters which are quite different from those of the other factories.[4] The tone of blue resembles Worcester, but is paler, and the foot-ring is roughly rectangular in section in contrast to the triangular foot-ring usual in Worcester. The later painting often resembled that on Flight's Worcester. In the later productions the slight "Salopian sprig" patterns imitating those of Chantilly[5] in strong violet blue are noteworthy. Towards the end of the century a dark underglaze blue, as well as a blue enamel, was much used in combination with the distinctive Salopian bright thin gilding (Plate 83 A),[6] again in the Worcester

[1] See p. 242 for his factory at Stoke-on-Trent.
[2] *Aris's Birmingham Gazette*, July 3, 1775.
[3] Vol. i, Plates III and IV.
[4] See Appendix, pp. 260, 264 and 269.
[5] The Chantilly mark is actually copied on a bowl at the V. & A.M. (see Appendix, p. 269). But this is painted in red and gilt as well as with blue sprigs.
[6] This gilding may, however, have been done in London at the workshop of Baxter, senr. See p. 212.

manner: striped patterns and wavy lines, and spirally fluted forms in the Flight and Barr style, were popular. A favourite gilt border consisted of interlacing ovals, or beading in classical style. Some finely pencilled slight floral patterns in black or brown, in combination with gilding, are peculiar to the factory. A jug in the Schreiber Collection (No. 682) with an inscription referring to the *Brimstree Loyal Legion* may reasonably be dated between 1794, when the Volunteer movement began, and 1802, when the Royal Arms (which are printed on the jug) were altered after the Peace of Amiens. The original copper-plate in Mr. Clifton Roberts' collection from which the inscription was printed bears also the words *Wenlock Loyal Volunteers* and is initialled *T T*, for Thomas Turner. An important instance of a Worcester pattern exactly copied is the "Royal lily" chosen by Queen Charlotte in 1788.[1] The Salopian versions are distinguishable by the tone of blue. To the same period belong some unusual European landscapes in underglaze blue, such as No. C 136—1921 in Mr. Alfred Darby's gift at South Kensington.

Painting in colours was sometimes very ambitious. The Worcester dry blue enamel was imitated, not very successfully, and exotic birds appear on some moulded cabbage-leaf jugs with mask-lip, but their colouring is inclined to be hot and the execution laborious and sticky-looking. The fruits and flowers are sometimes better, and distinct from the Worcester examples that inspired them. The mannerism of crowding the flowers into a tight mass is a noteworthy feature of Caughley painting (Plate 83 B). Simpler decoration of flowers or Chinese figures in colour recalls similar work at Lowestoft, though it is unlikely that either was conscious of the other; in both cases the painting was perhaps an unskilful imitation of Worcester. A sharp pink is distinctive in this Salopian painting, and

[1] See p. 167, footnote.

a hard shading of the petals in stiff lines [1] again recalls Lowestoft, from which the Caughley china may always be distinguished by its Worcesterish soapstone paste. Red-and-blue decoration in Lowestoft style was also done.

It is often asserted that the Worcester factory sent its wares by river to Caughley to be printed in blue.[2] There is no proof of the existence of such friendly relations as this would imply. On the contrary, the secession of Turner from Worcester is more likely to have been a cause of hostility. But some Salopian porcelain was, as I have said, decorated outside the factory by both Chamberlain and Grainger at Worcester, and this connection and the use of Hancock's plates are probably the circumstances that have given currency to the assertion.

[1] A teapot (No. 386) in Mr. Allen's collection shows this peculiarity in handling very clearly.

[2] Jewitt, 2nd edition, 1883 (vol. i, p. 162), states that "it is well known" that this took place, but gives no evidence in support of the statement.

CHAPTER X

LIVERPOOL

AMONGST THE POTTERIES WHICH WERE ACTIVE AT LIVERPOOL in the eighteenth century several appear from advertisements to have made porcelain as well as earthenware, and further evidence as to this has been given by the wasters and other material found by Mr. Peter Entwistle in 1921 in excavations on pottery sites in the city. There are also many traditions embodied in attributions at the Liverpool Museum and in collections in the neighbourhood, but in the absence of published details concerning the finds and of marks on the porcelain itself it is impossible in some cases at present to assign to particular factories the several classes reasonably regarded as of Liverpool origin. The following account will, I hope, provide a preliminary classification of a body of material which has hitherto stood in great confusion.

An advertisement of 1756 [1] proves Richard Chaffers to have been making porcelain at that date, at a pottery at Shaw's Brow. Samuel Gilbody,[2] W. Reid,[3] Seth, James and John Pennington [4] and Zachariah Barnes [5]

[1] Jewitt, vol. ii, p. 37.

[2] A print on a mug believed to be Liverpool has the inscription *Gilbody Maker* (see below, p. 193); and an announcement in Williamson's *Liverpool Advertiser* of July 3, 1761, also speaks of "china ware" belonging to the assignees of Samuel Gilbody. Thanks are due to Mr. Francis Buckley for this reference.

[3] Jewitt, vol. ii, p. 38, gives an advertisement dated 1756.

[4] Jewitt, vol. ii, p. 38.

[5] Jewitt, vol. ii, p. 24. Barnes was chiefly a tile-maker.

also appear from advertisements to have made porcelain at Liverpool in the second half of the eighteenth century.

RICHARD CHAFFERS (*b.* 1731, *d.* 1765) was in 1756 the owner of a soapstone mine in Cornwall, and the use of this ingredient in porcelain may well have been suggested to him by a workman named Podmore,[1] previously employed by Wedgwood and probably the Robert Podmore to whom special payments were made for his services as "arcanist" to the Worcester factory in 1751.[2] This Liverpool factory may thus almost be regarded as an offshoot of Worcester. The only documentary piece of Chaffers' porcelain is a mug in the Liverpool Museum, acquired from one of his descendants.[3] It is painted by the same hand as others in the Victoria and Albert Museum (such as C 938—1924), and another in Mr. Wallace Elliot's collection (Plate 80 A and C). Others of similar material and decoration, such as C 1040—1924 at South Kensington (Plate 80 B), may be confidently assigned to this factory, at which Chaffers was succeeded by Philip Christian. The free and charming brushwork seen in the decoration of this little group suggests the hand of a "delft" painter,[4] disciplined by the use of the brush on the absorbent surface of unfired tin-enamel. The clean and hard-looking but rather grey porcelain itself is not dissimilar to the soapstone porcelain of Worcester. It is noteworthy that Chaffers in his advertisement declared that every piece "had been tested with hot water", and this also points to the use of soapstone.[5] A pounce pot (or pepper-pot) of earthenware, not porcelain, in the same museum, is inscribed *Richard Chaffers*, and strangely dated 1769, four years after

[1] Jewitt, vol. ii, p. 35. [2] See p. 151.

[3] It is erroneously stated in Mrs. Willoughby Hodgson, *Old English China*, Plate 3, to be signed by Richard Chaffers.

[4] Liverpool had a flourishing "delft" industry.

[5] Chaffers' soapstone mine was eventually sold to the Worcester firm in 1776 (Binns, 2nd edition, p.313), and it is likely that at about this time, or a little before, the prevalent bone-ash paste began to be used at Liverpool.

the death of Chaffers the potter of that name. These mugs are of a distinctive form, a barrel-shape with a grooved foot, formerly believed to be peculiar to Liverpool, but, as I have shown,[1] probably used also at Longton Hall.

Mugs of this shape with black transfer-prints, though evidently made at Longton, have for long been ascribed wholly to Liverpool on account of the signature, *Sadler, Liverpool*, the name of a very active if commercially minded pottery-decorator with a "Printed Ware Manufactory" in Harrington Street. In a document[2] signed by Thomas Shaw and Samuel Gilbody and dated 1756, it was declared that as many as twelve hundred tiles had been printed in six hours by a process which John Sadler (*d.* 1789) and Guy Green were said to have invented. They seem to have contemplated patenting their process, but did not do so, perhaps because they had not invented it and it was in use elsewhere. The document speaks of trials made "in the past seven years", and, on the strength of this, priority has been claimed for Liverpool transfer-printing,[3] but no actual pieces can be ascribed to a date before about 1756, when the "King of Prussia" prints were probably made.[4] The statement in Moss's *Liverpool Guide* of 1790[5] that "copper-plate printing . . . originated here in 1752 and remained some time a secret with the inventors Messrs. Sadler and Green" is similarly discounted by the absence of pieces to which so early a date could be assigned. The Sadler prints were taken

[1] P. 125. [2] Published by Jewitt, vol. ii, p. 29.

[3] J. E. Hodgkin in *The Burlington Magazine*, vol. vi (1904–5), pp. 232 and 315. The advertisement of 1757 in the *Liverpool Advertiser* of a pamphlet on printing, referred to on p. 23, does not mention Liverpool among the places at which the method was practised, and we may infer that it had not then been long in use in the city or it would have been better known there.

[4] The enamel "dated" 1756 mentioned by Jewitt (vol. ii, p. 27) is apparently one exhibited at Liverpool in 1907 (Catalogue No. 115), which is merely signed *J. Sadler Liverp^{l}. Enam^{l}* and inscribed "Done from an Original painted at Berlin in 1756".

[5] Quoted in Jewitt, vol. ii, p. 27.

Painted in colours. About 1770. (*V. and A. Museum.*)
See p. 195.

A

B

C

About 1760. (*Mr. Wallace Elliot's and the V. and A. Museum Collections.*) See p. 191.

A

B

C

About 1760–70. A (dated 1773) and B are painted in blue; C in colours.
(Mr. Wallace Elliot's, Mr. Herbert Allen's and the Schreiber Collections.)

See pp. 194, 195.

A

B

Transfer-printed wares. About 1755–65.

(*Mr. Herbert Allen's and Schreiber Collections.*) See p. 193.

from the usual sources, and are, it must be confessed, often very poor indeed, compared with the best Worcester work. A distinctive quality of line may be recognised in such prints as the version of *La Cascade* on the saucer figured in Plate 82 (Schreiber Collection No. 787). Such pieces as these are probably of Liverpool manufacture, and the coarse, often blurred line indicates a special quality in this Liverpool glaze. *Frederick the Great*, *The Tea-Party*, *L'Amour* and other Worcester subjects are often repeated. A print inscribed "Frederick III. King of Prussia" (based on a portrait of Frederick the Great) on a cylindrical mug in the Liverpool Museum is signed *Gilbody*, *Maker* and *Evans Sct.* Another print, of William Pitt, is signed *T. Billinge*. A print used only by Sadler was the "arms" of the Society of Bucks (Plate 82), a body which was at first a convivial order, but from 1756 a charitable organisation.

Printing in underglaze blue was also practised at Liverpool, and a document for this is a jug in the British Museum (No. X. 12) inscribed *Frederick Heinzelman Liverpool*, with a date which has sometimes been read as 1799, but is more probably 1779. The rough printing in blue, chiefly of scroll-work and flowers, includes two birds of the kind called "livers", holding sprigs of liverwort in their beaks (they are taken from the arms of the city of Liverpool). There is also a border of hexagonal cell-diaper rendered in a peculiar way that helps to identify some other Liverpool china. Much of this ware roughly and thickly printed in heavy dark blue is traditionally ascribed to ZACHARIAH BARNES, but no evidence has yet been published in support of this. It dates for the greater part from the last quarter of the eighteenth century (Barnes was born in 1743), and the attribution is not improbably a true one.

A jug in the Liverpool Museum, painted in blue with classical figures allegorical of Agriculture, is recorded to have been acquired from a descendant of the PENNINGTONS. An admired blue is said to have been made by Seth Pennington, and the colour on this jug is of an unusual tone, rather bright, with a peculiar "sticky" appearance.[1] Punch-bowls painted with ships, such as were popular in Pennington's "delft" ware (there are examples at the Liverpool Museum), are said to have been made also in porcelain by the same family, and Mr. Wallace Elliot has a porcelain bowl with this decoration, depicting the ship *Swallow*,[2] evidently a Liverpool production and presumably Pennington's. The "sticky blue" may be seen in many examples at South Kensington. Perhaps the best example known to me is a fine cylindrical mug in the Schreiber Collection (No. 781: Plate 81) painted with a subject from *The Ladies' Amusement*. The free style of painting suggests the hand of a delft painter. It is interesting to recall that the mug was formerly considered to be an early Bristol piece[3] decorated by John Bowen, who also painted delft. A Liverpool origin is, however, suggested by the tone of blue, and especially by the form of the base, which shows the flat bottom common in Liverpool porcelain. Many other "sticky blue" pieces show the free style of the delft painters. A Worcester tradition such as I have proved for Chaffers' porcelain seems to inspire the numerous specimens with elaborate decoration evidently moulded from silver. The "Agriculture jug" at Liverpool is of this character, and the numerous and often very ugly sauce-boats, of a type usually ascribed by collectors to Worcester, illustrate the tendency very well. A large jug of this type in Mr. Wallace Elliot's collection with

[1] For this observation I am indebted to Mr. Bernard Rackham, who has also given me much other information about Liverpool porcelain. The distinctive character of the blue in this Liverpool painting, like the different shades found elsewhere, is probably to be explained by the local source of supply of the cobalt oxide ("zaffers", "sapher", "smales", "smalts") from which the colour was prepared. The Heinzelman jug mentioned above also shows a colour approaching the "sticky blue".

[2] Figured in *The Connoisseur*, vol. lxxix (Oct. 1927).

[3] It was also called Bow by Lady Charlotte Schreiber.

the additional interest of a date (1773) is figured in Plate 81.

CERTAIN OTHER CLASSES OF PORCELAIN PROVISIONALLY ascribed to Liverpool on various grounds may be here detailed:

Some pieces with blue borders crudely "marbled" in gold are represented by a set of five vases in the Clough Collection in Lancashire, and by two important large jugs in the Schreiber Collection (No. 783). The flower-painting on these is characteristic, and often seen on pieces attributed to Liverpool on other grounds. A bottle at South Kensington (Plate 79) shows these flowers and the marbling very well. The rather laborious style of figure-painting on some pieces of this class is seen again on a bowl (also with gilt-marbled blue border) which was formerly believed to be the work of Dr. Wall of Worcester.[1] The hunting-scene on one of the Schreiber jugs is identical with that in a probably Liverpool print on cream-coloured ware, and it is noteworthy that these two jugs were called Liverpool by Lady Charlotte Schreiber at a time when such an attribution would not have suggested itself without some further information as to the provenance of the pieces, evidence now unfortunately lost. The same gilt-marbled blue also occurs on a teapot at South Kensington (No. C 1181—1924), moulded with leaves at the foot and with a pattern of palm-tree columns forming compartments in which are painted flowers and exotic birds in Worcester style. There are other specimens of the family in Mr. Herbert Allen's collection (Nos. 497 and 498: Plate 81). Fragments moulded with the same pattern were found at Liverpool and help to confirm the attribution of this little class, which is often erroneously called Longton Hall[2] on the showing of the rather Staffordshire-like moulded patterns.

[1] See Hobson, *Worcester Porcelain*, Plate 5.

[2] As in an article in *The Connoisseur*, vol. xxxvi (1913), p. 2, where a similar specimen in the Stoke-on-Trent Museum is illustrated. Liverpool porcelain is frequently classified wrongly as Longton Hall and as Worcester.

Tin-glazed porcelain was evidently made at Liverpool, and fragments found at Liverpool have been proved to contain this ingredient. A mug at South Kensington (No. C 1434—1924) painted in blue and manganese (again in "delft" style) corresponds exactly with one of these fragments and has just such a glaze; its form—a tall and only slightly waisted "bell-shape" —is also found in Liverpool delft. Painting by the same hand appears in the "sticky blue" (compare a jug at South Kensington, No. C 643—1924) and we may perhaps regard this class also as Pennington porcelain.

A group of pieces, all crudely painted by the same hand with Chinese figures copied probably from a Worcester model, is represented at Liverpool by a tea-caddy with a printed border of the same pattern as that on the "Heinzelman" jug in the British Museum, already alluded to. A number of pieces by the same painter are at South Kensington; of these a bowl (C 1298—1924) and a jug (C 1299—1924) are marked with a monogram of H P in underglaze blue which can scarcely stand for either Seth or John Pennington. The bright red on these is distinctive. Painting in underglaze blue by the same hand is also seen, distinguished by the curiously lax cluster of circles that represents a tree in his Chinese landscape.

Fragments found on the pottery site seem to prove the origin of two other patterns which occur on porcelain otherwise resembling that thought to be Liverpool: a pattern including a stiff spray of red star-shaped flowers (compare the teapot at South Kensington No. C 1174—1924); and a heavily printed design in blue painted over in red with touches of yellow (compare another teapot at South Kensington No. C 1182—1924), probably from the same factory as the blue-printed pieces tentatively ascribed above to Zachariah Barnes.

A small class with Chinese figures printed in outline

and filled with colours resembles some Worcester porcelain,[1] but the borders of blue *lambrequins* often suggest a Liverpool origin for this disputed group of pieces.

THE PORCELAIN THUS ASCRIBED TO LIVERPOOL IS OF widely varying quality, with a general tendency to a rather heavy coarse paste having only slight translucency, and a blued glaze much disfigured by bubbles which are especially noticeable under the base, where the glaze commonly shows a bluish tone in the pools near the foot-ring. Among the characteristics of form are foot-rings undercut rather than bluntly triangular in section as at Lowestoft, the mug-shape with flat base and the tall bell-shape already mentioned. On the ground of paste and glaze and form of foot-ring we may assign to Liverpool a class with blue decoration of much merit by a painter with a very decided manner and a fondness for clusters of dots.[2] A group of these pieces is at South Kensington (a jug, No. C 822—1924, etc.). Similarly, a bowl in the same museum (No. C 1155—1924) with cut fruit in panels in a gilt-diapered blue ground of a type long regarded as Worcester,[3] must be regarded as a Liverpool imitation, on the showing of paste and glaze and form of foot-ring.

THE HERCULANEUM POTTERY[4] at Liverpool, established in 1796 on the right bank of the Mersey, made porcelain from 1801 until its closing in 1841. The productions are usually indistinguishable in style from contemporary Staffordshire wares and of little interest to the collector. They are generally marked with the name of the pottery and a "liver-bird". There are examples at South Kensington (with the "Miscellaneous porcelain" and in Mr. Herbert Allen's collection, No. 496).

[1] See p. 163.
[2] The hand is also recognisable on Liverpool delft.
[3] See Hobson, *Worcester Porcelain*, Plate LXIX.
[4] So named in emulation of the Etruria of Josiah Wedgwood.

CHAPTER XI

PINXTON

A short-lived porcelain factory was set up in 1796 at Pinxton in Derbyshire, about six miles from Mansfield, by John Coke (1775–1841), afterwards of Debdale Hall, with the help and probably at the instance of William Billingsley of Derby, who had invented a soft porcelain of high translucency. Billingsley left Pinxton not later than 1801, taking his recipes with him.[1]

[1] Billingsley went first to Mansfield, where he is supposed to have decorated porcelain brought in the white from Staffordshire. A covered cup with undistinguished decoration of gilt diaper, and a large jug with monochrome views of Nottingham Castle and Sherwood Forest, in the Cardiff Museum, are signed *Billingsley Mansfield*. He is said to have manufactured china a little later at Torksey in Lincolnshire, but no specimen of this has been certainly identified. A cup and saucer of heavy paste and crude decoration, in the Museum collection at South Kensington (No. C 437& A—1920), are traditionally said to have been made there by him or under his direction, though they bear little resemblance to his known work at Derby, Pinxton or elsewhere. A pottery was in existence at Torksey, or rather at the neighbouring hamlet of Brampton, but Billingsley may have had difficulty in securing the materials required by his recipe. The crude shape of the pieces would be accounted for by assuming them to have been thrown or moulded by a village potter unused to making table-ware. One would conjecture the painting to be an early work by one of his daughters, who are known to have helped in decorating his porcelain later on. Billingsley is also said to have attempted the manufacture of porcelain at Wirksworth in Derbyshire, but this too has never been established or the productions identified. In 1808 he took his recipes to Worcester. In conjunction with Samuel Walker, who had married his daughter Sarah, he is said to have installed at Worcester a reverberating enamel kiln in place of the box kilns until then in use. He left for Nantgarw three years later. Messrs. Flight, Barr and Barr had paid him a sum of money for the right to use his recipe, and a letter from them dated November 12, 1814, protesting against Billingsley's partnership with Dillwyn of Swansea, is reprinted in *Analysed Specimens*, p. 51. Billingsley had changed his name to Beeley, apparently

Coke sold the works to John Cutts in 1804; in 1808 the staff was reduced, but a coarse and opaque china of Staffordshire type continued to be made until the closing of the factory about 1813.

No mark was regularly used on Pinxton porcelain. The name of the factory, in script characters in gold, occurs on a mug in the British Museum (XII. 1).[1] A script P in red or black with a pattern number is sometimes seen. A crescent alone or with a sun with rays resembling a star (from the arms of Coke), and a bow and arrow, in purple or red, occur on unquestionable specimens of Pinxton china in the small collection at the Victoria and Albert Museum. Various impressed capital letters were found on unglazed fragments discovered on the site of the works, and a specimen marked with an impressed B, companion to a cup with a script P in red, was analysed by Mr. Herbert Eccles, and proved to contain much bone-ash as well as a high percentage of lead oxide due to the use of flint-glass in the frit.[2] A script B and 26 occur on a yellow-ground cream-jug in Mr. Wallace Elliot's collection, painted with Pinxton Church, so named; as the only other *script* letter found is P (for Pinxton), it is tempting to regard this as the initial of Billingsley.

Billingsley's very translucent and often beautifully white porcelain was here, as at Nantgarw later on, very liable to collapse in the kiln, and Pinxton pieces are often out of shape. A slightly wavy surface is often to be observed and this will sometimes help the collector to recognise Billingsley's Pinxton china: the paste is usually slightly greenish by transmitted light. The shapes were the simpler of the pseudo-classical forms popular at the time. Egg-cups and vases of similar

after leaving Torksey, though in the letter from Messrs. Flight and Barr he is still referred to by his full name. For details of his career at Nantgarw and later, see p. 202.

[1] The name, written in full, was, however, declared by Haslem (*Old Derby China Factory*, p. 227) to be a forgery.

[2] See *Analysed Specimens*, No. 19.

form are for some reason often met with. The styles of painting naturally resembled those current at Derby, whence most of the workmen came. Amongst the latter were W. Coffee, the Derby modeller, and several landscape painters, including James Hadfield and Edward Rowland. A Richard Robins from London was probably the subsequent partner of T. M. Randall at Spa Fields.[1] Cutts, afterwards the proprietor, was a landscape painter who subsequently painted Wedgwood's porcelain.[2] He is said to have been famous for his rapid execution, and carelessly drawn views of local scenery, often in Boreman's Derby style, are very common on Pinxton porcelain. A pale red and a yellowish green are distinctive features of the colouring. Coloured grounds—yellow, green and pinkish fawn, never very good technically—were much affected, again in the Derby fashion. Gilding was used very sparingly as a rule. The popular sprig patterns, particularly the so-called "Tournay sprig" in underglaze blue [3] and the "Paris cornflower" in blue, green and pink,[4] edged with a blue or brown line, are characteristic, and such specimens may safely be ascribed to Pinxton. Genuine pieces more elaborately decorated are naturally very rare. Billingsley's own flower-painting is not often recognisable. The painting on two goblet-shaped vases in the Schreiber Collection (No. 796) is probably his, and a rich floral border on a big ice-pail with a yellow ground at South Kensington (No. 308—1869) is traditionally said to be his work. Though this painting is noticeably different from Billingsley's work at Derby, the piece has a good pedigree and the tradition cannot be disregarded. Acquired in 1869, it was stated to have been given

[1] For fuller particulars of the workmen, see Jewitt, vol. ii, p. 140, and Haslem, pp. 239-246.
[2] See p. 248.
[3] V. & A.M. No. 1627—1871 (a large cup and saucer).
[4] V. & A.M. No. 3081—1901 (a plate); a characteristic goblet (No. 3085—1901) also has this decoration.

A

B

About 1790.

(*V. and A. Museum and Schreiber Collections.*) See pp. 187, 188.

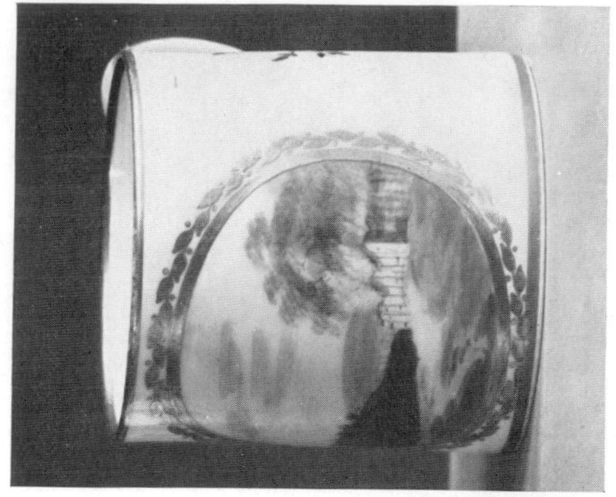

C

B

A

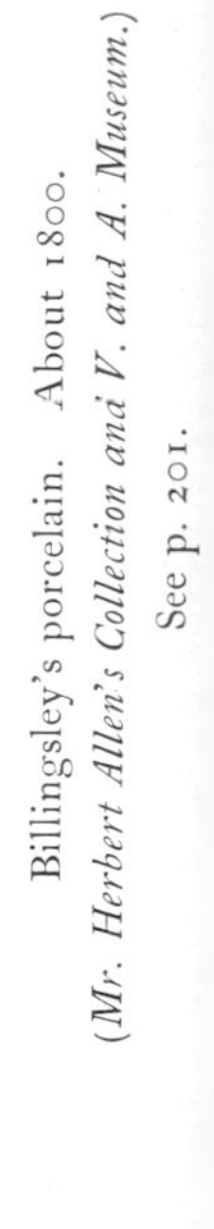

Billingsley's porcelain. About 1800.
(Mr. Herbert Allen's Collection and V. and A. Museum.)

See p. 201.

by John Coke to his father, the Rev. D'Ewes Coke of Brookhill Hall, where it remained for many years. An uneven yellow ground with scroll-work in brownish black similar to that on the ice-pail occurs on some cups and saucers at South Kensington formerly in the Jermyn Street Museum, where they were "authenticated" as Pinxton by John Haslem. Plate 84 B shows one of these with a characteristic little landscape in early Pinxton style. A beaker in Mr. Herbert Allen's collection, figured in the same plate, shows another style, and a cup and saucer in Mr. Wallace Elliot's collection [1] with a tiny landscape with sheep has the date 1796: a peculiar bright green is noticeable in the work of this hand, and a fragment found on the factory site, painted with deer, shows the same colour.

The later Pinxton porcelain may be well studied in Mr. Herbert Allen's collection. Some vases and a tea-service (Nos. 197 to 199 and 202) are typical of this, and may be compared with the beaker of the earlier, more translucent paste of Billingsley's making.[2]

[1] Figured in *The Connoisseur*, vol. lxxix (Sept. 1927).

[2] China money-tokens similar to those made at Worcester are said to have been made and issued by John Coke, and a specimen dated 1801 is described by Haslem, p. 243, and illustrated by Jewitt, vol. ii, p. 141.

CHAPTER XII

NANTGARW AND SWANSEA

A porcelain factory at Nantgarw, between Cardiff and Merthyr Tydfil in the valley of the Taff, was started in 1811 by William Billingsley of Derby and Pinxton, and his son-in-law Samuel Walker.[1] The famous porcelain made from Billingsley's recipe was a glassy soft-paste containing a considerable proportion of bone-ash.[2] It was highly translucent and of beautiful whiteness, but very liable to melt out of shape in the kiln, and therefore costly to produce. Financial difficulties led Billingsley to appeal for Government help, claiming that his porcelain was equal to the best soft-paste of Sèvres, and Lewis Weston Dillwyn, a Swansea potter, was asked by the Board of Trade to report upon the matter. Impressed by the fine quality of Billingsley's china, Dillwyn arranged for the manufacture to be transferred to his Cambrian Pottery at Swansea, in 1814.[3] Porcelain made from Billingsley's recipe, both at Nantgarw and Swansea, was as a rule marked with the name of the former and the initials C.W. (for China Works)[4] impressed in the paste, or more rarely,

[1] For the earlier history of Billingsley, see pp. 109 and 198.

[2] See *Analysed Specimens*, No. 21.

[3] Porcelain had not previously been made at Swansea. The "opaque china" made rather before this at the rival "Glamorgan Pottery" in the town was a fine earthenware.

[4] Formerly read as G. W. for "George" Walker. The potter's name, however, was Samuel. The suggestion that *C W* stands for *Cambrian Works* cannot be accepted, as the mark was used *before* the transfer to Swansea.

in red script characters. It is thus impossible to decide at which of the two places a particular piece was made, unless it is painted by a hand known to have been employed only at one or other of them.

Dillwyn found Billingsley's receipt too costly and unpractical, and by the introduction of a larger proportion of china-clay endeavoured to make a porcelain body which would be more stable in the kiln.[1] A porcelain in which ground flint was also substituted for the Lynn sand was first produced; this is known to collectors as the "duck's egg" body from its greenish translucency; it was usually marked with the word *Swansea*, impressed or painted in capitals or in script letters, in red or occasionally in gold.[2] About 1817 a new glassy body containing soapstone was introduced. This was markedly inferior to "Nantgarw" and "duck's egg"; it has a hard-looking, minutely pitted surface somewhat resembling pig-skin, with a smoky yellow translucency. Porcelain of this composition was usually marked with a trident, impressed. A rare variety of the same body, without the soapstone, is very glassy, with a dull white surface, and has a colourless translucency which Mr. Eccles has likened to "sodden snow". Of the porcelain with these bodies, collectors will value most highly the "Nantgarw", but the "duck's egg" also is a beautiful material.

By 1817 at the latest Billingsley and Walker had returned to Nantgarw.[3] Of the former's two daughters (who are said to have helped in the painting of his porcelain) the elder, Sarah, had died at Swansea in 1817; the younger, Lavinia, died shortly after his return to Nantgarw. In 1819 Billingsley took his recipes to

[1] See *Analysed Specimens* (pp. 47-50), in which extracts from Dillwyn's note-books are reprinted, showing his experiments towards a more workable formula.

[2] I have seen *Swansea* written in gold on hard-paste china; but the W had an unmistakably German form!

[3] Messrs. Flight and Barr of Worcester had previously (in 1814) protested against the use of Billingsley's recipe at Swansea. They did not, apparently, object to his manufacture of porcelain on his own account.

Coalport[1] at the invitation of John Rose, who had previously bought up the works at Caughley.[2] It is probable that Rose was aware of the high repute of the Welsh china and wished to limit its production to his own manufacture. Moreover, the London dealers had previously taken Coalport china in the white, to be decorated to their order, but were now preferring the Nantgarw and Swansea, thus injuring Rose's business.

After Billingsley's departure porcelain is said to have been made at Nantgarw until 1822 by William Weston Young (1776–1847), who had previously worked as a flower-painter at Swansea, with the assistance of another painter from Bristol, Thomas Pardoe, whose work will be described presently. Young's porcelain is not easily identified, but from entries in his diary[3] it seems to have been of the Swansea "trident" type.

In 1817 Dillwyn leased his Swansea pottery to Bevington and Company, whose names from this time occasionally appear as a mark on Swansea porcelain, which finally ceased to be made about 1823 or 1824. After Dillwyn's retirement an action (Roby[4] *v.* Dillwyn, 1821) was brought against him, it being alleged that the recipes for the finer porcelain had been withheld, whilst the quality of the stock transferred with the factory was of inferior quality—apparently for the greater part of the inferior "trident" body. A plate at South Kensington, painted by Baxter (No. 3491—1901) and given to the Jermyn Street Collection by Mrs. Dillwyn, is said to have been produced at the trial of the case.

Simple forms inclining to the classical style were the rule at both factories, and shapes for table-

[1] See p. 213 for certain pieces apparently made from the Nantgarw formula at Coalport. It has been suggested that the impressed *Nantgarw* mark was used at Coalport as well as at Swansea.

[2] See p. 185.

[3] See *Analysed Specimens*, pp. 20, 21.

[4] Roby, with John Bevington and George Haynes, had purchased Dillwyn's shares in the Cambrian Works.

ware were largely imitated from the Paris hard-paste which was very fashionable at the time. Plates moulded on the rims with flowers in low relief were popular. Flowers modelled in white biscuit and applied to decorative vases (there are two specimens in Mr. Herbert Allen's collection, Nos. 425 and 426) are often said to be the work of Goodsby, a modeller who came to Swansea from Derby, where such work was done. But there is no certainty about this. The initials *I.W.* which occur on a Swansea biscuit figure of a ram marked *Bevington*, at South Kensington (No. 3509—1901), are those of a modeller named Isaac Wood.

MOST OF THE PAINTING WAS OF FLOWERS IN THE naturalistic style of the time, in many cases obviously done in imitation of Billingsley's manner. The peculiar dark green enamel imitated from some Paris porcelain is almost peculiar to Swansea. Gilding of excellent quality, but rather liable to tarnishing, was done at both factories.

Of the painters' work which has been identified, that of Billingsley himself is not often seen on Nantgarw and Swansea china, though the roses on the sides of a sugar-bowl in Mr. Herbert Allen's collection (No. 430) are decidedly in his manner. Two plates exhibited at Swansea in 1914[1] are, however, almost certainly by his hand. It should be mentioned that much of the discussion of the painters' mannerisms by the late Robert Drane in Turner's book on the factories is based upon an initial confusion between the work of Billingsley and Pardoe.

For the greater part of the duration of the two

[1] Reproduced in the *Catalogue of a Loan Exhibition* held in 1914 at the Glynn Vivian Art Gallery, Swansea, pp. 10 and 11, and in Turner, Plate XXX. Much of the clean white china painted with rather large and blurred pink roses commonly attributed to him is not only not his work, but is not even Swansea china, but Coalport or Staffordshire porcelain of 1820–30. The romance associated with Billingsley and his porcelain has led to the attribution to Swansea of very much porcelain made elsewhere.

factories, Thomas Pardoe (*b.* 1770, *d.* 1823)[1] was living at or near Bristol, decorating porcelain and earthenware sent to him "in the white" from various places—from Worcester and probably Coalport as well as from the Welsh factories. His painting may be studied in a very important signed plate at South Kensington (No. 3142—1901) of unmarked china very like that of Worcester of the Flight and Barr period, and exhibited with the Miscellaneous Porcelain. Pardoe's rather "wet" style may also be seen on a Swansea sugar-bowl in a neighbouring case (No. C 286—1914). The well-known studies of plants copied from the *Botanical Magazine*,[2] with names written on the backs of the pieces, which were formerly believed to be the work of William Weston Young, are now recognised as early work of Thomas Pardoe. Young illustrated a work on natural history written by Dillwyn, and this circumstance has led to the attribution to him of all the plant-pieces, birds and butterflies painted on pottery with the names written on the backs of the pieces. But several styles are distinguishable on these. The handwriting of the names is a clue to the authorship of the painting, and Pardoe's trick of writing each letter separately helps us to recognise as his the hand commonly seen on services painted with "botanical" flowers. Young's more laborious style is, I think, never seen on porcelain, but is not uncommon on pottery.[3]

The style we call Lavinia Billingsley's is a rather artless one but has the pleasant quality of simplicity. Two plates at South Kensington, decorated with elephants (No. C 1026—1924) and with birds and butterflies (No. 3524—1901), are traditionally said to be and are very probably her work. The same hand may be recog-

[1] For details of his life, see W. J. Pountney, *op. cit.*, pp. 115, 116, and Turner, *op. cit.*, p. 179.

[2] Dillwyn was a devoted botanist and friend of Sir Joseph Banks, and favoured this kind of decoration.

[3] The butterflies are often his: the handwriting of the names provides a clue, as in the case of Pardoe.

nised on a cup and saucer in the same case with queer foliage and flowers (No. 3499—1901); and in Mr. Herbert Allen's collection in the Chinese figures on a pair of vases (No. 423) and in the birds and flowers on a large fruit-dish (No. 421).

Thomas Baxter (*b.* 1782, *d.* 1821) was a highly skilled and versatile painter who came to Swansea from Worcester in 1816,[1] and returned thither in 1819; at Swansea he excelled in "botanical studies" of plants, as well as in landscapes and figure-subjects in Sèvres style.[2] His work at Swansea may be studied at South Kensington on the well-authenticated plate (No. 3491—1901). His flower- and plant-pieces generally have a landscape or painted-over background of a quite peculiar kind.

Matthew Colclough, a bird-painter, (to judge by the examples traditionally ascribed to him) worked in a simple but naturalistic style, which should be distinguished from the more elaborate painting of birds done on Swansea china in London. Plates in the Schreiber (No. 801) and Victoria and Albert Museum Collections (No. 3490—1901) are in the style said to be his, whilst the birds on one (No. 419) in Mr. Herbert Allen's collection, formerly in the J. G. Mortlock Collection, were probably done in London for the dealer of that name. But the attribution of Turner's example (Plate XV. in his book) may be questioned. His authority is even more grotesquely untrustworthy than most of its kind. It seems that the specimen was "identified by Mr. Blank who knows the mannerism of this artist, who was a personal friend of his grandfather"! It has been suggested by Mr. E. M. Nance (whose forthcoming work on Nantgarw and Swansea should help to clear up many obscurities) that the supposed Colclough is the work of Baxter. The touch is similar, but not conclusively so, and it is difficult to explain why Baxter for

[1] For his Worcester work, see p. 180.

[2] But the vase figured in the *Swansea Exhibition Catalogue* (p. 6) apparently a forgery.

all his versatility should have been engaged on bird-painting at Swansea, though never practising it at Worcester, early or late. In favour of an attribution to Baxter, perhaps, is the simple gilt border which is the same on the authenticated Baxter plate and on those with the birds supposed to be by Colclough.

A well-authenticated specimen of the work of William Pollard is a mug at South Kensington (No. C 115—1915), acquired from one of his descendants. Turner states that Pollard died in 1854, aged fifty-one, and if these particulars are correct it is impossible that the very considerable quantity of porcelain painted by the same hand as this mug could ever have been executed by him before the closing of the factory. Doubts have, however, been expressed as to the correct reading of Pollard's age on the tombstone from which Turner's information was obtained. His flowers are as a rule loosely bunched; his mannerism of filling the spaces between the flowers with an indefinite purple-black may be observed on a large service and on other pieces in the collection at South Kensington. The Swansea plate figured in Plate 86 B is in his style. A very distinct and mannered style seen on both Nantgarw and Swansea-marked pieces is that of a painter generally known as "the Frenchman", whose hand has also been recognised on Paris porcelain made by Nast. A stiff spiky spray and an auricula or similar flower with the dark edge indicated by a hard broken ring, are peculiarities of his style. He is believed to have been the "de Junic" recorded as employed only at Swansea. If this highly conjectural identification is correct, pieces marked *Nantgarw* and painted by him provide a proof that this mark was used at the Swansea works.

The painting on a pot-pourri vase in Mr. Allen's collection (No. 428: Plate 86 A) closely resembles that on a plate signed by Henry Morris (*b.* 1797); [1] and a

[1] Turner, *op. cit.*, Plate IV.

A

B

About 1815.

A. *Mr. Herbert Allen's Collection.* B. *V. and A. Museum.*

See pp. 209, 210.

A

B

About 1815.
A, probably painted by Henry Morris; B, probably painted by William Pollard; mark, SWANSEA in red.
(*Mr. Herbert Allen's Collection.*) See p. 208.

cup and saucer in the Museum collection at South Kensington (No. C 378—1918) painted with a sea-shore scene with sailors, is perhaps an example of the work of George Beddow. A cup[1] traditionally said to be his work is by the same hand and shows his mannerism of shading in parallel, usually vertical lines.

MUCH PLAIN WHITE OR SLIGHTLY DECORATED NANT-garw and Swansea china was sent to London to be decorated by independent enamellers or to the order of the dealers John Mortlock, Pellatt and Green, and others[2] whose names were sometimes added to the marks. Of the numerous pieces of this class some are believed to have been decorated by Moses Webster, a painter from Derby employed by Robins and Randall of Spa Fields, Clerkenwell, London. A group of "outside enamelled" pieces at South Kensington includes several by his hand (Plate 85 B). The plates numbered C 76 and 77—1923 are also typical of his style, which has already been described.[3] An especially elaborate specimen of the London-decorated class is a plate in Mr. Herbert Allen's collection (No. 438), minutely painted with views of English mansions copied from engravings issued in the *Copper Plate Magazine* between 1792 and 1802. The figure-subject on another plate in Mr. Allen's collection was probably done by a painter named Plant (*d.* about 1850) who was employed by Sims, another "outside enameller" with an establishment in London. The rich basket of roses on a Nantgarw plate at South Kensington (No. 3519—1901) was declared by Haslem to have been painted by James Turner of Derby, working for Sims, who was himself an old Derby hand. Much of the Swansea and Nantgarw china smothered with soft indefinite roses may be put

[1] Turner, *op. cit.*, Plate X.

[2] Such as T. Bradley & Co., Neal and Bayley, Boucher and Gay, "Powell, 91 Wimpole Street" (Herbert Allen Collection, No. 434).

[3] See p. 114.

down to Sims and his painters. But by no means all the London-decorated Nantgarw china was decorated in costly fashion. I have seen a plate with the impressed mark, painted with a few slight sprays of flowers not unlike those on the specimen figured in Plate 85 A, inscribed underneath, *Mortlock*, in gold.

CHAPTER XIII

COALPORT

THE Coalport factory was founded by John Rose, who had been an apprentice of Turner at Caughley. After starting a pottery at Jackfield in Shropshire in 1780, he returned shortly afterwards to Coalport, a town on the Severn bank nearly opposite his former master's factory, which he eventually bought up in 1799. Porcelain was made at both factories under Rose's management until the older was finally closed, about 1814. The Swansea and Nantgarw porcelain manufactures were also acquired[1] a few years later by Rose, who died in 1841 and was succeeded by his nephew William. The firm is still in existence.

The manufacture was a very large one, and all grades of china were made. Only a small proportion of the pieces were ever marked; and of these many made towards the middle of the nineteenth century were close copies of Meissen, Sèvres and Chelsea models and bore the marks of those factories. These copies are quite likely to deceive the inexperienced collector, though their true origin may always be detected merely by an examination of the gilding, which is usually thin and highly burnished and always quite unlike the dull soft-looking gold of the earlier work; and there is naturally a quite different touch in the painting.

The earliest Coalport china cannot be separated from

[1] See p. 204 for an account of the circumstances of the purchase.

that of Caughley,[1] and the *C* and *S* of Salopian china were probably also used as marks. Paste and glaze may be presumed to have been similar, and underglaze blue painting and printing were chief modes of decoration. And it is quite possible that much of it was decorated outside the factory. The china shown on the work-table in Thomas Baxter's water-colour of his father's studio [2] in London includes not only a plate with a figure-subject of the kind done by Baxter himself, but also a number of pieces with decoration of a kind not usually believed to have been done outside the factories. Mr. Bernard Rackham has suggested to me that these pieces may have been sent only to be gilded at Baxter's workshop. They include spirally fluted cups and other pieces with simple conventional floral borders of a type common enough on both Worcester and Salopian china in the early nineteenth century, and also, strangely enough, a blue-and-white teapot or vase which could not have been painted anywhere but at a factory with "glost-ovens", since the decoration is under the glaze. A notice shown on the wall of the studio is headed *Coalport White China*, pointing to the probability that the porcelain made at Caughley after the purchase of the works in 1799 by John Rose of Coalport, as well as that made at Coalport in its earliest days, may have been sent for gilding (and perhaps sometimes painting) to Baxter in London. Many pieces of a kind usually attributed to Caughley [3] show gilding rather arbitrarily disposed over decoration in underglaze blue. And a well-known class of Chinese blue-and-white shows similar irrelevant gilding,[4] which from its resemblance to that on Salopian china is usually thought to have been done at Caughley. But Baxter is very likely to have been responsible for it.

When Billingsley came from Nantgarw to Coalport

[1] See p. 185. [2] See p. 180.

[3] A jug at South Kensington (No. C 51—1921) is an example.

[4] Tea-canisters are particularly common: No. 332—1907 at South Kensington is an example.

(he died there in 1828), his recipe was undoubtedly tried experimentally by Rose, and it is quite likely that the *Nantgarw* stamp was used at Coalport as it had been at Swansea, and the productions are thus likely to be mistaken. But pieces so marked in a style later than that of about 1820 are rarely seen. In Mr. Allen's collection, however, there is a little group of unmarked pieces (Nos. 414-416) that may well have been made at Coalport from the Nantgarw formula. The not uncommon wide-mouthed jugs, often dated and inscribed under the lip, painted with large indefinite pink roses and by custom miscalled Swansea, are almost certainly Coalport productions of about 1830, as is much else besides that goes by the name of Swansea. Some Coalport painting is even claimed as Billingsley's, but the only convincing example known to me (a plate at South Kensington, No. C 1025—1924) seems to date from the period *before* his Nantgarw venture. It bears the very unusual mark *Coalbrookdale* in red, suggesting that it was perhaps a piece sent to be painted by him outside the factory. The best Coalport porcelain from 1830 onwards was certainly of fine quality and highly translucent, and perhaps made from a modified Nantgarw formula. Some of the finest Coalport of the middle of the century was declared by Jewitt to be indistinguishable from Nantgarw.

Rose was awarded in 1820 the "Isis" Gold Medal of the Society of Arts for a leadless feldspathic glaze, and one of the factory marks [1] commemorates this. The characteristic Coalport "useful china" of the period 1820 to 1850 is mainly distinguished by its comparatively sparing decoration, in which the mannered flower-painting already mentioned in connection with Derby plays a leading part. Moulded patterns are much in evidence and gilding was lavish, but the white porcelain surface was not so completely smothered in decoration as at other factories. The rich dessert-

[1] Appendix, p. 272.

services which competed with those of Spode and Rockingham may sometimes be identified only by this characteristic, which is one of the few merits of early Coalport. The practice of using outlines for flower-painting printed in pink or purple is a distinguishing mark of some Coalport table-ware of this time. Coalport gilding was usually light in colour in contrast to that on Rockingham china.

The vases and decorative pieces were too often overloaded with moulded decoration; flowers modelled in the round were applied in profusion, and the "revived rococo" of the period 1820 to 1830 was especially distressing. In the crude and tasteless colouring a strong pink and a particularly unpleasant bright, rather yellowish green were prominent. The inkstand figured in Plate 96 is a characteristic specimen.

Towards 1845 not only were Sèvres models closely copied, but the Sèvres style was attempted in more or less original work. About the period of the Great Exhibition of 1851 the most "exquisite" of all the English painting in this manner was done by William Cook of Coalport, who specialised in groups of trophies as well as in flowers and birds. The cup and saucer numbered 3370—1901 at South Kensington and the plates in Mr. Allen's collection (Nos. 409 and 410) are good examples of a rather deceptive class which commonly bears the Sèvres mark. The imitation of Chelsea gold-anchor vases inspired the production of large pieces with figure-subjects in the manner of Boucher. A *rose Pompadour* ground (always miscalled at the time *rose du Barry*) was one of the proudest achievements of the factory, though poor enough in our eyes beside the Sèvres colour. A maroon-coloured ground is said to have been introduced by Samuel Walker, who had come to Coalport with his father-in-law. The egg-shell porcelain of almost paper-like thinness made in this period was, according to Jewitt, "a pure porcelain; one stone and one clay alone, without bone-ash".

A characteristic class of work practised at Coalport and elsewhere, much esteemed about the middle of the century, took the form of paintings in enamel on flat plaques of porcelain: highly finished naturalistic groups of flowers and fruit were especially favoured. Some work in this style was done by Jabez Aston and R. Eaton: examples are in Mr. Herbert Allen's collection (Nos. 403 and 626). The productions of the later nineteenth century lie outside the scope of this book.

CHAPTER XIV

SWINTON (ROCKINGHAM FACTORY)

PORCELAIN was made between 1820 and 1842 at Brameld's Pottery on the estate of the Marquis of Rockingham, at Swinton near Rotherham, Yorkshire, when the factory was in the hands of the three sons of William Brameld, who died in 1813. The eldest, Thomas, was according to Jewitt "a man of exquisite taste . . . intent on making Art-advances in his manufactory". Pottery of all kinds had been and continued to be made. The brown-glazed "Rockingham china" was, of course, not porcelain, but earthenware: the so-called Cadogan tea- or hot-water pots of this material, in the form of the Chinese peach-shaped wine-pot, were a celebrated Rockingham production.

Experiments were made in the manufacture of porcelain from about 1820. These were evidently not altogether unsuccessful, though financial difficulties led the proprietors to appeal in 1826 to Earl Fitzwilliam, who granted them a subsidy. From that date the factory took the name "Rockingham Works", with the right to use the Earl's crest (a griffin passant) as a mark. The production in that year of so difficult a piece of porcelain as the enormous "rhinoceros vase", made for the Earl and still at Wentworth House, shows that the potters were by no means without experience in porcelain manufacture. I reproduce here (Plate 96) the companion vase in the Victoria and Albert Museum[1] as

[1] No. 47—1869. The vase is upwards of three feet high.

an excellent illustration of the taste of the period. It is recorded to have been painted by Edwin Steele, son of Thomas Steele of Derby,[1] himself employed at Swinton for a short time. Other examples of Edwin Steele's work at Swinton are in Mr. Allen's collection (Nos. 596, 598 and 601). Amongst the other painters were William Corden, also of Derby; the Speights, father and son, the latter of whom specialised in heraldic decoration; Brentnall, Collinson and Llandig were fruit- and flower-painters; and one Bailey is named by Jewitt as "principal butterfly painter". Their styles, however, are seldom distinguishable, as no documentary pieces have been preserved.

In 1830 the factory received an order from William IV. for a large dessert-service,[2] now in Buckingham Palace, and from this date until the end of the reign styled itself "Royal" and "Manufacturer to the King".

The "Rockingham" porcelain was of good quality and its decoration not more florid than was usual in the period. The "Derby style" was followed rather than that of Coalport, but unmarked pieces are often not easy to identify. A certain light feathery touch in the details of painted decoration often distinguishes Rockingham dessert-services from those made by Spode and at Coalport. The lavish gilding sometimes includes delicate lace-patterns of a kind not found elsewhere: the gilding itself is generally darker than on Coalport, inclining to a coppery tone. The coloured grounds were not very distinctive; a deep thick *gros bleu* inclining to violet, and a thick smooth opaque green, however, were peculiar to the factory, as was the so-called "Rockingham glaze" of manganese brown, used on the teapots already mentioned. A large cup and saucer with this glaze is in the collection of Rockingham china at South Kensington (No. 3165—1901). A neutral grey ground was also much favoured.

[1] See p. 113.

[2] Numbering 200 pieces, said to have cost £5000.

Rockingham coloured figures were often on a larger scale than those of other factories, and coarsely enamelled with broad half-translucent washes. Certain smaller shepherdesses and the like are easily mistaken for Derby. The toy houses in porcelain with encrusted vegetation have a North of England "peasant" flavour that is charming by contrast with the more ostentatious work done at the factory.

It should be mentioned that undecorated Rockingham china was bought and painted by Allen of Lowestoft.[1]

[1] Jewitt, vol. i, p. 502. See p. 132.

CHAPTER XV

PLYMOUTH AND BRISTOL

We have seen that as early as 1745 [1] William Cookworthy (*b.* 1705, *d.* 1780), a Quaker chemist of Plymouth, was acquainted with the nature of the clay used by the Chinese in the manufacture of true porcelain, and it is probable that his search for it in Cornwall was rewarded at the latest by 1758,[2] when Tregonning Hill, the place of his discovery, was mentioned in Borlase's *Natural History of Cornwall* as the source of a fine white clay. In the meantime the use of Cornish soapstone as an ingredient of soft-paste may well have been due to Cookworthy's researches.[3]

In 1765 a further consignment of china-clay from America was sent to Richard Champion by his brother-in-law, Caleb Lloyd of Charleston, South Carolina. This was the same "unaker" that had been sent twenty years earlier and used at Bow, and we find the young Champion, a member of a Bristol family of merchants and then twenty-two years of age, already interested in the manufacture of china. Champion wrote in reply in the same year of a "new work just established" attempting to make porcelain with Cornish materials; "the body is perfectly white within," he wrote, "but not

[1] See p. 54.

[2] In an undated memorandum, probably written before the patent was taken out in 1768, he speaks of having found the china-clay and stone "nearly twenty years ago".

[3] See p. 149.

without, which is always smoky". Champion promised to try the American clay, but pointed out that it was useless without the fusible china-stone. This last, a variety of granite or feldspar known in Cornwall as "moorstone" or "growanstone", was found by Cookworthy at a slightly later date in the tower of St. Columb Church,[1] though the first specimens obtained proved impure and the desired whiteness on melting was not obtained, the presence of iron causing reddish stains. A suitable variety, which showed greenish spots comparable to the green tone described by Père d'Entrecolles, was eventually found near St. Austell, and a patent for porcelain manufacture with these materials was taken out by Cookworthy in 1768.[2] A note-book written by one John Allen of Liskeard, quoted by Lady Radford,[3] states that the factory was started by a company subscribing "fourteen shares of £15 or £20 each . . . held . . . three by William Cookworthy and one by each of the other partners, *viz.* Philip Cookworthy, Richard Champion, John and Joseph Harford, William Phillips, T. Were and Sons, John Bulteel, William Wolcott, Joseph Fry, and Thomas Franks [*sic*]. Some of these afterwards advanced further sums and the undertaking seems to have been attended with loss." The last-named subscriber was a Bristol potter; the others were prominent Bristol men or relatives of Cookworthy. Thomas Were, a brother-in-law, had, before 1767, advanced money on account of "William Cookworthy on the china affair or the Plymouth Porcelain Company: To Bill remitted on China affair at Bristol £30."[4]

[1] There is a legend to the effect that Cookworthy observed some stones which had fused at a bell-casting, and so obtained a clue for the discovery of *petuntse* (quoted from a manuscript diary of 1797 by Rev. John Skinner, in a well-documented article by Lady Radford in the *Devonian Year Book*, 1920, p. 31).

[2] Specification No. 898, March 17, 1768.

[3] *Loc. cit.*, p. 36.

[4] Quoted by Lady Radford, *loc. cit.*, p. 34.

Cookworthy's account of his discovery [1] is well worth reading for its demonstration of his scientific method, as well as for its interest in connection with a landmark in the history of English china manufacture. A diligent study of the *Letters* of Père d'Entrecolles [2] was evidently the inspiration of his research; the lime and plant-ash used in his glaze were in fact prepared in precisely the same manner as at Ching-tê Chên.

The factory was at first conducted at Coxside, Plymouth,[3] with the assistance of Thomas Pitt, afterwards Lord Camelford.[4] The close association of Plymouth and Bristol parties in the concern from its beginning makes it difficult to decide the exact date of the transfer of the manufacture to Bristol, but it was probably about 1770. Some decoration, at all events, seems to have been carried out at Bristol from this date, since an advertisement in a Worcester newspaper of 1770 invited painters desiring work at the "Plymouth New Invented Patent Porcelain Manufactory" to apply to Thomas Frank at Castle Street, *Bristol*.[5] In this

[1] Quoted from G. Harrison's *Memoir of William Cookworthy*, pp. 199-207, in Hugh Owen's great work, *Two Centuries of Ceramic Art in Bristol*, pp. xv-xxii. Owen's book is not free from errors, but these and its typographical eccentricities do not seriously affect its importance as a contribution to the history of English pottery.

[2] See p. 149.

[3] It was contended by R. N. Worth (*Transactions of the Devonshire Association for the Advancement of Science, Literature and Art*, 1876, p. 480) that it was conducted at a bakery near Cookworthy's house in High Street, Plymouth, but it is more likely that early experiments only were made there. A former employee asserted that the works were at Coxside. See a letter quoted by Lady Radford, *loc. cit.*, p. 37.

[4] Interesting details about the discovery are given in a letter from Lord Camelford quoted in Polwhele's *History of Cornwall*. He refers to the discovery on an estate of his of a "certain white saponaceous clay, and close by it a species of granite or moorstone, white with greenish spots, which he (Cookworthy) immediately perceived to be the two materials described by the missionary Père d'Entrecolles". The use of the first person plural elsewhere in this letter proves Lord Camelford's connection with the manufacture.

[5] R. W. Binns, *A Century of Potting in the City of Worcester*, p. 87. Frank was, as I have mentioned, a partner in the Plymouth company, but even so, it is unlikely that application to Bristol would have been invited for a Plymouth factory.

year, too, Thomas Were and Sons sold their share "to the proprietors of the New China Manufacture at Bristol—where the work is intended to be carried on".[1] A drawing by Champion of a kiln, dated 1770, was published by Owen,[2] and the removal from Plymouth may well have been due to Champion's insistence. The latter in his evidence given before Parliament a few years later claimed that he had been connected with Cookworthy's manufacture "nearly since the time of the patent"; and we have seen that his interest in the subject dated from 1765 at the latest. The dissolution of a partnership between "Joseph Harford and R. C." is mentioned in 1769 in the diary of his sister, Sarah Champion. A later entry, in 1771, speaks of the "china work" carried on at Castle Green; and premises there were in the rate-book for that year with William Cookworthy as occupier. Cookworthy was then an old man, and in 1773 the patent rights and business were finally purchased by Champion, who styled the works the Bristol China Manufactory. John Brittan was his foreman.

The patent expired in 1775, and Champion's application for an extension was opposed by Josiah Wedgwood and other Staffordshire potters, whose natural self-interest was cloaked in pretensions of zeal for the public welfare. Champion was granted certain rights over the sale of the Cornish minerals and their sole use in translucent porcelain; but others were allowed the free use of the clay and stone in opaque pottery. This set-back and the ambitious nature of much of the Bristol china prevented it attaining any commercial success. Champion, too, was an ardent Whig politician, and his divided attention probably handicapped his work as a potter. In any case, such a

[1] Lady Radford, *loc. cit.*, p. 40.

[2] P. 18. The words written on the drawing, "The Last Burning of Enamel Nov. 27 1770", may refer to the impending removal. Several pieces marked with the same date may also have been inscribed with the event in view.

manufacture could scarcely have been successful without royal or princely patronage or a Government subsidy, such as were enjoyed by the Continental factories of the same order. Financial difficulties obliged Champion to sell the patent rights in 1781 to a company of Staffordshire potters, who continued the manufacture of the more simply decorated wares at a factory opened in the following year, called the New Hall, at Shelton.[1]

For a short time after this date Champion was Deputy Paymaster-General to the Forces under his friend Edmund Burke, but changes of Government deprived him of the post and finally led to his emigration in 1784 to a farm in South Carolina, where he died on October 7, 1791, aged 48.

MARKS WERE BY NO MEANS ALWAYS USED AT PLYMOUTH and Bristol, though the sign for tin (which is also that for the planet Jupiter), resembling the numerals 2 and 4 conjoined, in underglaze blue, gilt or enamel, occurs fairly often on the earlier pieces. It referred, no doubt, to the ancient tin-mining industry of Cornwall, and reveals the chemist in Cookworthy. But it was evidently used by him also at Bristol. There are a number of pieces in existence bearing this mark together with that commonly employed later at Bristol, a cross painted in enamel or gold.[2] An early vase in a set in the Schreiber Collection (No. 710) has a cross incised in the glaze, whilst the others have the tin-mark. A capital B in blue enamel was also used at Bristol, occasionally in combination with the cross.[3] This and the crossed swords in underglaze blue in imitation of

[1] See p. 240. It is sometimes said on the authority of the inaccurate Simeon Shaw that the sale took place in 1777; but Owen pointed out that this is disproved by Champion's figure made in memory of his daughter, who died in 1779. Shaw, it may be noted, attributed the failure of the Plymouth and Bristol manufacture to ignorance of the "principles of combinative potency"!

[2] A milk-jug in the British Museum (No. VIII. 50) and a basin painted in blue in the Schreiber Collection (No. 692) are examples.

[3] A coffee-pot formerly in the Trapnell Collection bears both marks.

Meissen were often accompanied by numerals, commonly believed to be painters' marks. I shall discuss these presently in connection with the painting on Bristol china. It is noteworthy that the porcelain figures seldom bear a factory mark: of the thirty examples in the Schreiber Collection, not one has the mark.

To distinguish Plymouth china from Bristol is not always easy, and the hard porcelain made at the two places would be more scientifically as well as more conveniently classified, as it may be by style, into Cookworthy's and Champion's, representing the earlier and later productions.

THE IDENTIFICATION OF THE UNMARKED CHINA attributable to one or other of the two factories is of course simplified by the fact that it is hard-paste. Some training of the collector's eye is required before the distinctive quality of this true porcelain can be surely recognised, but with a little experience it is seldom necessary to use a file. Whilst the glaze is often pitted and milky with numerous minute bubbles [1] and quite unlike the glassy covering of soft-paste, the body with its compact texture is not unlike a kind of very hard glass. In colour, both Plymouth and Bristol show a constant tendency to a brownish smoke-staining, never quite overcome, and when this is absent in Bristol china, the glaze is cold and glittering. Technical short-comings mark much of the work, both early and late. Grit has often adhered to the foot-ring. The presence of slight spiral ridges in "thrown" pieces is a common defect (known as wreathing), due to unskilful work: a vase or cup unevenly wetted or compressed by the thrower's fingers has shrunk unequally in the kiln. Handles are often askew from the same cause. A rib, or ring in relief, under the base of the plates and dishes was a device used to support them

[1] According to the patent quoted by Jewitt, vol. i, p. 376, and Owen, p. 392, the Bristol glaze contained also tin-ashes, which would give it opacity.

A B C

D E

F G H

About 1770.

A and C are painted in colours; F and H in underglaze blue.

(*Schreiber and V. and A. Museum Collections.*) See pp. 226, 228, 229.

Asia, from a set of the Continents. About 1770.
(*Schreiber Collection.*) See p. 229.

in the kiln. Plates were a weak point in the Bristol manufacture, and are consequently rare.[1] Warping and fire-cracks are common; figures lean forward quite literally overcome by the heat of their firing. Analysis has shown [2] that the fluxing material in Bristol china is even less than in the Chinese or Meissen, and the very high temperature required for its firing was obviously hard to obtain and control. Lord Camelford, writing in 1790 of the former Plymouth factory, spoke of the difficulty that had been experienced in apportioning the ingredients; Champion, speaking of a later time, declared that no two specimens of the Cornish china-stone behaved alike. To the relative infusibility of glaze is due the fact that the enamels, baked on at a second firing, are seldom perfectly incorporated but stand out as a superficial incrustation. An obviously *fused* appearance, due to the imperfect control of the firing of the ware, is seen in the details of many figures, and this, with the common smokiness, distinguishes the pieces usually regarded as Plymouth. But Bristol was also liable to the same faults, though to a slighter extent. The same shortcomings are commonly seen in the hard-paste porcelain of the small German factories in Thuringia, where figures were made in the same period. These are often erroneously classified as English.[3]

One of Cookworthy's earliest productions, a mug in the British Museum (No. VII. 9), is painted in underglaze blue with the Plymouth arms and has the inscription *March 14 1768 C.F.*, the initials presumably standing for *Cookworthy fecit.*[4] A tradition in the Cookworthy family insists that the earliest blue-painting was

[1] Wedgwood was aware of this weakness, and pressed the point in his case against the Bristol patent. His own "Queen's ware" plates could be made perfectly true.

[2] Church, p. 81.

[3] As are several items in the *Catalogue of the Trapnell Collection* and in Owen. The collector should compare the exhaustive and fully illustrated *Alt-Thüringer Porzellan* (Kloster-Veilsdorf, Ilmenau, Limbach, etc.) of R. Graul and A. Kurzwelly (Leipzig, 1909).

[4] The date is three days before that of the patent.

done by the inventor himself. If this is true, the British Museum mug is a most likely specimen, perhaps done as an exhibit, since it bears a date before that of the patent. Prideaux[1] repeated a legend, apparently the creation of Simeon Shaw, to the effect that Cookworthy had invented a new process of making cobalt-blue direct from the ore. However this may be, the underglaze colour on Plymouth china is invariably of blackish or greyish tone. Notwithstanding this shortcoming the Plymouth blue-and-white is often decidedly attractive in an unpretentious way, and shows an individual treatment of the Chinese motives, as in the mugs figured in Plate 87. Quasi-classical borders were, for some reason, a feature of this blue-and-white: those on two cups and saucers in the Schreiber Collection (No. 693) include the classical ox-skull. Painting in red-and-blue in Chinese style was also practised at Plymouth; a jug (C 1259—1924) and a mug (C 1253—1924) at South Kensington are examples. Another blue-and-white mug, inscribed *Josiah and Catharine Greethead March 13 1769* and important for its date, is in the Schreiber Collection (No. 694), where the collector may see what is undoubtedly the finest existing series of Cookworthy's porcelain.

Lady Charlotte Schreiber had the good fortune to purchase many fine pieces which had been preserved by members of Cookworthy's family.[2] Many of these, like most of the figures, were unquestionably presentation pieces, and do not at all represent the average quality of the Plymouth and Bristol work. The enormous tea- and coffee-pots (Schr. Nos. 735 and 736), 9¾ in. and 11⅛ in. high, bearing the Plymouth mark in gold, were evidently show-pieces of this kind: they are ambitiously but unskilfully gilded on a marbled blue ground apparently imitated from

[1] *Relics of William Cookworthy*, p. 7.

[2] The collections of John Prideaux, Miss Fox and Miss Tregellis were all inherited in this way.

Worcester porcelain. They are often held to be work of the Bristol period,[1] though their flower-painting links them with certain early vases, and like them they were evidently made by way of displaying the new porcelain to Cookworthy's friends. The sets of vases (or *garnitures*[2]), of which there are two in the Schreiber Collection (Nos. 710 and 711), show very well the difficulty with which the porcelain was made: the pieces which purport to be uniform vary in size and are sometimes distorted; one of the pieces was chipped before it was painted, but none the less was considered worth decorating, a leaf having been painted over the chip. To the same class of show-pieces belongs a claret-ground tea-pot in the same collection (No. 737), also marked in gold. The ground-colour is mottled and scarcely successful.

Of the less pretentious pieces, a noteworthy document, given by Mr. Sydney Whiteford to the Plymouth Museum, is a small sauce-boat inscribed *Mr. Wm. Cookworthy's Factory Plym^o^ 1770*. Sauce-boats from the same mould are at South Kensington, in the Schreiber and Museum Collections (Nos. 724 and 725 and 3096 and 3097—1901); two of these are painted in colours on either side with a cock, presumably from the crest of the Cookworthy family—a cock gules.

These earlier things are not only marked by imperfections in the paste, but a muddy tone is also characteristic of certain of the enamel colours. A brownish-crimson appears very often, particularly on the slight *rococo* scroll-work for which the elderly Cookworthy evidently retained a liking. Chinese subjects and patterns, as a rule decidedly crude, were apparently copied from Worcester porcelain.

The T° mark, ascribed to "Mr. Tebo", to which

[1] Compare Owen, p. 79, and Church, p. 79.

[2] Two beakers and three covered vases after the fashion of the so-called *garnitures de cheminée* made in China for export to Europe.

such frequent reference has already been made in this book,[1] reappears on porcelain which must be ascribed to the Cookworthy period. Shell-salts were evidently a favourite invention of this "repairer", for we find them again in Plymouth porcelain: Plate 87 includes an unusually effective example with the shells and coral arranged with some approach to rhythm. The reappearance on these salts of the familiar "dishevelled birds" of Bow and Worcester has already been discussed.[2] Painting perhaps by the same hand is seen on a Bristol plate in the Schreiber Collection (No. 755), though this may have been done, as asserted by Owen, as a careful copy to match a Bow service.[3] Though white Plymouth porcelain can never have been available in London for this purpose to any considerable extent, the survival of undecorated pieces shows that it was not impossible for Giles to have obtained them.

It is remarkable that Longton models were sometimes used for Plymouth figures. The latter may, of course, have been moulded from actual Longton specimens, but the coincidence (or partiality) has never been satisfactorily explained. Another suggested explanation is that Cookworthy purchased the Longton moulds at a sale at Salisbury in 1760.[4] Instances of this identity of moulds are the *Boys with a Goat* (Schr. No. 702), and the *Seated Musicians* (Schr. No. 683: Plate 87 D and E), though these are unlikely to be the work of the same "repairer" as the Longton figures[5] since the flowers and accessories are quite different. Some of the Plymouth and Bristol figures, however, seem to be original compositions, and in spite of all shortcomings rank with the finest ever made in England.

[1] P. 66, where I have explained the improbability of his having modelled the Bristol *Seasons*, and p. 70.

[2] As on the specimens at South Kensington (Nos. 210, 211 and 212—1864).

[3] A Bow plate in the Schreiber Collection (No. 107) is similar.

[4] See p. 129.

[5] Such as C 707 and 708—1925 at South Kensington.

Among the best are the *Continents*, of which a complete set with a good pedigree is in the Victoria and Albert Museum (Nos. C 553 to 556—1920). Further examples of the splendid *Asia* and *America* are in the Schreiber Collection (Nos. 697: Plate 88, and 696). The grave *Shepherdess* (Plate 89) is a well-known "Plymouth" model, and the little naked boys as *Seasons* (Schr. No. 699: Plate 87 A and C) are very delightful things, obviously of the earlier period. There are also the figures of birds and beasts, of which several are at South Kensington (Plate 87 B).

These earlier figures may readily be distinguished from the others by their scrolled *rococo* bases, often picked out in the distinctive "Plymouth" brown-crimson: the later "Bristol" bases are, by a curious anomaly, of the indefinite *rockwork* favoured at Sèvres and elsewhere in the Louis Seize period. We have a rare piece of evidence of the conceiving of some of the most ambitious Bristol figures in Champion's instructions to the (unfortunately anonymous) modeller of the *Elements* and *Seasons*, published by Owen,[1] and reprinted by Mr. Rackham in the Schreiber Catalogue. Writing of the *Elements*, Champion says: "As I have an inclination to fancys of this kind, I chose to write to you as wish to have some elegant Designs. I have seen the four Elements which are made at Derby they are very Beautifull the Dress easy, the forms fine, two in particular Air and Water are the charming figures. I apprehend that you made the models & therefore hope that from your execution the following fancies will not look amiss." Then follows a description of the figures as he wished them made. This connection between Derby and Bristol seems to have been generally overlooked. A set of Derby *Elements* appears in the extant price-list as the work of Stephan, who was modelling for Duesbury from 1770 onwards. There is no record,

[1] Facsimile (of Champion's manuscript) No. 4. Complete sets of the figures are in the Schreiber Collection (Nos. 742 and 743).

however, that Stephan ever went to Bristol, though there is a legend that another workman, described as "Thomas Briand of Derby", was responsible for the biscuit plaques to be mentioned presently. A connection with Derby is suggested by the very marked similarity of the figures of children made at both factories. With their large heads, smirking expressions and affected attitudes they are all clearly of the Acier-Sèvres family. But as many of the English figures seem to be original models, and the style is so distinctive, a single modeller is suggested for both factories. The Bristol children as *Seasons* (Schr. No. 745: Plate 89 B) show the style very well, whilst the *Boy and Girl carrying dogs* closely follow a Derby model.[1] The grown-up *Seasons* and *Elements* for which Champion's instructions have been preserved show much less of the contemporary Derby style, and do not seem in the least like Stephan's work. Mr. Rackham has suggested that the Derby *Elements* referred to were perhaps the earlier figures of which the white *Pluto* conjecturally ascribed to the factory on page 87 was the *Earth*: the Bristol *Elements* show the same excellent lively movement. The *Seasons*, of which I reproduce the stately *Autumn* (Plate 89), are clearly the work of the same hand. The *Shepherds* and *Shepherdesses*, *Children with Dogs* and the fine *Venus and Adonis*, may all be seen in unequalled specimens in the Schreiber Collection. Many of the best have the T° mark.

A form evidently favoured by "Mr. Tebo" was the large "frill vase" with applied masks, acanthus foliage and festoons of flowers. Bow specimens of the type sometimes bear his mark, as do certain Worcester vases[2] almost identical in form with two Bristol specimens in Mr. Herbert Allen's collection (Nos. 444 and 446). One may assume that the "repairer"

[1] Compare the Chelsea-Derby pair, Schr. No. 349.

[2] No. 125 in the Frank Lloyd Collection and No 571 (Plate 74) in the Schreiber Collection are examples.

would take from factory to factory the simple moulds for masks and flowers required to do the applied decoration on such vases as these. It was formerly believed that "Tebo" modelled most of the Bristol figures, but the coincidence of the mask on a Bristol jug with the head of *Winter* in the *Seasons*, remarked upon by Mr. Rackham, does not imply that the "repairer" (who might mould a jug) was also the modeller of the figure. It may well be that the mask was cribbed by the repairer who moulded the figure from a model made by another. Another Bristol type found at Worcester, and perhaps due to "Mr. Tebo", is the basketwork dish moulded with vine leaves in relief. An ambitious type, eloquent of Champion's determination but scarcely successful, is represented by two large vases painted with birds in panels reserved on a light scale-blue ground, and mounted in *ormoulu*, in Mr. Allen's collection (No. 447).

Much more successful than these are the large hexagonal vases with painting on a white ground, of which there are fine examples both at South Kensington (Schr. No. 750: Plate 90) and at the British Museum (VIII. 18), painted with birds in distant landscapes in a very personal manner. These show strong Sèvres influence and are by the same hand as some well-known painting on Worcester porcelain.[1] Their painter was almost certainly the "Mons. Soqui" mentioned by Harrison in his *Memoirs of Cookworthy*, and the "excellent painter and enameller from Sèvres" referred to by Prideaux.[2] Landscapes, without birds, by the same hand are sometimes seen. Some smaller and very charming examples often bear the "Plymouth" mark: one such—a coffee-cup in the Schreiber Collection (No. 723)—is painted *en camaieu* in a very pleasant blue and crimson. Other specimens with his painting in the same collection are two coffee-cups

[1] See p. 171.

[2] *Relics of William Cookworthy*, p. 5.

(No. 722), and an early vase (No. 712) showing his undeveloped style. The painting on the great hexagonal vases is perhaps the best of his work at either Bristol or Worcester.

The beauty and interest of much of the Plymouth and Bristol painting goes far to compensate for the imperfections of the china itself. Owen gives a list of workmen[1] and the names of some other painters have been preserved in the apprentice-lists.[2] There were doubtless several skilled painters found amongst the "lads of genius" who were offered "encouragement" in an advertisement of 1775. As usual in English porcelain, one can do little more than bring together the work of certain hands: to ascertain their names is unfortunately beyond hope. The most celebrated of all the painters was Henry Bone (*b.* 1755, *d.* 1834), the son of a Plymouth cabinet-maker and afterwards a fashionable miniaturist. He is sometimes said to have been apprenticed at Plymouth, though he was only fifteen years of age when the works were transferred to Bristol, and Owen asserts that he was apprenticed to Champion in 1772 for a period of seven years. The monochrome bird-painting just mentioned has been attributed to him, but, as Mr. Rackham has shown,[3] the "tin" mark on some of these indicates a date before 1773, when Bone was only eighteen years old, and such accomplished painting could scarcely be the work of so young a man. Moreover, there is good reason to regard this as the work of the Frenchman already discussed. Owen asserted that all the pieces decorated by William Stephens were marked with the numeral 2, and since the several pieces of one service were sometimes marked with different numerals, he inferred that these could not be pattern numbers,

[1] William Fifield, a well-known painter of Bristol pottery, is sometimes said to have worked for Champion, but he was not born until 1777.
[2] Owen, pp. 289 and 299; Jewitt, vol. i, p. 397, and Pountney, p. 224.
[3] *The Burlington Magazine*, xxv (1914), p. 104.

A

B

C

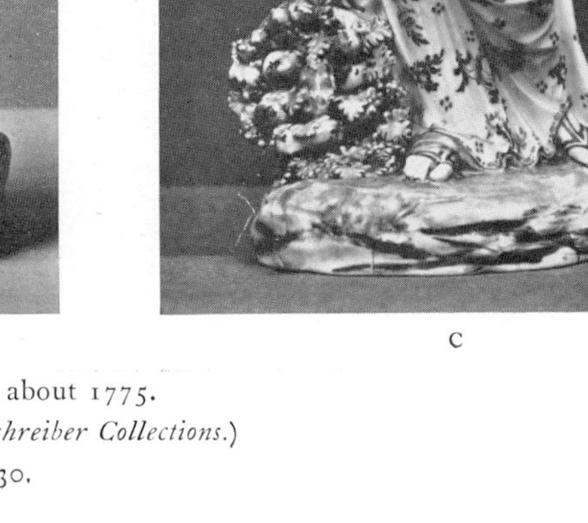

A, about 1770; B and C, about 1775.
(Mr. Herbert Allen's and the Schreiber Collections.)
See pp. 229, 230.

About 1775.
(*Schreiber Collection.*)
See p. 231.

A

B

C

Table-ware, painted in colours. About 1775–80.
(*Schreiber and V. and A. Museum Collections.*)
See pp. 235, 236.

A

B

C

Table-ware, painted in colours. About 1775–80.
(Mr. Herbert Allen's, V. and A. Museum and the Schreiber Collections.)
See pp. 233 to 236.

but must be the marks of Champion's apprentices, of whom William Stephens was believed to be the second. Owen thence conjectured that the mark of Henry Bone, the first, would be 1. There is good reason to abandon this theory. It is likely that numbers indicating seniority, if ever used at all, would vary with changes in the staff. And the numeral 1 appears on the plate painted with "dishevelled birds" mentioned above.[1] Moreover, the numeral 2 occurs on a saucer (No. 3121—1901) and a plate (No. 3109—1901) at South Kensington, handled in very different styles. Further, the painter of the plate just mentioned was evidently also the painter of the very beautiful monochrome flowers in pale-blue enamel on a cup and saucer (No. 3118—1901) in the same case, but this is marked 6. Again, a cup and saucer in the Herbert Allen Collection (No. 470) are both painted with the same pattern and evidently by the same hand, but the cup bears the numeral 3 and the saucer 1. Numerals in gold are also likely to be gilders' numbers rather than enamellers'. In view of his subsequent career and the statement of his biographer that he painted landscapes and flowers on china, it is more likely that Bone's work is to be found in such things as the charming crimson landscapes which decorate a teapot at South Kensington (No. C 109—1919), with the initials *HMB*; or perhaps the little oriental sea-shore scene on a cup and saucer in Mr. Allen's collection (Plate 92).

Champion made a number of handsome china services for his friends.[2] The wife of Edmund Burke was the recipient of one of these, on his election as Member of Parliament for Bristol, largely with Champion's assistance, in 1774. A cup and saucer

[1] Other examples marked with the numeral 1 are a tureen and cover at South Kensington (No. 3116—1901) and a tea-cup and saucer (VIII. 26) at the British Museum.

[2] A full list of these services is given in the *Catalogue of the Alfred Trapnell Collection*, pp. xxii-xxvii.

from the service is in the British Museum (No. VIII. 20), painted with figures and the arms of Burke impaling Nugent. A Bristol china service decorated with the favourite green festoons and a monogram of two S's was also made for presentation by Burke to Mrs. Smith, the wife of one of his supporters. Specimens are at South Kensington (No. 8122 and A—1862) and the British Museum (No. VIII. 25). The "Robert Smyth" service, made for the wedding in 1776 of the fifth baronet of that name, of Colchester, has the monogram R S composed of tiny flowers: an example is in Mr. Allen's collection (No. 464), which also includes a cup and saucer with the initial C, below a ring, composed of forget-me-nots. The "Mark Harford" service [1] was made for a member of a Bristol family associated with Champion's factory from the first. The earliest-dated Bristol-marked pieces are two coffee-cups in the Schreiber Collection (No. 763) with the initial *I. H* and the date 1774.[2] The service from which these came was traditionally believed to have been made for Joseph Harford, whose partnership with Champion was mentioned above, but Owen pointed out that the initials are more likely to be those of Joseph Hickey, a friend of Edmund Burke and London agent for the factory. A service made for William Cowles, a merchant of Castle Green, Bristol, is represented in the Schreiber Collection by a group of pieces, some of them bearing the Bristol cross and the date 1776.[3]

For the rest, the "useful ware" made at Bristol during Champion's proprietorship varied from elaborate things like these services [4] to the simple "cottage china" for which Champion, with more foresight, could

[1] Illustrated in Pountney, Plate L.

[2] These have the curious feature of the Bristol cross-mark *inside* the cups.

[3] Apart from these services, a rather crude pattern with festoons of flowers in green and black in "cottage style" (such as the cup and saucer, Schr. No. 770) has become known for some unexplained reason as the "Horace Walpole pattern".

[4] The beautiful "cabaret" sets are among the most sought after of Champion's wares.

undoubtedly have secured a large market. For his porcelain was genuinely "useful", as his advertisements claimed,[1] capable of good service, and standing sudden changes of temperature as well as the fine earthenwares of Staffordshire. Wedgwood and his fellows were well aware of this and doubtless feared its competition. In the British Museum are two tumbler-shaped cups (No. VIII. 39), produced as evidence in Champion's case before the House of Commons in 1775, and it is noteworthy that these are marked with the Meissen crossed swords. Champion constantly insisted on the kinship between his china and the "Dresden", and the mark was perhaps innocently meant to show that the specimens were indistinguishable from the German. In a surviving catalogue of an auction-sale of Bristol china held by Christie in 1780,[2] there are repeated references to "Dresden" and "French" patterns. Champion's models are clearly indicated in a letter of 1776, where he claims that his china equalled "the Dresden in strength", "in elegance perfectly resembling the beautiful manufacture of Sèvres". The ribbon and festoon patterns of the latter were a principal decoration (Plates 91 and 92); the laurel and husk (the so-called mignonette) pattern was especially in favour, as was the grey *camaieu* painting of the same factory (Plate 91). These are combined on a cup and saucer in the British Museum (No. VIII. 21), also said to have been shown in the House of Commons. Much of the flower-painting is the work of two hands. One of these, with a fluent style of brushwork, was the painter of the pale-blue monochrome flowers on a cup and saucer already

[1] A Bristol advertisement of 1776 included the following: "The Bristol china is superior to any other English Manufactory [*sic*]. Its texture is fine, exceeding the East India and its strength so great that water may be boiled in it. It is . . . distinguished from every other English China which being composed of a Number of Ingredients mix'd together the principal part being glass occasions it soon to get dirty in the wear, renders it continually liable to Accidents and in every respect only an Imitation and therefore is stiled by Chemists, a false Porcelain."

[2] Reprinted in Nightingale, p. 101.

referred to (No. 3118—1901 at South Kensington), and of the dish figured in Plate 91. The other arranged his flowers in tighter bunches, with less emphasis on the slender curving stems which are characteristic of the style previously mentioned: a teapot (Plate 92) shows the general effect of his painting. The severely classical cups of cylindrical form are worthy of comparison with the best contemporary work at Sèvres and Derby: the small cup with gilt S-shaped scrolls (Plate 91) is typical of some pretty things in the same style.

The "cottage china", which is particularly well represented in Mr. Herbert Allen's collection, was slightly decorated with festoons and sprigs, without gilding. It is often unmarked and at times scarcely distinguishable from the New Hall porcelain that succeeded it. In general, however, the Bristol colouring is distinctive. Pinks tended, as at Plymouth, to be brownish; a clear yellow, an uncommonly wet and juicy red and a bright translucent leaf-green are characteristic of this as of other Bristol (and Plymouth) china. Bristol shapes are subtly different from others. The globular teapot copied from the Chinese and adopted also at Lowestoft, Liverpool and Worcester, tended at Bristol to have straighter sides, sometimes even slightly incurved (Plate 91); jugs and even cups have the same outline, and a double curve in the handles, not seen elsewhere, is also common. A twig handle with tiny buds is peculiar to Bristol, as is the double-twig of a kind most often associated with Leeds and Staffordshire earthenware; longitudinally ribbed and simple loop handles flattened only on the inner side are also characteristic.

Transfer-printing was but rarely used, but a few poorish things are met with, the prints roughly coloured over. A teapot of characteristic shape in the Victoria and Albert Museum (No. C 1177—1924) is crudely painted in colours over a design of Chinese figures printed in outline. A print of birds washed over in colours is sometimes seen (specimens are at South Kensington and the British Museum). All these seem to be of the "Plymouth" period. A rare jug with a decidedly Salopian-like black print of a Chinese lady and boy, in the Schreiber Collection (No. 779), was for long regarded as Chinese porcelain printed at Caughley, but has the Bristol "wreathing" and smokiness. The crude, skimpy handle suggests an imperfect piece on which a trial of transfer-printing has been made. It is not impossible that such pieces as this were done at the instance of Robert Hancock, after he had left Worcester in 1774. The glaze of hard-paste is of course not fusible enough for printing to be readily successful. Some specimens printed in underglaze-blue with flowers (such as the mug in the Schreiber Collection, No. 730) have a decidedly Worcesterish look. Underglaze-blue painting is seen on a pair of strainers in the Schreiber Collection (No. 729).

STANDING APART FROM THE OTHER BRISTOL PRODUCTIONS are the biscuit plaques with modelled and applied flowers and portrait busts, shields of arms and the like in relief, which Champion delighted to make for presentation to his friends. It was stated by Owen [1] that a plaque inscribed *G G* and said to have been made for Gabriel Goldney bore a pasted-on label inscribed in his handwriting, "Specimen of Bristol china modeled by Thomas Briand of Derby 1777," to whom, in the absence of other evidence, this class of work is consequently ascribed.[2] The British Museum is especially rich in these plaques, many of which have the interest of quite certain documentation.[3] One of the specimens

[1] P. 87.

[2] It is not quite certain, however, that the "*G G*" of the plaque is the Gabriel Goldney of the label, who may well have been a nineteenth-century Bristol citizen of the same name, partner in Pountney and Allies' Bristol pottery in 1836. In this case, the attribution may be no more than a surmise, made long after the event, though possibly recording a tradition not to be disregarded.

[3] A full account and classification of the plaques is given in an article by Dr. Philip Nelson in *The Connoisseur*, vol. vi (1903), p. 139.

in the British Museum (No. VIII. 3) survived with little damage a fire at the Alexandra Palace which reduced many valuable specimens of soft-paste china to shapeless lumps.

At a much later date, about 1845–50, somewhat similar panels were made by Edward Raby for the Water Lane Pottery at Bristol, then under the management of J. D. Pountney, who died in 1852. These are sometimes mistaken for early specimens, but they were of a softer paste, with the ground occasionally stained blue on the surface. In the rare instances of a blue ground in Champion's plaques the paste was stained throughout before firing. The latter, moreover, usually have a very slight but perceptible gloss or "smear" due to vapourised glaze in the kiln. Champion used a similar biscuit to make models of birds' nests with eggs: specimens of these are in the British Museum (No. VIII. 9) and in Mr. Herbert Allen's collection (No. 485), which also includes some of Raby's work.

CHAPTER XVI

STAFFORDSHIRE

It is a matter for wonder that among Staffordshire potters for nearly twenty years after William Littler none ever attempted the making of china figures. Perhaps the hazards of soft-paste forbade them, but the commercial success of the Cannock-born Duesbury should have made the attempt seem worth while. We have at all events no figures that can reasonably be considered of Staffordshire origin until about 1790, a date we may assign to those rather rustic but attractive pieces in the style of the Ralph Woods, which some have wished to claim for Lowestoft on the evidence of some fragmentary moulds found on the site. Style and colouring make it highly improbable that these were made anywhere but in Staffordshire: they are in fact the porcelain counterparts of the Wood figures in earthenware. A pair of figures of this kind in a private collection in the Isle of Wight bears a mark *W* * * *, stated by Chaffers without any reason given to be that of Aaron Wood. There is no positive evidence that any of the Woods ever made porcelain, but from the style of the figures they may well be the work of Voyez or another of their modellers. They are in the later, opaque-coloured manner. The *W* * * * mark is found also on several bulb-pots of hard-looking porcelain of cold and greyish tone, painted with landscapes in Pinxton style and apparently dating from about 1800,[1]

[1] Marked specimens are in Mr. Arthur Hurst's collection. An

as well as on a plate of cream-coloured earthenware in Leeds style in the Victoria and Albert Museum (No. 3537—1901). These widely differing pieces suggest the work of a "general potter" such as Enoch Wood, rather than Aaron Wood, who indeed could not have made pieces in so late a style. Mr. Broderip's gift to the Victoria and Albert Museum includes a fine little group of these Staffordshire figures, which are for the greater part of decidedly soft paste: Plate 93 shows some of these. Figures of a harder material are sometimes met with, rather later in date and usually of the insipid classical models which had largely replaced the more vigorous rustic subjects by the end of the century. Figures in porcelain of about 1800 of the "flat back" type are occasionally seen marked *Neale & Co.*: Mr. Bernard Middleditch has one of these.

The patent of Richard Champion for the manufacture of hard-paste porcelain was purchased in 1781 by a company of five Staffordshire potters: Samuel Hollins, Jacob Warburton,[1] William Clowes, Charles Bagnal and Anthony Keeling, who began operations at the pottery of the last-named at Tunstall. In 1782 the works were transferred, after a disagreement amongst the partners, to an establishment at Shelton, near Hanley, called the NEW HALL. The company (which styled itself the "New Hall China Manufactory") was as much interested in the sale of the materials over which it held patent rights as in the manufacture of china from them, and by about 1810 hard-paste had been given up in favour of a glassy-looking dull white porcelain. A specimen of this has been analysed [2] and proved to be essentially a bone-porcelain of the modern

unmarked specimen is at South Kensington (No. 3077—1901). I have lately seen a porcelain group with an impressed number evidently referring to a *Ra. Wood*-marked item in the list of moulds published in F. Falkner, *The Wood Family of Burslem*.

[1] Jacob Warburton is said to have invented and patented a process of printing in gold (Hobson, *Catalogue*, p. 145), and is stated by Simeon Shaw to have been "distinguished for his moral and convivial habits of mind".

[2] *Analysed Specimens*, No. 43.

Staffordshire type. Wares of this period were usually marked with the name of the factory in a double circle, printed in red or brown. The earlier porcelain had seldom been marked, except occasionally with pattern-numbers preceded by *N* or *No.* in script characters. The firm came to an end in 1825.

The hard-paste of New Hall is sometimes not easily distinguishable from the Bristol "cottage china". It seems probable, too, that it was sometimes marked with the Bristol cross. The slight patterns are often very charming, though the material itself was seldom free from imperfections and was often cold or grey in tone. A straight-sided silver-shape teapot (Plate 94 A) was very popular at New Hall and almost peculiar to the factory.[1] Sprigs and festoons were much in favour as before at Bristol: black, red and pink enamels predominate in contrast with the green, red and yellow of Bristol. But the style of the patterns was common also to several other Staffordshire factories: Minton's earlier pattern-books include much that is very similar.[2] Somewhat crude but bold designs, not without character, are seen on the later New Hall: birds and landscapes in which pink and silver lustre[3] were used have a rustic quality that is decidedly refreshing in contrast with the pretentious work done at Worcester and other contemporary china-factories. Simple formal patterns in lustre, with white lines taken out with a point, are equally satisfying. Other patterns are decidedly modern in their feeling for the stylisation of floral motives and are very attractive.[4] The colour of the paste and its peculiar glassy translucency serve to identify this later porcelain when it is unmarked. There is a very full representation of New Hall, both early and late, at South Kensington (Plate 94).

[1] Compare that at S. Kensington signed *Ralph Clowes Newhall fecit.*

[2] Some characteristic New Hall patterns have also been ascribed, probably in error, to a factory at Wirksworth in Derbyshire. See p. 255.

[3] From gold and platinum.

[4] Black monochrome was sometimes used.

Of all the Staffordshire factories New Hall alone inherited any part of the eighteenth-century tradition. Little can be said in praise of the other Staffordshire productions of the early-nineteenth century, and though we are beginning to respect some of the moral qualities of the Victorians, too long overshadowed by their defects, those qualities were scarcely compatible with artistic expression in porcelain. It is astonishing now to read the complacent eulogies of contemporary productions uttered by that painstaking antiquary, Llewellynn Jewitt.

The still-existing firm founded in 1796 at Stoke-on-Trent by Thomas MINTON (1765–1836) may point to an honourable record of well-meant effort in the nineteenth century, not least in porcelain manufacture. Minton was a pupil of Turner of Caughley and later engraved copper plates for pottery-printing under the first Josiah Spode. He died in 1836, and for five years his son Herbert carried on the business in partnership with John Boyle, under the style of "Minton and Boyle". Herbert Minton died in 1858. Colin Minton Campbell continued the factory in partnership with Michael Hollins, and later with the grandsons of Thomas Minton. In 1883 the present company was formed. The marks used were numerous: some of them are reproduced in the Appendix to this book.

Porcelain of normal Staffordshire body was made from about 1798. Most of the current styles were adopted in the usually unmarked productions of the first twenty years: in particular, simple and effective designs of types in use at New Hall figure largely in the firm's pattern-books of this period. The only mark used in this early period was a monogram of two S's (not unlike the Sèvres mark) with M below them, in blue enamel. Minton's Japan patterns were perhaps cleaner and generally in rather better taste than those of his rivals at Derby, Worcester and Spode's. Good stipple-printing was done; and the excellent slight landscapes in monochrome are again in later New Hall style. The only distinctive early Minton style is one represented at South Kensington by a bowl (No. 312—1869) with bold gilding on a strong blue ground and panels of rather crude flowers in hot colouring. Mr. Allen's collection includes three vases (No. 517) in the same style. The "Minton and Boyle" period was one of prosperity, and to this belong the numerous services marked with the name and number of the pattern in a scrolled cartouche, sometimes with the initials *M & B*. The well-known "Amherst Japan", first made for Lord Amherst, Governor of India, is on Minton's "stone-china".

From 1841 begins the modern period, which lies outside the scope of this book. If the standard of invention seldom rose above the academically respectable, the work was always refined and sometimes beautiful. The numerous imitations of Sèvres[1] were at least as good as those of Coalport and Copeland's. A number of French artists joined the staff, amongst them Léon Arnoux (*d.* 1902), who came in 1848 and was a leading figure in the direction of the work. Turquoise grounds were constantly made with success, and the Parian biscuit invented by Copeland was used to great advantage;[2] such reliefs as those by Carrier (afterwards Carrier-Belleuse) on the service made for the wedding of King Edward VII. in 1863 are undeniably accomplished.[3] The clever work of Marc-Louis Solon in *pâte sur pâte* is too well known and too recent to need more than mention.

The SPODE factory at Stoke-on-Trent was founded by Josiah of that name, who was born in 1733, and

[1] The earlier work in Sèvres style, with turquoise ground, is not easily recognised with certainty. Robins and Randall (see p. 257) did similar work, and sometimes used Minton's porcelain. Compare Herbert Allen Collection, No. 523, etc.

[2] Though George Cocker of Derby was allowed to repeat his popular successes. *Glazed* Parian (compare the dessert dishes and cruet-stand in Mr. Allen's collection, Nos. 529 and 530) has a distinctive silky appearance.

[3] A centre-piece and two candelabra from this service are at present on loan at the Victoria and Albert Museum from H.M. the King.

in 1749 an apprentice of Thomas Whieldon. At first earthenware only was made; the factory rapidly became prosperous, and a London warehouse in Fore Street, Cripplegate, proving too small to deal with the firm's business, large premises were taken in 1779 at the Theatre Royal, in Lincoln's Inn Fields and Portugal Street. A second Josiah Spode (*b.* 1754, *d.* 1827) succeeded to the management on his father's death in 1797; about 1813[1] he took into partnership the firm's traveller William Copeland, and in 1833 the factory passed into the hands of the latter's son, William Taylor Copeland, by whose descendants it is still conducted. The third Josiah Spode (*d.* 1829) seems to have taken little active part in the management. The firm was Copeland and Garrett from 1833 to 1847; then "W. T. Copeland, late Spode". Several marks are given in the Appendix.

Porcelain does not seem to have been made until the time of the second Josiah Spode. It has been contended on the evidence of the water-marks on certain pattern-books that porcelain was made at an earlier date,[2] but from the style of the surviving specimens none can be dated much before the beginning of the nineteenth century. The younger Spode is generally believed to have discovered the most satisfactory formula for bone-china, using a proportion of bone-ash in place of some of the china-clay in a formula otherwise similar to that for hard-paste.[3] Spode's formula seems to have enabled him to abandon the former preliminary "fritting" of some of the ingredients. The Spode body has remained the English standard to the present day. Natural feldspar, distinct from the partly

[1] An inscription on a bowl in the British Museum (XIV. 8) is signed *Spode & Copeland Manufacturers Feby. 1813.*

[2] Water-marks naturally give only the *earliest* possible date for the designs upon them, which may be many years later.

[3] It should be mentioned, however, that so great an authority on the chemistry of pottery as Professor Church declared that Spode's formula was a matter of common knowledge in Staffordshire long before his time, and Martin Barr of Worcester undoubtedly experimented in the same direction not much later than 1795.

feldspathic china-stone, was used also in porcelain which from its style dates from the later years of the Spode management: this bears the distinctive "Felspar" mark. A third type of body, intermediate between porcelain and earthenware and introduced in 1805, was named "stone china".[1] The last-named type also bore a distinctive mark, but much of Spode's china had only a pattern number, though *Spode* in red or gold is not uncommon.

Practically nothing is known of the workmen responsible for Spode's designs or their execution, and the few names that have been recorded cannot be associated with particular specimens. This is hardly to be regretted, as no English porcelain is more clearly the product of the bad taste of the early years of the nineteenth century, particularly of the period following the Napoleonic wars, and of the commercialism that pandered to it. It is scarcely conceivable that a sensibility capable of appreciating the delicate art of eighteenth-century china can fail to be repelled by the vulgarities of most of Spode's wares. His commercial success was evidently enormous, and the great house built by him at Penkhull Mount is depicted on a characteristic vase (No. 372—1899) at South Kensington, with a dull claret-coloured ground, white flowers in applied relief and the heavy raised gilding said to have been the invention of his chief enameller, Henry Daniel.

A large collection which had been preserved in the

[1] Among the many other Staffordshire firms who also made "stone china" (which was usually decorated with Japan patterns), C. J. Mason, the brother of George Miles Mason, took out a patent in 1813 for an "ironstone china" which was especially hard and was alleged to contain slag of ironstone. The Masons' business was later acquired by Ashworth's. Jewitt says of Ashworth's ironstone wares that they "include priceless Art treasures . . . deserving to be in every home of taste". "Turner's patent stone china" is sometimes met with. Ridgway's of Cauldon Place made excellent porcelain as well as stone china. Jewitt's comment on the "toilettes Victoria" "used by the Imperial Family", and other of Ridgway's productions, is that they "achieved results never before attempted or attained as to magnitude and finish of goods". Staffordshire "ironstone china" was both cheap and durable, and quickly secured a very large market at home and abroad.

Spode family was presented to the South Kensington Museum in 1899 and 1902 by Miss H. M. Gulson, niece of a fourth Josiah Spode. This and Mr. Herbert Allen's collection illustrate most of the types made at the factory. These were very numerous; in fact most other factories' styles were adopted and no well-marked Spode style can be said to have emerged. Paste and glaze were technically excellent, but not as a rule distinguishable from other Staffordshire or from Rockingham china. The mannered flower-painting associated with the Steeles and the later Derby porcelain (but perhaps not invented there), the designs wholly in gilt, again like Derby, and some very weak figure-painting were among the themes. Modelled and applied flowers like those of Coalport and Derby were occasionally used, and imitations of the Meissen *Schneeballenvasen* were made in this way. Some carefully finished naturalistic birds and landscapes were evidently reserved for the most costly pieces. The Japan patterns in red, blue and gold were among the earliest productions; at their best and least pretentious they were neat (Plate 95 B), but the more showy kinds were as hideous as Bloor's later "Derby Japans", which are closely akin to them. Black stipple-prints of very good quality included the usual landscapes, and printed flowers were occasionally done with pleasant effect.

Spode's "stone china" was obviously for the greater part intended as common useful ware: much was in fact made to match the heavy dishes of blue-and-white still being imported in quantity from China. But the very free adaptations of Chinese designs, with simple washes of colour over printed outlines, often have originality and force as well as a sincerity which is entirely lacking in the more pretentious pieces. Some very exact copies of Chinese *famille rose* were also made on Spode's "stone china": a Chinese plate and a Spode copy are shown side by side in Mr. Herbert Allen's collection (No. 640) at South Kensington.

The best of Spode's later porcelain, made towards 1830 (and often bearing the "Felspar" mark), and the earlier Copeland tend towards the revived Sèvres style, affected also at Coalport and Rockingham. The rich dessert services of this period are at least handsome. Several of the coloured grounds were distinct from those of the rival factories: a soft greenish or pinkish grey, a pale green, a canary yellow, a deep rich fawn, and a very pale biscuit-colour were of shades peculiar to Spode's. Flowers painted in reserve on a gilt or dark-blue ground were much done at Spode's (Plate 95 A and C). Other and less attractive coloured grounds used in this and earlier periods included a hideous matt blue (usually decorated with gilding), a dull pink and a heavy lifeless claret colour.

Messrs. Copelands' productions are beyond the scope of this book, but it is interesting to note that Jewitt, writing of some of them in 1878, declared that "in this ware it is a literal truism to say, Perfection can no farther go . . . the vases and other decorative articles . . . take rank with the finest productions of any age or any country". Parian porcelain was produced in 1846 after an attempt to find the secret of the earlier Derby biscuit. It was largely used to imitate marble sculpture on a small scale. Some very carefully painted pieces made by Copelands about the time of the Great Exhibition of 1851 show that the firm shared in the general wish to outdo Sèvres in exquisiteness. A cup and saucer at South Kensington (No. 2701—1901), marked *Copeland and Garrett*, is a creditable production of this kind.

A large pottery was conducted by the firm of DAVENPORT, at Longport near Burslem, from 1793 until 1882, and much surviving porcelain dating from the early-nineteenth century bears their mark. It is without much character, though usually good, technically. Collectors are in the habit of regarding Davenport as a "dark horse", capable of anything. The styles adopted were very various, and the material, whilst sometimes as grey as late Worcester, is occasionally almost as white and translucent as Nantgarw. The Derby styles were much followed, however, and richly gilt borders of formal patterns and naturalistic flower and fruit painting in Derby style were characteristic. The famous Derby painter of fruit, Thomas Steele, seems actually to have worked at Davenport's, and two plates at South Kensington (Nos. 2550—1901 and C 289—1914) are unmistakably by his hand. Figure-subjects on two plates in Mr. Herbert Allen's collection (Nos. 515 and 516), in the style of Chamberlain's Worcester but attributable to Davenport's on the showing of their borders, are signed W. Fletcher, an artist otherwise unknown. Jesse Mountford, the Derby landscape-painter, is recorded to have moved to Longport, and Joshua Cristall, the water-colourist, is stated by Jewitt to have served an apprenticeship to John Davenport.

The firm of WEDGWOOD made porcelain for a short time, according to some recent authorities only between 1812 and 1816.[1] But the quantity surviving and the number of patterns suggest that the facts are, as stated by Church and the earlier historians of the Etruria works, that porcelain was made from about 1805 to about 1815 on the initiative of Thomas Byerley (*d.* 1810), nephew of the first Josiah Wedgwood and a partner in the firm. Useful ware was chiefly made, and it is without much distinction. The careless landscapes which appear on much of it are obviously by the hand of John Cutts of Pinxton, who is known to have worked for Wedgwood's.[2]

From about 1820 porcelain was produced as an article of commerce at very many other Staffordshire

[1] Porcelain manufacture was of course revived at Wedgwood's in more recent years, about 1872.

[2] Mr. John Cook of the Works Museum at Etruria has kindly sent me a copy of a letter addressed by Cutts to Wedgwood and dated from Pinxton in 1812.

Figures in the style of the Ralph Woods. About 1790. (*V. and A. Museum.*) See p. 240.

A

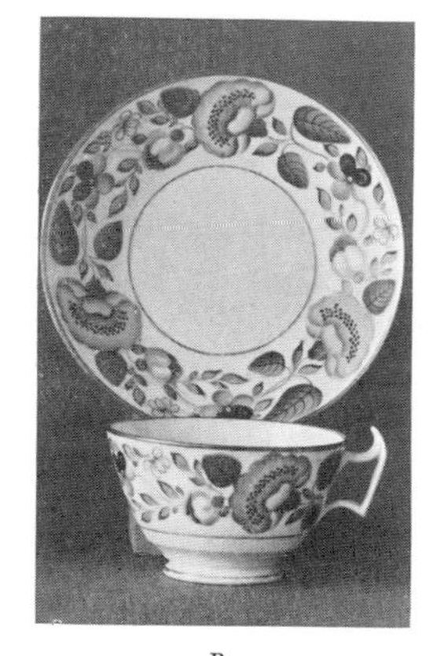

B

C

D E

Table-ware in New Hall styles. About 1800–20.
(*V. and A. Museum.*)
See p. 241.

A

B

A. Spode's porcelain. About 1810–20. B. Coalport. About 1830.
(*V. and A. Museum.*) See pp. 214, 246, 247.

Rockingham: "The Rhinoceros Vase". About 1826.
(*V. and A. Museum.*) See p. 216.

factories. Few of these wares were marked, and they are rarely worth the collector's attention.[1] It is satisfying, however, for him to be able to assign an approximate date, if not a factory, to stray pieces of nineteenth-century porcelain that may come his way, but a key to dating can scarcely be given. Styles had (and have) a way of persisting in the provincial and country markets long after the passing of their metropolitan vogue. The collector will perhaps be helped by the brief outline I have given in the Introduction. Several marks of minor factories are given in the Appendix, with a note of the classes of porcelain on which they appear.

[1] It may be remarked here that the charge of artistic insignificance in the nineteenth-century wares is by no means due to the familiar contempt for the insufficiently antique. The period of the Napoleonic wars marks a definite break with the old traditions of craftsmanship. The financial and cultural impoverishment they caused left the industrialising process, already well begun by Wedgwood, irrevocably complete.

CHAPTER XVII

MISCELLANEOUS FACTORIES AND LEGENDS

THE obscure beginnings of English porcelain have naturally permitted the wildest conjectures regarding supposed early specimens. The originally vague significance of the word "china", which we now take to mean porcelain only, is doubtless responsible for some of the myths. It was current in the seventeenth and eighteenth centuries for several sorts of ware, particularly blue-and-white, and its use does not necessarily imply porcelain as we now understand it. I have already explained how JOHN DWIGHT and FRANCIS PLACE came, partly in this way, to be credited with the making of some unquestionably Chinese porcelain.[1]

An often-quoted early report of porcelain-manufacture appeared in a publication of 1716 [2] and spoke of "a try'd and infallible method" by which ground-up oriental china was mixed with gum-water and burnt oyster-shells. Mr. Hobson described this as Gilbertian, but admitted that Dossie's *Handmaid to the Arts* (1758) indicated that powdered Chinese porcelain was actually an ingredient in some of the earlier soft-pastes. And Mr. William Burton [3] thinks the recipe not so absurd

[1] See p. 3.

[2] Quoted in Hobson, *Catalogue*, p. xvi, from *Essays for the Month of December 1716*, by a *Society of Gentlemen* (said to be the work of Aaron Hill).

[3] *English Porcelain*, p. 8. Burnt oyster-shells have of course been used as a source of lime, and gum-water was apparently used in early porcelain manufactures to remedy a lack of plasticity in a paste containing little clay.

as it seems. Dossie said he had seen "near London" eleven mills at work, grinding Eastern china for this purpose, but the porcelain made was "grey, full of flaws and bubbles". We cannot certainly recognise the productions from this and the description may not be altogether accurate, but it is interesting to recall that casks of "broken India china" were sent from Chelsea to Derby in 1790.[1] Perhaps some of the alumina in the analyses of English soft-paste is due to this ingredient. But we may be certain that artificial porcelain was not made in any quantity by the "try'd and infallible method" of 1716, or at all events not at that date.

Another mystery has been made round the efforts in England of the Comte de BRANCAS-LAURAGUAIS, who in 1766 took the first step towards an English patent for hard-paste, but never entered his specification.[2] He discovered *kaolin* at Alençon in 1758, and is believed to have found it also in Cornwall about the time of his application for a patent. His productions in France, of dates between 1764 and 1768, bear a monogram L.B. or L.R.[3] and include a plate painted in *famille rose* style,[4] as well as busts and reliefs, all said to be greyish and full of imperfections. A breakfast-cup and saucer and a plate in Mr. Allen's collection (No. 624), painted with flowers in natural colours, has the mark L.P. in monogram in blue and has been claimed as Brancas-Lauraguais porcelain. But it is of nineteenth-century date and probably Continental, and the mark decidedly suspect as a later addition. Brancas-Lauraguais's English porcelain is, I am afraid, a myth.

[1] ". . . in 1790 and previous thereto." W. Bemrose, *Bow, Chelsea and Derby Porcelain*, p. 37.

[2] Jewitt, vol. i, p. 114.

[3] A list of his productions is given in Comte Xavier de Chavagnac and E. Grollier, *Histoire des manufactures françaises de porcelaine*, pp. 403-405. Owen, p. xxiii, described a tea-bottle declared to be of Brancas-Lauraguais porcelain, "marked in red . . . B.L.", which has since been lost sight of.

[4] Illustrated in E. Hannover, *Pottery and Porcelain*, vol. iii, Fig. 478.

An imperfect knowledge of London topography may well have assisted in the creation of some of the legendary factories. The eastern suburbs and outskirts of London were perhaps as little known to the citizens in the eighteenth century as they are to-day. The exact site of the Bow factory may not have been described to or understood by the gossips of the time, and Jonas Hanway [1] may have heard of the Bow factory from two different sources and not realised that the STEPNEY of one informant was the same as the Bow of another. A confusion between the locality of the factory and of the church familiarly called Bow Church [2] would facilitate the mistake. A similar error would account for the reference to different factories at STRATFORD and Bow, in an account in the *London Chronicle*, 1755, of the departure of some china-makers for Scotland.[3]

I have in the course of this book given instances of errors in the gossip repeated by Simeon Shaw in his *History of the Staffordshire Potteries*, and we need attach little importance to his tale [4] of a second Chelsea factory started in 1747 by some disgruntled Staffordshire workmen whose services had not been appreciated at the other Chelsea works. Mr. William King has pointed out that according to Shaw's dates their establishment, if it ever existed, must have lasted until 1754, and it is strange that we have no further record of it. As Mr. King says, the tale is probably no more than a piece of misplaced local patriotism on the part of Shaw.

Dr. Pococke [5] spoke of the "china and enamel manufactory" at York House at BATTERSEA, and Rouquet,[6] after describing the Chelsea works, referred

[1] He wrote in his *Travels* (1753), vol. iv, p. 228, after visiting Meissen in 1750, "It is with great satisfaction that I observe the manufactures of Bow, Chelsea and Stepney so improved".

[2] See p. 57 for an apparently mistaken reference to Bow Churchyard.

[3] Quoted in Hobson, *Catalogue*, p. xviii.

[4] *Op. cit.*, p. 167.

[5] *Op. cit.*, vol. ii, p. 69.

[6] *Op. cit.*, p. 143.

to a neighbouring "manufacture de porcelaine" where certain pieces were printed ("en camayeux par une espèce d'impression"). Both writers probably saw porcelain being printed at the Battersea enamel factory and inferred that it was also made there. I have elsewhere [1] mentioned the resemblance of certain Bow prints to those of Ravenet, and the possibility that both Chelsea and Bow porcelain may have been occasionally decorated at Battersea. Or the "porcelaine" may have been white-enamelled copper! Similarly we may explain the BIRMINGHAM china of an advertisement of 1757 quoted by Nightingale [2] as a mistaken reference to South Staffordshire enamels. Dr. Pococke's presumed confusion of the two materials at Battersea will perhaps justify us in disregarding his report [3] of a former china-manufacture at the "Sturbridge" (STOURBRIDGE) glass-works, which had been discontinued, however, at the time of his visit in 1751.

More persistently and ardently supported by local patriots are the supposed porcelain factories at ISLEWORTH, Wirksworth and Church Gresley. For the first of these we have no written evidence relating to porcelain [4] until 1795, when Lysons spoke of a "china manufactory" there; but that author was probably not concerned to distinguish porcelain from earthenware. The traditional ascription to Isleworth of two pieces formerly in the Jermyn Street Collection [5] and now at South Kensington is quite certainly mistaken: they are both of Lowdin's Bristol or Worcester china. A saucer, also at South Kensington (No. 3774—1901), painted in blue with the initials CHS surmounted by a crest consisting of a portcullis, is of different character. A similar plate in the possession

[1] P. 73. [2] P. lxv. [3] Vol. ii, p. 223.

[4] Pottery was evidently made in some quantity at an earlier date. Black and other ware is supposed to have been made.

[5] The little mug figured in Plate 55 F (No. 3147—1901), and a bowl (No. 3777 — 1901) with the same pattern. Two Worcesterish bowls in the British Museum (Nos. XVI. 1 and 2) have been similarly ascribed.

of the Earl of Jersey at Osterley Park (near Isleworth) has the monogram of Sarah Child (*b.* 1764, *d.* 1793), heiress of Robert Child of Osterley and mother of Sarah, Countess of Jersey. The traditional ascription of these pieces to Isleworth is more respectable, but they may equally well be Worcester or Salopian porcelain.

Of an attempted manufacture at CHURCH GRESLEY near Burton-on-Trent there is much circumstantial evidence, but of its productions in porcelain little indeed. It is said to have been established in 1794 by Sir Nigel Bowyer Gresley, who engaged amongst others William Coffee, the Derby modeller;[1] it was sold to W. Nadin in 1800 and finally closed in 1808. A mug, painted in blue, in the British Museum (XIII. 1),[2] formerly ascribed to Church Gresley on traditional grounds, is almost certainly a Bow piece. A showy service with yellow panels alternating with panels of coloured flowers,[3] also attributed to the factory, is very like Flight and Barr's Worcester, and in any case too "slick" and accomplished to have been made at a factory that is admitted to have been a failure, technically and commercially.[4] That the pattern is known as the "Church Gresley pattern" would merely imply that it was ordered (of the Worcester firm) by someone from that place: it was a Worcester practice so to name their patterns. A vase claimed as Church Gresley by a descendant of the second proprietor [5] is a Continental production of a well-known type. Its date is shown by its style to be nearer 1820 than the period

[1] But by 1795 he had "finished all there was to do there" (Jewitt, vol. ii, p. 98).

[2] There are others similar at South Kensington (Nos. C 841—1924 and C 1307—1924).

[3] The pattern is also on a service at Windsor Castle, made for Edward, Duke of Kent, who visited the Church Gresley works. Hence the mistake?

[4] "The china always came out of the ovens cracked and crazed." See a letter quoted by Jewitt, vol. ii, p. 156, and Haslem (*Catalogue*, p. 48) says that it was "so soft that it came out of the oven every shape but the right".

[5] In *The Expert*, May 25, 1907.

given for the factory. Church Gresley must therefore be considered to be another myth.

Similar traditions, probably mistaken,[1] have given some porcelain to a WIRKSWORTH factory. Fine white china-clay in the neighbourhood may well have tempted potters to start a pottery in the district, but of porcelain made from it there is no sure record. The Catalogue of a Fine Art and Industrial Exhibition held at Derby in 1870[2] is full of praise for Wirksworth china, but states that the factory came to an end in 1777. Jewitt[3] quotes a document confirming this, and also mentions the story that William Billingsley started a porcelain factory at Wirksworth at some time between 1804 and 1808. The discovery of wasters proves, indeed, that porcelain of some sort was made there, but what it was like and whether it was made in any quantity are questions still unanswered. Most of the pieces traditionally said to have been made at the factory[4] appear to be of late eighteenth- or early nineteenth-century date. They are too late in style to have been made before 1777, and do not in the least resemble, either in paste or decoration, the china made by Billingsley, either at Pinxton just before the dates given for his supposed Wirksworth factory, or later at Nantgarw. On the other hand, they closely resemble Staffordshire porcelain[5] of New Hall type, and none

[1] Traditions about pottery orally transmitted usually prove to be of very doubtful value. An excellent instance of this is provided by the legend which led Lady Charlotte Schreiber to attribute to Plymouth the Chelsea bust of George II. It was acquired as a replica of one "that belonged to the late Dr. Cookworthy of Plymouth which came to him from the manufacturers and which he has left as an heirloom in his family". (*Lady Charlotte Schreiber's Journal*, vol. i, p. 57.)

[2] By W. Bemrose and A. Wallis.

[3] Vol. ii, pp. 142-144.

[4] See articles by T. L. Tudor in the *Transactions of the Derbyshire Archæological and Natural History Society*, 1916, p. 117, and in *The Connoisseur* vol. li (1918), p. 25; but see also Bernard Rackham in *The Burlington Magazine*, vol. xxix (1916), p. 339.

[5] The resemblance said to exist between the supposed Wirksworth and Lowestoft depends only on the use of certain diapers of Chinese origin such as were common also on Staffordshire porcelain well into the nineteenth

of them corresponds with the porcelain wasters found on the factory site. Plate 94 D shows a cup and saucer of one of the patterns said to be Wirksworth. One sugar-bowl claimed for the factory, with handles in the form of twisted rope,[1] is not quite like anything made in porcelain elsewhere, though closely similar to Leeds earthenware, and it may be a genuine Wirksworth piece.[2] But apart from this problematical piece it seems that little if any Wirksworth china has yet been authenticated. The fact that so little of the presumed New Hall china is marked must, however, warn the collector to regard the question as still an open one. I have already alluded[3] to another Billingsley tradition, regarding a cup said to have been made by him at TORKSEY, rather earlier than the supposed Wirksworth venture.

These myths survive by virtue of the quantity of unmarked and to most people problematical early china in existence. On the other hand, factories have sometimes been invented to account for marks, actually those of dealers, which occasionally appear on pieces. I have already mentioned several examples of these.[4] A puzzling mark on a Derby coffee-cup in the British Museum collection (No. III. 24) and a Worcester teapot in the Frank Lloyd Collection (and many other extant pieces) is that of Coombs, a china-repairer of Bristol, who fixed together broken parts with frit and re-marked the pieces in enamel colour. He is known to have worked between 1780 and 1805.

I have already had much to say of the "outside enamellers" who decorated porcelain but did not make it. For those disturbers of the collector's peace Duesbury and Giles, in particular, I must refer the reader

century. But the paste of genuine Lowestoft is entirely different from that of the supposed Wirksworth specimens.

[1] Illustrated in Tudor, *loc. cit.*

[2] I have not had an opportunity of examining this piece and presume that it is actually of porcelain.

[3] P. 198. [4] Pp. 209 and 272.

to the earlier pages,[1] where I have discussed the doubts about some Bow, Chelsea, Derby and Worcester attributions, due to their activities. By the nineteenth century porcelain was more generally marked and the enamellers give less trouble. Allen of Lowestoft, Thomas Pardoe, Thomas Baxter and his father, and the Donovans of Dublin have been spoken of. There are examples of the work of the last-named in Mr. Herbert Allen's collection (No. 588) and in the British Museum (No. XIV. 10); on the latter, Donovan's mark is added to that of Minton's factory. Thomas Martin Randall (*b.* 1786, *d.* 1859) and Richard Robins,[2] of Spa Fields, not only decorated English china for the London dealers, but painted in the most costly Sèvres manner much white Sèvres china bought up in Paris in 1813 by Baldock and Garman when the *pâte tendre* was abandoned at the French national factory. Lightly decorated Sèvres porcelain was even stripped of its painting with acid and redecorated with more pretentious designs. Much of the supposed Sèvres china in English collections was painted by Robins and Randall, who used also in the same way white china obtained from Minton's.[3] Randall is stated by Jewitt to have himself started a manufacture of soft-paste about 1825, at MADELEY in Shropshire, and there made imitations of Sèvres. Sims was another enameller who took Nantgarw china in the white;[4] Zachariah Boreman, after leaving Derby, is said to have worked for Sims, himself an old Derby hand. Cartwright, Battam,[5] Anderson and Muss are other decorators mentioned by Haslem,[6] who had good opportunities to obtain in-

[1] Pp. 56, 61, 171.

[2] P. 209.

[3] A sugar-basin with a Sèvres mark in the Allen Collection (No. 531) is an example of this kind of fake. A family named Bevington of Hanley is also said (see Rhead, *British Pottery Marks*, p. 35) to have made colourable imitations of Sèvres in quantity about 1870.

[4] P. 209.

[5] Afterwards with Copeland's.

[6] P. 209.

formation about these establishments. Muss employed amongst others the celebrated John Martin (1789–1854), who painted the very striking picture illustrating *Paradise Lost* on a plaque of Flight and Barr porcelain in the Allen Collection (No. 312).

APPENDIX A

MARKS

The following tables include all the well-established factory-marks in their characteristic forms. In all cases where a reasonable doubt exists in the attribution of a mark, attention has been drawn to the fact in the text, which should always be consulted. Workmen's marks, numerals and initial-letters could, of course, be added to indefinitely, but this would not help the collector in identifying his specimens.

"In blue" in every case means in underglaze blue: marks in blue over the glaze are described as "in blue enamel".

CHELSEA

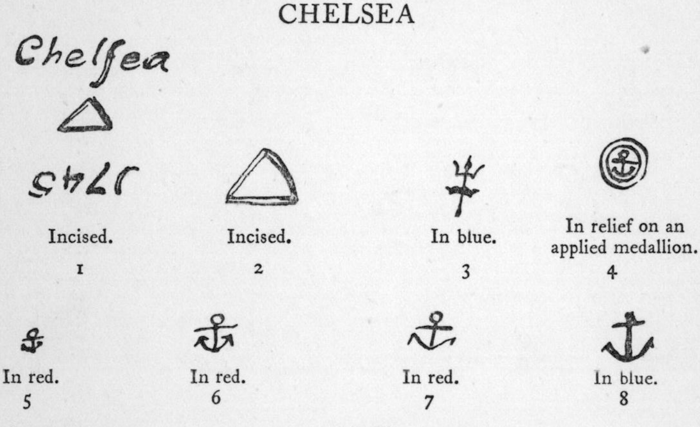

(1) 1745. (2) From 1745 to 1750.
(3) About 1750 (see p. 21).
(4) From 1750 to 1756 and perhaps earlier.
(5) to (8) About 1753 to 1756 and occasionally later. Imitated also at Derby, Bow and Worcester. A red anchor, as a rule much larger than these, was used at Venice (Cozzi factory); an anchor, usually printed, was also a Davenport mark (see p. 274). A list of factories using an anchor as a mark, on earthenware as well as porcelain, is given in Rhead, *British Pottery Marks*, p. 13.

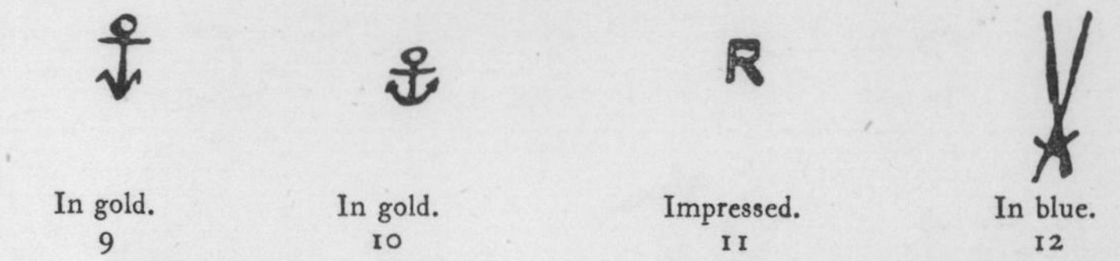

(9) and (10) From 1758 to 1769. Found also on Derby, and copied on imitations of Chelsea made at Coalport and on modern Tournay and German copies of Chelsea figures and of the Derby figures of the 1760's, formerly believed to be Chelsea.

(11) "Repairer's mark" (not Roubiliac's, see p. 26). About 1760-65.

(12) Imitation Meissen mark on a cup of about 1750, in the Schreiber Collection.

BOW

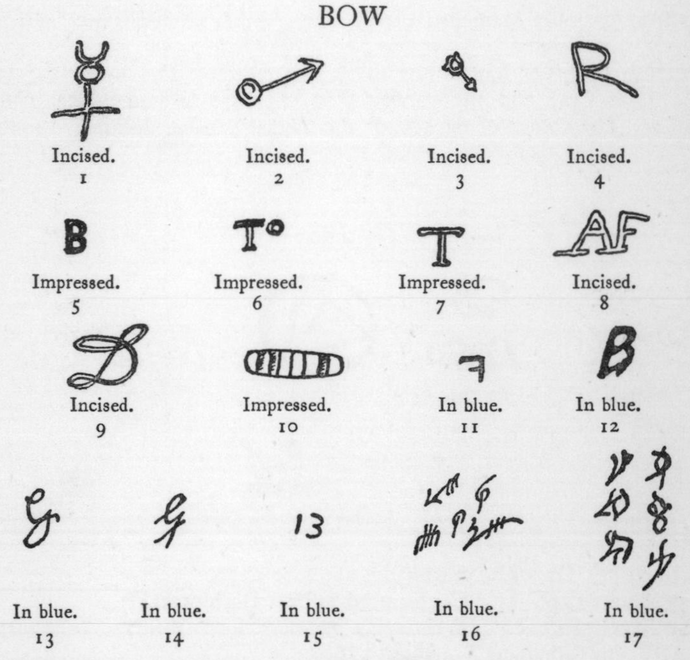

(1) to (3) On early pieces, probably before 1750.

(4) to (10) Presumably "repairers'" marks. About 1750 to 1760.

(11) to (17) On blue-and-white china. About 1755 to 1765. For No. 11, see pp. 76 and 156. Compare Nos. 16 and 17 with the Worcester mark No. 7 and the Caughley mark No. 11: the crossed swords sometimes accompany them.

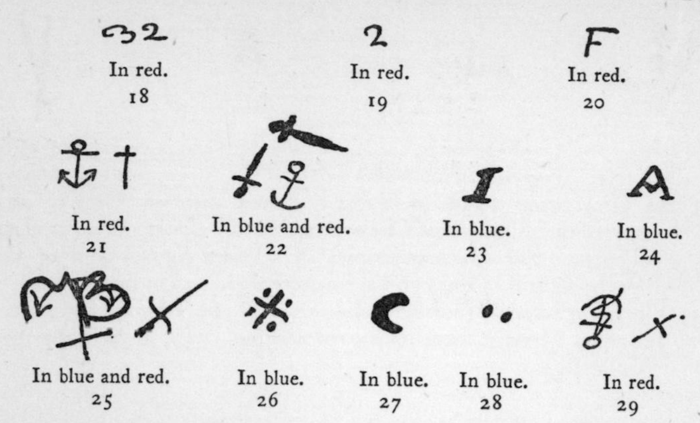

(18) to (20) On enamelled useful wares; other numerals and initials also occur.

(21) to (29) On figures and other late pieces. The heavy dagger in (22) and the cursive *B* in (25) are in underglaze blue. The colour of the anchor and dagger is often decidedly brown rather than red. About 1760 to 1775.

DERBY

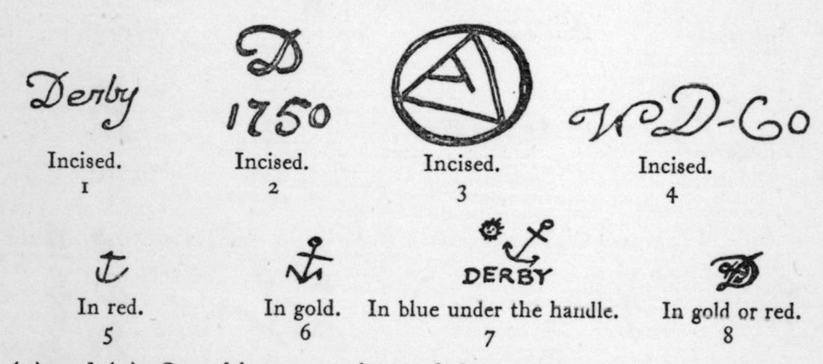

(1) and (2) On white cream-jugs of about 1750.

(3) About 1750–55. Conjectured to be a Derby mark.

(4) Much reduced. Presumably standing for "William Duesbury and Company". About 1760.

(5) Forged Chelsea mark on a plate of about 1760.

(6) Forged Chelsea mark on a figure of Lord Chatham (Schreiber Collection).

(7) Reputed mark of Richard Holdship on a printed mug (but see p. 93).

(8) The normal "Chelsea-Derby" mark on useful wares. About 1770–84.

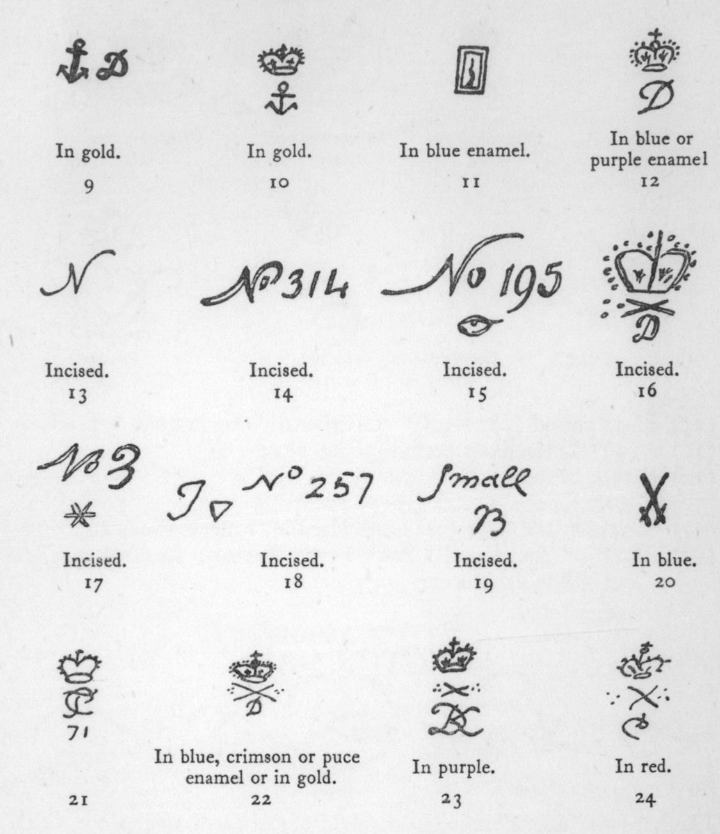

(9) Rare Chelsea-Derby mark on a service of the pattern figured in Plate 41 A.

(10) About 1770–80.

(11) About 1770–80: on an early "Japan" pattern (Plate 42).

(12) For a few years before 1784.

(13) to (19) Marks on figures. The numbers are model-numbers. The symbols are those of "repairers" (see p. 105). In (19) "B" may mean "best" or "biscuit". A similar script N occurs on useful wares.

(20) Forged Meissen mark.

(21) Forged Frankenthal mark on copies of gold-striped pieces (see p. 98).

(22) About 1784 to about 1810.

(23) Duesbury and Kean period (1795–96).

(24) Bloor period (1811–48). Occasionally also in gold or black.

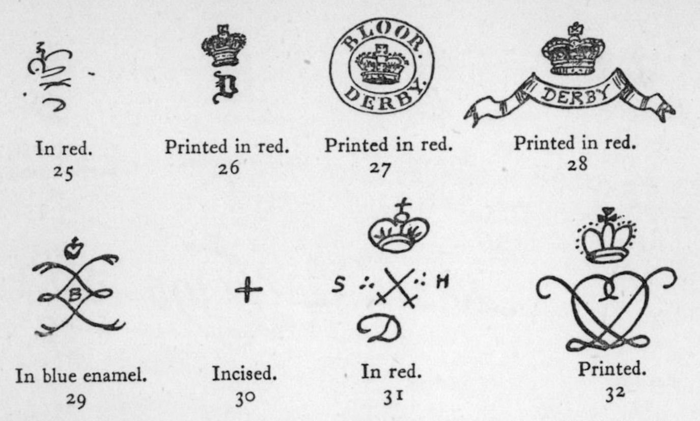

In red. 25 | Printed in red. 26 | Printed in red. 27 | Printed in red. 28

In blue enamel. 29 | Incised. 30 | In red. 31 | Printed. 32

(25) Bloor period (1811–48). Occasionally also in gold or black.
(26) to (28) Later Bloor period (about 1820–48).
(29) Forged Sèvres mark on late Derby.
(30) George Cocker's mark (see p. 106).
(31) Stevenson and (also Sampson) Hancock's mark: about 1850–70.
(32) Mark of the Royal Crown-Derby Factory, founded in 1876 and still in existence.

LONGTON HALL

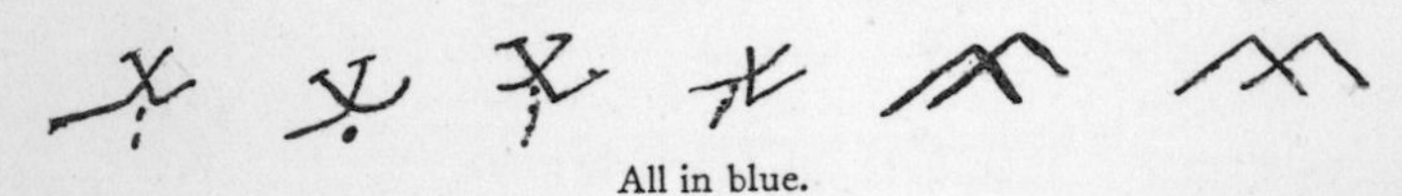

All in blue.

The last two "marks" occur in the field of the decoration (see p. 121). Perhaps imitated from the conventionalised distant mountains of a Chinese landscape.

LOWESTOFT

All in blue.

The thin crescent with open ends (No. 7 in the line) is printed, on blue-printed pieces: the other marks are painted. The first four are examples of the Lowestoft marks written inside the foot-ring. The crescents and the W are copies of Worcester marks: the crossed swords, a Lowestoft version of the Meissen mark.

BRISTOL (Lowdin's Factory) AND EARLY WORCESTER

Bristoll — Impressed in relief. 1

Bristol — Impressed in relief. 2

Bristoll 1750 — Impressed in relief. 3

In red. 4

In blue. 5

In blue. 6

In blue. 7

In blue. 8

In blue. 9

In blue. 10

In blue. 11

In blue. 12

In red. 13

In blue, below the handle. 14

In red. 15

In brown. 16

In blue, below the handle. 17

In blue. 18

BX — Incised. 19

Incised. 20

Incised. 21

Nos. 4 to 18 are probably workmen's marks: some of them are found also on Worcester porcelain (see p. 147). No. 18 occurs on a mug of the "scratched cross" family. There are many others.

Nos. 19 to 21. For the significance of these incised marks, see pp. 147, 148.

WORCESTER

"Dr. Wall" Period (1751–83)

In red. 1

In blue. 2

In blue. 3

In blue. 4

In blue. 5

In blue. 6

In blue. 7

In blue. 8

(1) to (8) Workmen's or painters' marks: 1751 to about 1770. There are many others; see also Bristol (Lowdin's), above. The Chinese characters (No. 7) should be compared with the Bow (Nos. 16 and 17) and Caughley (No. 11) marks of a similar kind.

In blue. 9	In red. 10	Printed in blue. 11	In gold, black or blue enamel. 12
Printed in blue. 13	 In blue. 14	 In blue. 15	 In blue. 16
 In blue. 17	Printed in blue. 18	 In blue or black. 19	 In red. 20
 In blue enamel. 21	 In blue. 22	 In blue. 23	 In blue. 24

(9) In slightly varying forms: in use until about 1795.
(10) On enamelled wares: 1770–90.
(11) On wares printed in underglaze blue.
(12) Chiefly used in the Flight period, but occasionally also (as on the "Duke of Gloucester's" service) in the earlier period, 1770–80.
(13) On blue-printed wares.
(14) to (17) On all classes of porcelain 1755–83. There are many other slightly varying forms.
(18) On blue-printed wares only.
(19) This occurs on black-"pencilled" china, and also on pieces of "Lowdin's" type painted in colours.
(20) Seen occasionally on enamelled wares after about 1768, probably added by a Chelsea painter working at Worcester. A specimen analysed by Mr. Herbert Eccles has this mark (see *Analysed Specimens*, No. 29). The anchor in *gold* is very rare, but occurs on a pale-claret-ground cup and saucer painted with "dishevelled birds", in the British Museum (see p. 172).
(21) On transfer-printed wares coloured over, perhaps added by Giles (see p. 162).
(22) Imitation Meissen mark common on many classes of china. The number between the blades is sometimes "91" (or 16). Almost the only mark ever seen on black-printed wares, usually unmarked.
(23) and (24) Imitations of the Tournay, and Chantilly, Sèvres marks.

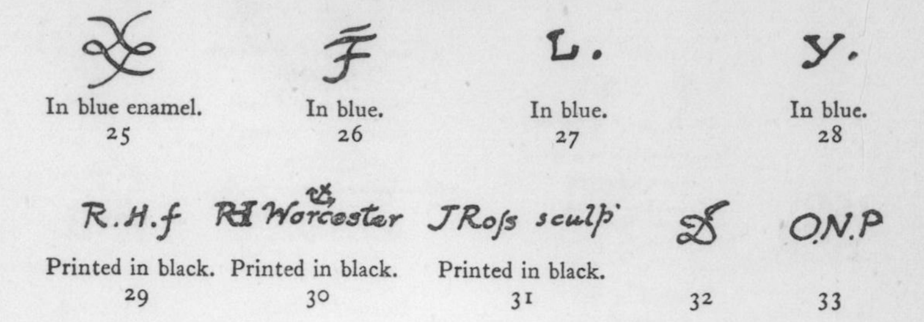

In blue enamel. 25 | In blue. 26 | In blue. 27 | In blue. 28

Printed in black. 29 | Printed in black. 30 | Printed in black. 31 | 32 | 33

(25) and (26) Imitations of the Sèvres and Fürstenberg marks.
(27) and (28) Probably workmen's marks; both occur on an enamelled piece of about 1775.
(29) Initials of Robert Hancock.
(30) Monogram and rebus device of Richard Holdship: but see p. 160.
(31) Signature of James Ross.
(32) Initials of John Donaldson on painted decoration.
(33) Initials of O'Neale (*O'Neale pinxit*) on painted decoration; the name is sometimes written in full.

"Flight" to "Flight and Barr" Periods (1783–1840)

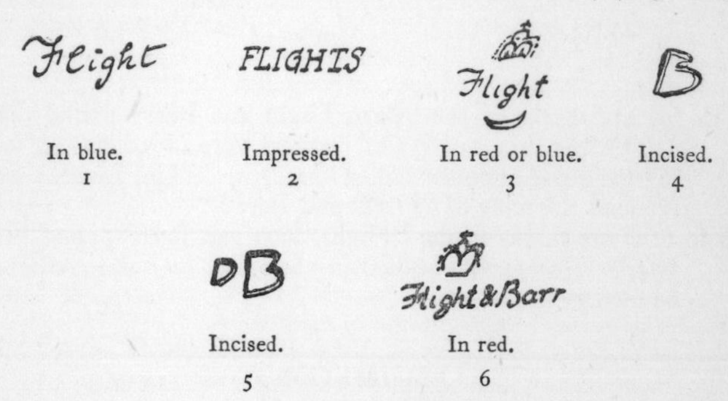

In blue. 1 | Impressed. 2 | In red or blue. 3 | Incised. 4

Incised. 5 | In red. 6

(1) to (3) Marks of the "Flight" period (1783–1792). No. 2 is rare. The crown (No. 3) was added after the granting of a royal patent in 1789. *Flight* and a crescent is sometimes found in red, blue or gold.
(4) to (6) are marks of the "Flight and Barr" period (1792–1807). (4) and (5) indicate experimental pastes introduced by Martin Barr; stated by Binns not to have been used after 1803, but an incised B occurs on a flower-pot in the Schreiber Collection (No. 678) to be ascribed to the year 1809.

B.F.B.

Impressed.

7

BARR FLIGHT & BARR
Royal Porcelain Works
WORCESTER
London House
No 1 Coventry Street

Printed in red or black.

8

Barr Flight & Barr
Worcester
Flight & Barr
Coventry Street
London
Manufacturers to their Majesties & Royal Family

In red or black.

9

FBB

Impressed.

10

Flight Barr & Barr
Worcester.

In red or black.

11

Printed in red or black.

12

(7) to (9) are marks of the "Barr, Flight and Barr" period (1807–1813): the Prince of Wales' feathers were added in 1807 following the royal appointment of that year. The London branch retained the style of "Flight and Barr".

(10) to (12) are marks of the "Flight, Barr and Barr" period (1813–1840). Joseph Flight died in 1829, but his name continued to be used in the marks.

CHAMBERLAIN'S

Chamberlains
Wors No 276

In red.

1

Chamberlains
Worcester
403

In purple.

2

Chamberlains
Worcester

In gold.

3

(1) Early mark, about 1800.

(2) and (3) About 1810–20: the gold mark was used on the more ambitious productions.

Chamberlain's
Worcester
& 63, Piccadilly,
London.

Printed in red.
4

Chamberlain's
Regent China
Worcester
& 155
New Bond Street,
London

Printed in red.
5

Chamberlains

Incised.
6

CHAMBERLAINS

Impressed.
7

Chamberlain
Worcester.

In red.
8

CHAMBERLAIN & Co.
WORCESTER
155 NEW BOND St.
& No. 1.
COVENTRY St.
LONDON.

Printed in red.
9

(4) The Piccadilly premises were in use by Chamberlain's for the period 1814–16 only.

(5) The crown was used after the beginning of the Regency in 1811, when the "Regent china" body was introduced by Chamberlain's for occasional use: this body is very translucent and somewhat resembles Nantgarw china, but is harder. No. 5 above was the special mark used upon it. A plate at South Kensington (No. 3301—1901) is an example. The Bond Street address dates from 1816, and there are various other marks including it. The words "Royal Porcelain Manufacturers" began to be used in 1820 on the accession of George IV.

(6) and (7) Late marks, about 1845–50. (7) occurs on pieces with a very hard paste and thick raised gilding.

(8) About 1845. The smaller and more laboured writing distinguishes this from the earlier mark.

(9) The two addresses indicate the period between 1840 (when the two Worcester firms were amalgamated as "Chamberlain and Company") and 1845, when the Coventry Street house was given up. Also used in script characters.

Modern Period

Printed or impressed.
1

Printed.
2

Impressed.
3

Printed.
4

(1) and (2) Marks of Kerr and Binns (1852–62). The second of these was used only on pieces of exceptional quality: the date (here "52" for 1852) was added in gold.

(3) and (4) Marks of the Royal Worcester Porcelain Company, founded in 1862 and still in existence. WORCESTER impressed sometimes appears with these.

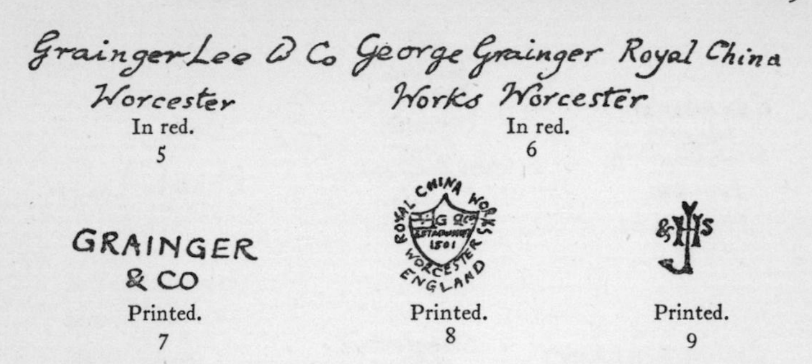

In red. 5 — In red. 6

Printed. 7 — Printed. 8 — Printed. 9

(5) to (7) Marks of Grainger's factory, founded in 1801.

(8) Modern "Grainger's" mark used by the Royal Worcester Porcelain Company.

(9) Mark of James Hadley, a rival modern Worcester firm started in 1896 and absorbed by the older company in 1905.

CAUGHLEY

(SALOPIAN)

S — In blue. 1

S — Printed in blue. 2

C — In blue or (rarely) in gold. 3

C — Printed in blue. 4

S × — In blue. 5

In blue. 6

In blue. 7

Printed in blue. 8

In blue. 9

In blue. 10

In blue. 11

In blue. 12

Nos. 6 to 8 are of course imitation Worcester marks. The fretted square is rarely seen.

Nos. 9 and 10 are typical disguised numerals. Others occur.

No. 11 occurs on a powdered-blue plate in the Victoria and Albert Museum (No. C 1301—1924) in combination with the mark *Salopian* impressed. Compare Bow (Nos. 16 and 17) and Worcester (No. 7) marks of this character.

No. 12 is an imitation of the Chantilly mark of a hunting horn.

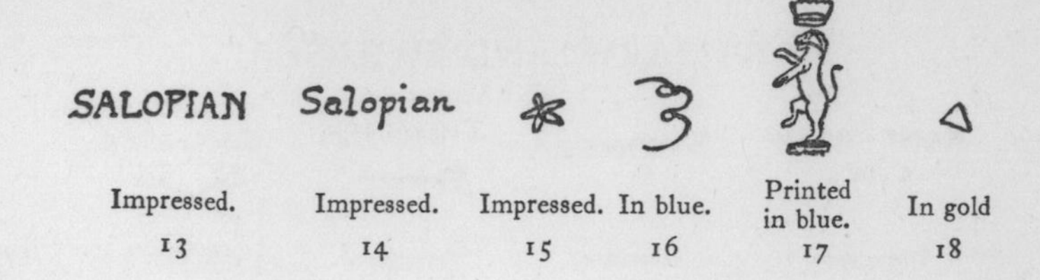

Impressed. 13 — Impressed. 14 — Impressed. 15 — In blue. 16 — Printed in blue. 17 — In gold 18

LIVERPOOL

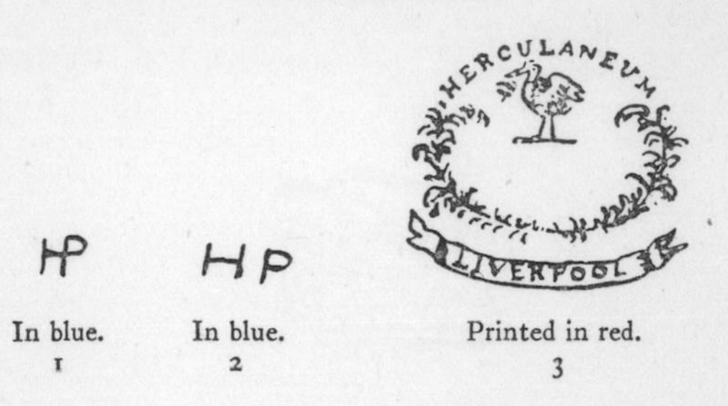

In blue. 1 — In blue. 2 — Printed in red. 3

Nos. 1 and 2 occur on enamelled pieces of about 1765.
No. 3 is the mark of the Herculaneum Factory (about 1800–41).

PINXTON

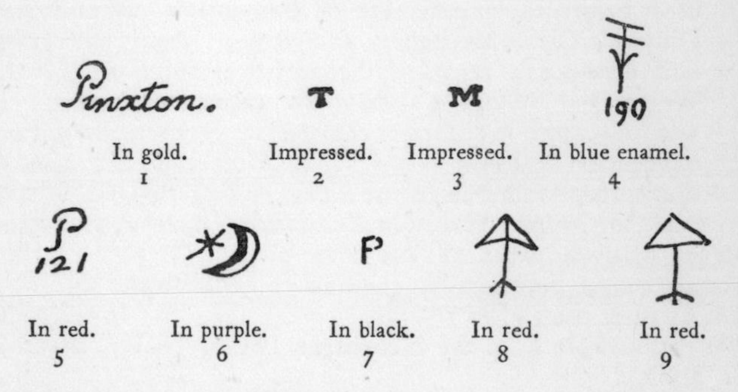

In gold. 1 — Impressed. 2 — Impressed. 3 — In blue enamel. 4

In red. 5 — In purple. 6 — In black. 7 — In red. 8 — In red. 9

The word *Pinxton* in full (No. 1) is rare, but occurs on a mug in the British Museum (No. XII. 1). The impressed capitals are usually early: the arrows late.

NANTGARW AND SWANSEA

NANT-GARW C.W.	SWANSEA	SWANSEA (with trident)	SWANSEA (with crossed tridents)
Impressed. 1	Impressed. 2	Impressed. 3	Impressed. 4

SWANSEA	*Swansea*	DILLWYN & CO. SWANSEA.	BEVINGTON & CO.
In red and other colours. 5	In gold (rarely), red and other colours. 6	Impressed. 7	Impressed. 8

Printed in red.
9

(1) Used at both Nantgarw and Swansea, and perhaps also at Coalport on Billingsley's paste. The letters *C.W.* (which are sometimes absent) most probably stand for "China Works" and not for "Cambrian Works" as asserted by Solon, since the mark was used before the transference of Billingsley's manufacture to Dillwyn's Cambrian Pottery at Swansea. Jewitt and Haslem both erroneously regarded the initials as those of "George" Walker, but Billingsley's son-in-law was named Samuel. The word *Nantgarw* in red script characters is very rare, but is known to occur on authentic pieces. Mr. Herbert Eccles states that the word pencilled in colour occurs on forgeries and imitations made at Coalport (*Swansea Exhibition Catalogue*, p. 23.)

(2) to (6) Swansea marks, 1814–17: see p. 203.

(7) Rarely seen on porcelain but common on earthenware.

(8) On Swansea china after 1817.

(9) On earthenware from the Glamorgan Pottery (Baker, Bevan and Irwin).

COALPORT

Printed in red. 1	In blue. 2	In blue. 3	In blue. 4
In gold. 5	In blue or gold. 6	In blue enamel. 7	In blue enamel. 8
In gold. 9	In blue. 10	In blue. 11	In gold. 12.
Printed. 13.			

(1) From 1820 onwards.
(2) to (5) Second quarter of the nineteenth century.
(6) Middle of nineteenth century.
(7) to (11) Imitations of the Sèvres, Chelsea and Meissen marks. An *impressed* anchor is stated by Jewitt (vol. i, p. 290) to have been used at Coalport.
(12) From 1861 onwards. The letters enclosed are the initials of the names of the factories absorbed—Caughley, Nantgarw and Swansea.
(13) Modern mark. The year in this, 1750, is the date of foundation claimed for the factory and not the date of the porcelain bearing the mark.

The very rare early mark *Coalbrookdale* has been mentioned in the text (p. 213). Rather later marks include various forms of the abbreviation *C. Dale*, as well as the names of the London dealers, Daniell and Sparks. A formal rose (for John or W. Rose) is also said to have been used.

SWINTON (ROCKINGHAM FACTORY)

Printed in red or brown.

The griffin mark was used only after the factory began to be assisted by Earl Fitzwilliam in 1826. The word *Royal* prefixed to the name of the factory indicates a date after 1830. The words *Manufacturer to the King* naturally occur only up to the date of the death of William IV (1837). The name *Brameld* in relief on an applied medallion occurs (but rarely) in conjunction with the printed mark.

PLYMOUTH

In blue, blue enamel, red, or gold.	Incised through the glaze.	In blue.
1	2	3

No. 2 occurs on one of a set of vases and beakers in the Schreiber Collection (No. 710), the others of which are marked with No. 1.

T and T° impressed (see Bow No. 6 and page 227) and *K*, impressed, also occur.

BRISTOL

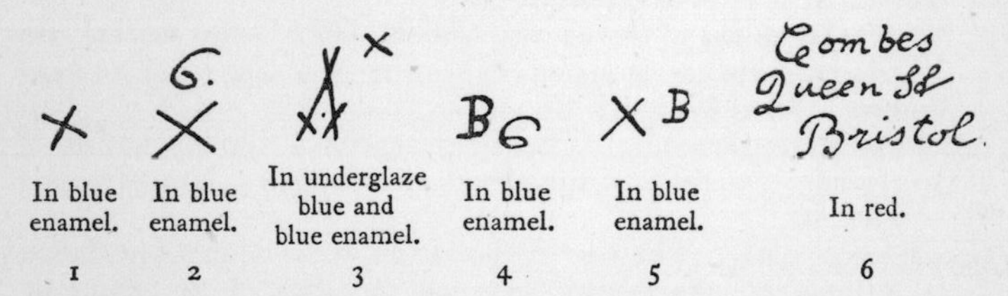

In blue enamel.	In blue enamel.	In underglaze blue and blue enamel.	In blue enamel.	In blue enamel.	In red.
1	2	3	4	5	6

No. 3 has the crossed swords in underglaze blue, and the small cross in blue enamel.

No. 6 is one of the marks of a china-repairer who added his name in red enamel to pieces he had mended with fusible vitreous cement. The name was sometimes spelt *Coombs*, and dates between 1780 and 1800 were often added (see p. 256).

The T° mark also occurs.

STAFFORDSHIRE

Adams: a Tunstall and Stoke family including four members named William Adams made pottery of many kinds during the eighteenth and nineteenth centuries, notably jasper ware and blue-printed earthenware. About the second quarter of the nineteenth century porcelain made by Adams of Greenfield, Tunstall, was marked

W A & S

Marks on "ironstone" and other wares included the name of the firm (which still exists) in full, sometimes with other matter.

Alcock: S. Alcock of Hill Top, at a pottery established about 1830, made biscuit figures and other wares sometimes marked

S A & Co

or with the name in full, sometimes accompanied by devices suggesting the name given to the service upon which they appear.

Allertons, of Longton, established 1831, made porcelain as well as the lustred wares for which they are well-known. The wares were usually marked with the name in full.

Ashworth, see Mason.

Booths, of Tunstall, a still-existing firm, sometimes marked its wares, which included copies in earthenware of Worcester china,

T B & S

for T. Booth and Sons.

Bourne: The name of Charles Bourne of the Foley pottery is said to appear on porcelain of early nineteenth century date.

Brownfield: W. Brownfield of Cobridge used the mark of the "Staffordshire knot" (from the county arms), with the initials W. B., on porcelain dating from the last third of the nineteenth century. The knot is of course common to many modern Staffordshire marks.

Copeland, see Spode.

Davenport, of Longport.

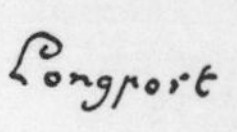

With the exception of No. 4 all are printed, usually in red.

Green: The name of T. Green of Fenton is sometimes found as a mark on porcelain of the middle of the nineteenth century.

Hilditch and Sons of Longton made porcelain in the early nineteenth century marked

Printed in red.

Mason: George Miles Mason and his brother C. J. Mason are chiefly famous for their "ironstone-china" (see p. 245) patented in 1813. The name

MILES MASON

impressed, sometimes abbreviated, appears on porcelain of about 1800–10, and the imitation Chinese seal character given below was also used on some of the early pieces.

Printed, usually in blue.

The "ironstone" patent was purchased by F. Morley in 1851, and passed into the hands of the Ashworths (a still-existing firm) whose name appears in the marks.

Mayer and Newbold of Lane End used their initials as a mark on china dating from about 1835.

M&N

In red.

Mintons:

780	M	Devon M&B		MINTON
In blue enamel.	In blue.	Printed.	Printed or impressed.	Impressed.
1	2	3	4	5

(1) and (2) are early marks, 1800–30.
(3) Minton and Boyle (1836–41).
(4) After 1851.
(5) After 1865.

Since 1842 certain signs have been used to indicate the year of manufacture. A list is given in G. W. Rhead's *British Pottery Marks* (London, 1910), p. 181.

Neale: Porcelain figures and useful wares are occasionally found marked with the name of this Hanley firm

NEALE & CO.

NEALE & WILSON impressed also occurs as a mark on a plate painted with fruit, of about 1790, in the Cardiff Museum.

New Hall:

N421

In red or crimson.
1

Printed in red.
2

(1) 1782 to about 1810.
(2) About 1810 to 1825.

Patent Mark: From 1842 to 1883 pottery designs could be registered at the Patent Office. In the following specimen mark, X is a code-letter for the year of registration.

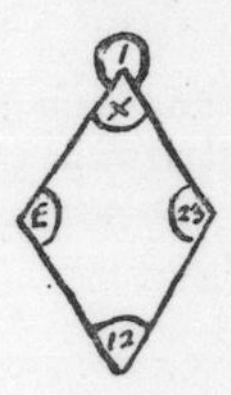

Printed.

Ridgway: The firm of Ridgway of Cauldon Place, Stoke-on-Trent, flourished especially during the period of the management of John, a son of Job Ridgway, the founder, from 1814 to 1859. The name of the firm appeared in most of the marks. The following mark is typical of those in which the initials only are used. It dates from the period 1815–30.

Printed.

Shorthose, of Hanley, a general potter, marked some printed porcelain of about 1800–23 as follows:

Shorthose & C°

Spode and *Copeland:*

In red. 1 — In red. 2 — Printed in purple. 3

In red. 4 — Printed in blue. 5 — Printed in blue. 6 — Printed in green. 7

(1) and (2) On various porcelain about 1800–33.
(3) Generally late: about 1825–33.
(4) to (6) First quarter of nineteenth century.
(7) About 1840.

Turner of Lane End.

Turner's Patent

On red.

The mark above occurs on a crudely decorated stone-china plate, of early nineteenth-century date, at South Kensington. A mark on a porcelain bowl in the British Museum, *Lane End 1786*, is probably Turner's.

Wedgwood of Etruria. Porcelain was made at Etruria only in the early nineteenth century (see p. 248), never under the management of the first Josiah Wedgwood.

WEDGWOOD

Printed, usually in red.

Wood of Burslem. No mark is unquestionably to be associated with Aaron or Ralph Wood the elder, but the following may refer to Ralph the younger or Enoch Wood (see p. 239):

W ✳ ✳ ✳

APPENDIX B

TABLE SHOWING THE ULTIMATE ADOPTION OF BONE-ASH AS AN INGREDIENT IN ALL THE ENGLISH PORCELAIN BODIES.

Glassy porcelain: ×××××× Hard-paste porcelain: ~~~~~~

Soapstone porcelain: oooooo Porcelain containing bone-ash: ——————

	1745	1750	1755	1760	1765	1770	1775	1780	1785	1790	1795	1800	1810	1815	1820	1825
CHELSEA	×	×	×	—	—	—										
BOW	×	—	—	—	—	—	—									
DERBY		×	×	×	×	—	—	—	—	—	—	—	—	—	—	—
LONGTON HALL		×	×	×												
LOWESTOFT				—	—	—	—	—	—	—	—	—				
EARLY BRISTOL AND WORCESTER		o	o	o	o	o	o	o	o	o	o	—	—	—	—	—
LIVERPOOL			o	o	o	—	—	— ?								
CAUGHLEY							o	o	o	o	o					
COALPORT												—	—	—	—	—
PINXTON											—	—	—			
NANTGARW AND SWANSEA														—		
PLYMOUTH AND BRISTOL						~	~	~								
NEW HALL									~	~	~	~	—	—	—	—
SPODE AND LATER STAFFORDSHIRE												—	—	—	—	—

Notes: (1) The very small percentage of phosphoric acid in the analyses of some Longton Hall specimens may be due to other ingredients than bone-ash, and in any case the paste is essentially of glassy rather than of bone-ash type.

(2) The paste used after about 1800 in Staffordshire and elsewhere was a hybrid feldspathic porcelain containing china-clay and bone-ash.

(3) The change to a bone-ash paste at Liverpool may be presumed to have taken place when Chaffers' soapstone mine was sold in 1776.

INDEX